Place in Literature

Place in Literature

Regions, Cultures, Communities

Roberto M. Dainotto

Cornell University Press   Ithaca and London

First published 2000 by Cornell University Press

Printed in the United States of America

LIBRARY OF CONGRESS CATALOGING-IN-PUBLICATION DATA

Dainotto, Roberto Maria, 1962–
   Place in literature : regions, cultures, communities / Roberto Maria Dainotto.
      p. cm.
   Includes index.
   ISBN 0-8014-3683-4 (cloth)
   1. English fiction—19th century—History and criticism.   2. Place (Philosophy) in
literature.   3. Hardy, Thomas, 1840–1928—Settings.   4. Gaskell, Elizabeth Cleghorn,
1810–1865—Settings.   5. Italian fiction—19th century—History and criticism.
   6. Regionalism in literature.   7. Local color in literature.   8. Community in literature.
   9. Culture in literature.   10. Setting (Literature) I. Title.
   PR878.P525 D35 1999 2000
   823'.80932—dc21
                                                                                    99-038957

Cornell University Press strives to use environmentally responsible
suppliers and materials to the fullest extent possible in the publishing
of its books. Such materials include vegetable-based, low-VOC inks
and acid-free papers that are recycled, totally chlorine-free, or partly
composed of nonwood fibers. Books that bear the logo of the FSC
(Forest Stewardship Council) use paper taken from forests that have
been inspected and certified as meeting the highest standards for
environmental and social responsibility. For further information, visit
our website at www.cornellpress.cornell.edu.

Cloth printing   10 9 8 7 6 5 4 3 2 1

Contents

Acknowledgments

Finishing a first book, so I have been told, often results in feelings of delight and joy. My particular delight is that of recognizing, after the work is done, the generosity of those who provided their assistance and contributions and helped me to give this work shape and consistency. My first thank you then goes to Timothy Reiss and Richard Sieburth, who helped me the most. Without their ideas and questions, this would have been a different book — and a feebler one for sure. For the future, I may only hope for readers of such passionate erudition, and for such intellectual stimulation. I am also grateful to Margaret Cohen and Jennifer Wicke for their help with theoretical issues, and to Barbara Spackman for having questioned my refusal to question some of Verga's more questionable assumptions regarding the "objectivity" of his regionalism. If Verga *still* escapes my criticism, it is not because I *did* not follow her advice, but because I *could* not. Call it *omertà*, if you wish, but have you ever heard of a Sicilian doubting Verga?!

What I understand of Heidegger's and Husserl's "regional" aesthetics is the fruit of lengthy conversations with Martin Reichardt, whom I also thank for some great Thai lunches. Filippo Acquachiara, *infermiere per professione intellettuale per vocazione*, found and passed along to me much of the material I used for the chapter on Gentile and Fascism. Roee Rosen was kind enough to read parts of my original draft and show expressions of encouraging enthusiasm. He should perhaps reconsider sainthood. I would also like to thank Daniel Javitch for his ready answers to rhetorical riddles and for generously sharing with me anything he could find on maps and literature. Since this might not be the appropriate context in which to thank him also for his continuous help and encouragement during graduate school and "post-doc" exile, I shall refrain from doing so.

A very special acknowledgment, in a book devoted to space, goes to Eugenio Somaini, Antonio Somaini, and Maggie Cardelus, who offered me nothing less than the space — literally! — to write the following pages. My wife, Edna, helped me every time her knowledge was needed, and shared with me all the hardships that accompanied the writing of this book. Happy that it is finally over, she is now fine, doing well, and regaining the lost weight.

I finally thank Bernhard Kendler and the staff of Cornell University Press for believing in this book.

Preliminary versions of the following material were presented as "All the Regions Do Smilingly Revolt: The Literature of Place and Region," published in *Critical Inquiry* 22 (1996): 3; "What Is a Region? The Aesthetic of Regionalism between Place and Commonplace," read at the conference *Theory and Practice of Critical Regionalism in the Development of European Architecture* (Stockholm, Sweden, July 11–13, 1997); "Regional Paradises in Victorian England: Topos and U-topos," read at the *VII International Conference of the British Comparative Literature Association* (Edinburgh, July 12–15, 1995); "*Tramonto* e *Risorgimento* in Gentile's Dialectics of Nationhood," read at the conference *Making and Unmaking Italy: The Cultivation of National Identity around the Risorgimento* (University of California at Berkeley, November 14–16, 1997); and "At the Theater of Mangiafoco: The True Story of Pinocchio's Relocation in Padania," read at the conference *The Relocation of Languages and Cultures: A Transnational and Transdisciplinary Workshop* (Duke University, May 6–10, 1997).

A last *grazie* goes to my mother for having made everything possible, and to my father, to whose memory I dedicate this work.

Place in Literature

all the regions
Do smilingly revolt; and who resist
Are mock'd for valiant ignorance,
And perish constant fools.

— WILLIAM SHAKESPEARE, *Coriolanus*

Introduction:

The Literature
of Place and Region

All things have their place,
Knew we how to place them . . .

— GEORGE HERBERT

"Can you imagine what it would be like if there were no places in the world? None whatsoever! An utter, placeless void!" With a ghastly opening such as this, Edward Casey's *Getting Back into Place* could be taken here as an exemplary case of a more general, maybe epochal commitment to restore the category of place at the core of intellectual reflection.[1] Place, as its author reminds us, is our ontological origin: " 'life-stories' have a geography too," Edward Soja had already declared in 1989, thus inaugurating a new epoch with his *Postmodern Geographies*.[2] For Casey, place is the origin of our thought as well: thinking, like being,

1. Edward S. Casey, *Getting Back into Place: Toward a Renewed Understanding of the Place-World* (Bloomington: Indiana University Press, 1993), ix.
2. Edward W. Soja, *Postmodern Geographies: The Reassertion of Space in Critical Social Theory* (London: Verso, 1989), 14.

1

can hardly happen in a void. That is why "the prospect of no-place is dismaying," and why for Casey the neglect of place from traditional theoretical speculations is appalling. Thank God, and despite such neglect, places *do* exist: in fact, they have even begun to abound in today's discussions, to the point that it is hard to remember any such interest on the topic after at least Heidegger — perhaps even Kant.

The book that begins here intends to look with a somewhat colder eye at the "return to place" that characterizes so much of our contemporary theory. It eludes one question — What can we gain from a return to place? — that many, today, seem quite eager to answer. It entertains, instead, another: What have we lost by our "getting back to place"?

What we have lost, to begin with, is a *historical* perspective. Place, as much as we see its theorists claiming to the contrary, is fundamentally a negation of history. To claim that culture springs from a place means, after all, to naturalize a process of historical formation, and along with history to negate the historical forces, struggles, and tensions that made a culture what it is.

The discourse of place, to put it differently, attempts to substitute a latently ideological tool of analysis — history — with an allegedly natural one — place. If history, as described by a classic fruit of nineteenth-century historicism such as the *Communist Manifesto*, "is the history of class struggles"; and if history, as Walter Benjamin adds, is the "tool" of whichever class is the "victor" and the barbaric silencing of the other,[3] — then "place" serves a fictional objective. It is a fiction that there is no victor at all, that a plurality of stories coexist in space, and that writing *of* "places" is the writing *from* a place of freedom. Yet, as Lefebvre remarks:

> What is happening here is that a powerful ideological tendency . . . is expressing, in an admirably unconscious manner, those dominant ideas which are perforce the ideas of the dominant class. To some degree, perhaps, these ideas are deformed or diverted in the process, but the net result is that a particular 'theoretical practice' produces a *mental space* which is apparently, but only apparently, extra-ideological.[4]

3. Karl Marx and Friedrich Engels, *The Communist Manifesto* (Harmondsworth, Eng.: Penguin, 1985), 79; Walter Benjamin, "Theses on the Philosophy of History," in *Illuminations*, trans. Harry Zohn (New York: Schocken Books, 1969), 255.

4. Henri Lefebvre, *The Production of Space*, trans. Donald Nicholson-Smith (1991; reprint, Oxford: Blackwell, 1995), 6.

The theoretical compulsion to put all cultures, so to speak, in their place *seems* to service the multicultural utopia of a coexistence of different cultures. What this contiguous arrangement of cultures in space actually does, instead, is to bracket away the very question of hegemony — the historical process whereby one culture acquires authority over all others and puts them "in order."

The general objective of this book, then, is not simply to denounce the latent ideological construction of "place" but also to question the epistemological validity of "place" as a category of cultural understanding. Can place ever recover the silenced cultures of "marginality" if it loses sight of the very historical reasons — barbaric reasons, no doubt — that made such cultures marginal in the first place? Or does it not risk to naturalize the very drama of their marginalization? It is from such a perspective that this book suggests that an epistemology of place is possible only from the place of Benjamin's "victor" — and as an occultation, precisely, of the barbaric history that has led to the victory.

My focus will be, primarily, literature. In the questioning of traditional aesthetic values once mistaken as universal, literary theory has also rediscovered the new episteme of place — and, along with it, what Homi Bhabha has called the "location of culture."[5] If the old modernist intellectual, fundamentally a *deraciné*, saw literature as a "strategy of permanent exile" and fundamental displacement — *ostranenie* in Shklovsky's formulation, *atopie* in Barthes's[6] — the new intellectual rather likes to pose as a topologist: S / he speaks *from* one specific place of cultural production, and *about* a localized "geography of the imagination"[7] within whose borders a given literary utterance may remain significant, relevant, and even intelligible. "Positionality"[8] — you might have heard of it — is the magic word, and you'd better take it literally.

Exemplary of this reaction against an "old" a-topic literature, and rep-

5. Homi K. Bhabha, *The Location of Culture* (London: Routledge, 1994).

6. George Steiner, *Extraterritorial* (New York: Atheneum, 1971); Viktor Shklovsky, "Art as Technique," in *Russian Formalist Criticism: Four Essays*, trans. Lee T. Lemon and Marian J. Reis (Lincoln: University of Nebraska Press, 1965); Roland Barthes, *Roland Barthes Par Roland Barthes* (Paris: Éditions du Seuil, 1975).

7. Guy Davenport, *The Geography of the Imagination* (Berkeley: North Point Press, 1981), 269–270.

8. Michael Awkward, *Negotiating Difference: Race, Gender, and the Politics of Positionality* (Chicago: Chicago University Press, 1995).

resentative of the "new" culture of place, regional literature is a most illustrious protagonist of this *fin de siècle* project of localizing the aesthetic. Revived by the frenzy of the *Europe des règions* and by the fear of placelessness brought about by an incipient globalization,[9] regionalism is not only a kind of "literature 'set in' or 'about' places";[10] it is, furthermore, an attempt to find a *new* place from which to study literature, and from which to engender a different, "changed ecology"[11] of cultural production. The challenge to an "old ecology," implicit in the generalized requests for a change, has also issued from a disciplinary crisis: distrustful of the concept of "nationalism," criticism must now rethink the whole of the humanities in a frame other than the traditional nineteenth-century model of national literature. Regionalism, in this sense, offers a new place from which to conceive a new literature — or, as W. H. New remarks (and isn't it true that *nomina numina sunt*, after all?), it provides "a more appropriate frame within which to read literature than . . . nationalism."[12]

Nationalism, as Edward Said tells us, is "an act of geographical violence." Against the superimposition of the unified map of the nation on all kinds of internal differences, "concrete geographical identity" ought now to be restored.[13] Following closely this postcolonialist principle, regionalism, too, begins from the assumption that "nationalism is a political imposition on art . . . which, deriving from a nineteenth-century notion of national 'identity,' cultivates a notion of cultural unity . . . which is scarcely people's actual political experience."[14] Against such ideas of cultural unity, regionalism thus promises a novel critical framework striving to comprehend all "social variations affected by economics, gender, race, creed, region, and so on [which] have their effects upon language and hence upon the voice and structure of literature."[15] As nationalist "Grand

9. See Marc Augé, *Non-Places: Introduction to an Anthropology of Supermodernity*, trans. John Howe (London: Verso, 1995).

10. Raymond Williams, "Region and Class in the Novel," *The Uses of Fiction: Essays on the Modern Novel in Honour of Arnold Kettle*, ed. Douglas Jefferson and Martin Graham (Milton Keynes, Eng.: Open University Press, 1982), 59.

11. Edward W. Said, "Yeats and Decolonization," *Dia Art Foundation: Discussions in Contemporary Culture. Remaking History* 4 (1989).

12. W. H. New, "Beyond Nationalism: On Regionalism," *World Literature in English* 23.1 (1984): 13.

13. Said, "Yeats and Decolonization," 10–11.

14. New, "Beyond Nationalism," 13.

15. New, "Beyond Nationalism," 13–14.

Narratives"[16] are no longer capable of accounting for the diversities of such modes of cultural identification as class, gender, or race, a "regional" outlook at the very "structure of literature" remains the only alternative to the "imposed" cultural unity of national literature.

Borrowing the language and analytic tools of postcolonial discourse, regionalism thus depicts itself as some kind of liberation front busy to set marginal and vernacular cultures free from an all-equalizing nation. In the introduction to the volume *Stories from the New Europe*, the editor Scott Walker, for instance, cheerfully welcomes the "blossoming . . . [of] regional identities" throughout the old continent and calls for a resistance to "political pressures to unify [local realities] under artificial boundaries [i.e., the nation-state]."[17] "Artificial boundaries," "political pressures," "political imposition," and a sense of "imposed national 'identity'" — all these are the burdens of an old cultural ecology centered on the nation. Against it, regionalism will decolonize the place of literature and recover residual forms of cultural identity ready to resurface in what Jules Chametzky has called "our decentralized literature."[18]

The regionalist co-optation of postcolonial theory may, from its very outset, make us a little suspicious. As Paolo Fadda has noted, in the arbitrary translation of specific colonial experiences into the postindustrial situation of the West, what remains of "postcolonialism" is merely a rhetorical apparatus of antinationalist tropes — the rhetoric, indeed, of regionalism.[19] It is often the case that the flag of regionalism is impugned in the West not by the exploited regions, which in fact need to rely on welfare measures provided by the nation-state, but by the exploiting ones, which would rather do away with the costs of welfare. After the Italian Lombard League presented its project of "strong regionalism," proposing that Italy be divided into nine regions, Alfredo Pasini, mayor of the League in the city of Pordenone, was asked to comment on his leader's incitements to secession. The leader of the League, Umberto Bossi, had just ar-

---

16. Jean François Lyotard, *The Postmodern Condition: A Report on Knowledge*, trans. Geoff Bennington and Brian Massumi (Manchester, Eng.: Manchester University Press, 1984).

17. Scott Walker, ed., *The Graywolf Annual Nine: Stories from the New Europe* (St. Paul, Minn.: Graywolf Press, 1992), ix.

18. Jules Chametzky, *Our Decentralized Literature: Cultural Meditations in Selected Jewish and Southern Writers* (Amherst: University of Massachusetts Press, 1986).

19. Paolo Fadda, "La retorica dell'autonomia," *l'Unione Sarda* (1 settembre 1995).

gued for the possibility of "taking arms" against "colonial Rome" and the "Italian justice" (and of not paying taxes) with words that sounded more proper to a war of colonial liberation than to Italian parliamentary politics. Pasini's disarmingly candid answer was that "sometimes Bossi exaggerates with his provocations, but this is part of a marketing operation [*operazione di marketing*]."[20] It might in fact be nothing but a rhetorical, or marketing, operation to paint the economically privileged regions of the Italian northeast with the postcolonial colors of the exploited victim of colonization!

Historically, it was a region of such economic privilege — the industrialized Basque region of Spain — that imported the discourse of postcolonialism into regionalist grounds. The theory of "oppositional regionalism" was developed in Frederico Krutwig's *Vasconia* (1962) under the direct influence of the decolonization process engaged in by Cuba. Krutwig's suggestion was that because Cuba had seceded from the Spanish Empire, the very notion of Spain as an essential unity was then put into question. He concluded that the Basque "countries," too, once considered as part of an indivisible Spain, could now be considered as "colonies" whose fight against Spain was somewhat legitimated by the Cuban successful secession.[21] The basic assumption of the "internal colonization" theory, which from "oppositional regionalism" has started to inform regionalism *tout court*, is that within a nation there exist distinct (ethnic) groups — with specific traditions, languages, and cultures — colonized by and subjected to the power of a centralized state.

Whereas nationalism remains perceived today as the "political imposition" of what Benedict Anderson has called an "imagined totality,"[22] re-

20. Alfredo Pasini, interviewed in Guido Passalacqua, " 'Umberto, frena sul razzismo,' " *La repubblica* (30 aprile 1997): 7.

21. See Marianne Heiberg, "Urban Politics and Rural Culture: Basque Nationalism," in *The Politics of Territorial Identity*, ed. Stein Rokkan and Derek W. Urwin (London: Sage Publications, 1982). For the application of "internal colonization theory" in France, see Robert Lafont, *La revendication occitane* (Paris: Flammarion, 1973); and M. Hechter, *Internal Colonialism: The Celtic Fringe in British National Development* (London: Routledge & Kegan Paul, 1975). See also John Loughlin, "Regionalism and Ethnic Nationalism in France," in *Centre-Periphery Relations in Western Europe*, ed. Yves Mény and Vincent Wright (London: George Allen & Unwin, 1985), 222.

22. Benedict Anderson, *Imagined Communities: Reflections on the Origin and Spread of Nationalism* (London: Verso, 1983).

gionalism rises as an alternative to such imagined — let alone imposed — "colonial" identity. Yet, if nations are inventions, and their unity is, as the saying goes, "artificial,"[23] are we to assume that regionalism could offer instead a more "natural" collective identity than nationalism? A naive form of regionalism relies, in fact, on the alleged "existence of a local unitary group" — a group that can be defined clearly in terms of space, place, and region.[24] As Lucio Gambi points out, this sort of regionalism takes for granted that "those who inhabit a certain place" also share a sense of "homogeneity, and therefore cultural and economic identity."[25] The question is obvious: How is this homogenized notion of regionalism, different from that of nationalism, to take into account the way in which as many variables as "gender, creed, race, class, and so on [affect] the structure of literature"? Does not the very idea of "region" impose, as Werner Sollors notes, a "homogenization . . . of the investigated region itself"?[26]

At any rate, these sorts of questions, however pertinent, threaten to obscure an even more essential one: What is regionalism? Or, for that matter, as W. J. Keuth puts it: "What is a region? This is the fundamental question, and an obvious place to begin is with dictionary definition. Here, however, the *Oxford English Dictionary* proves somewhat unhelpful. . . . The relevant definitions are disappointingly vague at the edges."[27] As a matter of fact, a dictionary, in the specific circumstances, may prove quite useless: etymology tells us that "region" is a jurisdiction (or regimentation) of the king — *regis* in Latin. Not very helpful. Worse, there are *climatic* regions

23. Giovanni Rombai, "L'Italia come espressione geografica. Stato e autonomie locali dopo l'unificazione nazionale," in *La chioma della vittoria. Scritti sull'identità degli Italiani dall'Unità alla seconda Repubblica*, ed. Sergio Bertelli (Firenze: Ponte alle Grazie, 1997), 48.

24. Massimo Severo Giannini, "Il riassetto dei poteri locali," *Rivista trimestrale di diritto pubblico* 21 (1971): 454–455.

25. Lucio Gambi, "Le 'Regioni' negli Stati preunitari," in *Studi di storia medievale e moderna per Ernesto Sestan* (Firenze: Olschki, 1980), 885.

26. Werner Sollors, "The Ethics of Wholesome Provincialism," in *Beyond Ethnicity: Consent and Descent in American Culture* (New York: Oxford University Press, 1986), 177.

27. W. J. Keuth, *Regions of the Imagination: The Development of British Rural Fiction* (Toronto: University of Toronto Press, 1988), 3–4. "What is a region?" is of course a bit of a parodic use of Ernest Renan's Sorbonne lecture of 1882, "Qu'est-ce qu'une nation?" (in Homi K. Bhabha, ed., *Nation and Narration* [New York: Routledge, 1990], 8–22).

extending over entire continents, *cultural* regions limited to small areas, and *economic* regions that never coincide with administrative ones. Then there are *linguistic* regions, too, that group together — to make things more complicated — also noncontiguous areas. . . .

One would gladly come to terms with the limitations of a dictionary if geography could, at least, give us some hints as to what a "region" is. But not even geography, alas!, is spared this sense of puzzlement and confusion when it comments on the topic. A. Frémont writes: "In general, the region presents itself as a middle space, less extended than the nation and the great space of civilization, but wider than the social space of a group."[28] Less extended or wider, the confines of the region remain rather blurry. The borders of this "middle space" escape conceptualization. Its essence, between group and nation, seems vague altogether. What place is a region? Where does it lie? The borders of regions such as Bosnia-Herzegovina in the former Yugoslavia, or Trentino-Alto Adige in Italy, are not, after all, natural facts of the terrain that geography can discuss. They are, rather, contingent historical creations, ephemeral "inventions" themselves. Geography, too, is at a loss.

Amid this general perplexity, one must admit that literary theory at least has its own certitudes: whatever a region might be, regionalism remains a "better frame" than nationalism to understand literature. Eli Mandel articulates for us this passage from theoretical aporia to programmatic confidence: "The theoretical basis of literary regionalism is rather less firm than the historical . . . but a sense persists that writers work out of a locale or area, boundaries of some sort of defining sensibility."[29] Given the fleeting nature of its object, the theory of regionalism itself needs to be a little slack. Yet, one advantage immediately compensates for such inaccuracy: "a sense persists that writers work out of a locale or area." Mandel's "region," or, for that matter, the region of literary regionalism — which is reminiscent of the "phenomenological geography" of Carl Otwin Sauer and Yi-Fu Tuan and is indebted to the "ecological thinking" of Gregory Bateson — seems to be, from its very outset, a "complex integration of na-

28. A. Frémont, *La région, espace vécu* (Paris: Presses Universitaires de France, 1976), 138; translation mine.

29. Eli Mandel, "Writing West: On the Road to Wood Mountain," in *Another Time* (Erin, Ontario: Press Porcépic, 1977), 68.

ture and culture."[30] Artistic "sensibility" merges into a whole with its "locale or area" to form an ecosystem isolated from all external pressures. The inventions of nationalism, let alone the impositions of history and the pressures of politics, have undoubtedly been left out.

In partial agreement with David Jordan's suggestion that "the term 'regionalism' has been used recently in a metaphoric sense to allude to any marginalized 'space,'"[31] I, too, believe that regionalism is a rhetorical figure of difference and opposition. Yet, I think that this figure is only at a superficial level pointing to the "margin." Rather, regionalism remains primarily the metaphor of a desire for an original and free literariness that has survived the instrumental impositions of nationalism and politics alike. "Regional" is a pastoral sensibility untouched by the evils of history and sheltered from the latter within the "boundaries of some sort" of place. To put it bluntly, regionalism is the figure of an otherness that is, essentially, otherness *from*, and against, history.

A certain impulse to invent a better world outside of "history" and its most immediate signs of social decay seems quite proper to the pastoral as a genre.[32] The invention of the archaic *place* of the Golden Age, from Theocritus to Sidney, clearly denounces a sense of uneasiness in front of the perceived decadence brought about by the unfolding of time. Yet, in the sort of recuperation of place that is more proper to regionalism, the agon is directed no longer against a vague concept of "history" (understood as some sort of teleology of the Fall) but rather against the more precise epistemological horizon of historicism. At the same moment that the rhetorical tradition of the pastoral is recuperated in the rustic depictions of "a beautiful relation between rich and poor,"[33] historicism — the idea that

30. E. Relph, *Place and Placelessness* (London: Pion, 1976), 3; see also Carl Otwin Sauer, *Land and Life: A Selection from the Writings of Carl Otwin Sauer*, ed. John Leighly (Berkeley: University of California Press, 1965); Yi-Fu Tuan, *Space and Place: The Pespective of Experience* (1977; reprint, Minneapolis: University of Minnesota Press, 1989); and Gregory Bateson, *Mind and Nature: A Necessary Unity* (New York: Dutton, 1979).

31. David M. Jordan, *New World Regionalism: Literature in the Americas* (Toronto: University of Toronto Press, 1994), 9.

32. Harry Levin, *The Myth of the Golden Age in the Renaissance* (Bloomington: Indiana University Press, 1969).

33. William Empson, *Some Versions of Pastoral*, 3d ed. (1935; reprint, London: Hogarth Press, 1986), 11.

cultures have a limited historical life — is replaced by the naturalizing — and eternalizing — idea that cultures are bound to, and sheltered by, their "place."

This agon against history should not pass unnoticed here. New's assertion, quoted above, that nationalism derives "from a nineteenth-century notion of national 'identity'," and Scott Walker's remark that "over half of all nations were formed in the past forty years,"[34] sound like eager attempts to pin down nationalism and national literature to a historical accident. It might not be mere chance that such eagerness forgets to see regional literature also as a historical invention: regionalism, the new science of "a locale or area," might be "less firm" than history but is certainly above it. Regionalism is, in fact, the metaphor of a pure origin so indifferent to and defiant of historical accidents as to show, in Walker's words, "an amazing resilience in the face of a long history of military and / or political repression."[35]

Long live regionalism! What we are handling is a figure *standing for* an immanence that historical events can at best hide behind some "inventions" but that remains everlastingly alive and there — in the place. The figure of a "resilient" origin surviving the impositions of history seems in fact not at all a new one in the discourse of regionalism. Already John Crowe Ransom, writing his seminal essay "The Aesthetic of Regionalism" in the Thirties, could recall his regionalist illumination, occasioned by a visit at the Indian Pueblo of Albuquerque, in the unmistakable rhetoric of resilience:

> So this was regionalism; flourishing on the meanest capital, surviving stubbornly, and brilliantly. In the face of the efforts of the insidious white missions and the aggressive government schools to "enlighten" these Indian people, their culture persists, though in the most part it goes back to the Stone Age, and they live as they always have lived.[36]

Fifty years later, Jim Wayne Miller in his "Outlook for Regional Studies" would go back in time — if not to the Stone Age — to maintain that regionalism is "part of our past, but it is also part of our future — and it of-

---

34. Walker, *Graywolf Annual Nine*, x.
35. Walker, *Graywolf Annual Nine*, x.
36. John Crowe Ransom, "The Aesthetic of Regionalism," in *Selected Essays of John Crowe Ransom*, ed. Thomas Daniel Young and John Hindle (Baton Rouge: Louisiana State University Press, 1984), 45.

fers a much needed vision of life in the country and in the globe."[37] The fact that regionalism is not part of our *present* might be a symptom of its metaphoric essence: as a desire, regionalism is a hypothesis of what *could* have existed and *could* be realized again in the future. As such, regionalism tightly fits the figure, contiguous to metaphor, that Derrida calls *differance*: because the "region" *is* not, it always defers itself to a hypothetical future that is the coming back of an original past — the realization, in other words, of what it was always supposed to be.

Resilience, persistence, stubborn survival of modes of living "*always lived*": these are the features of our metaphoric regionalism. Neither the colonial "insidious" work of the white missions nor the historical "aggressiveness" of government schools can ever bend this desire for a pure region. To draw my conclusion from David Jordan's suggestion, I would say that "regionalism" is a figural reading of a literary text, interpreted *as if* it were the expression of a sensibility bounded to the local, and therefore set free from historical and political impositions. Grafted on the usually realistic surface[38] of the kind of literature it privileges, regionalism grows on it as an allegorical branch that supplements the naturalistic description with a symbolic and moral vision (the "much needed vision" of what *could* be) of suprahistorical freedom.

37. Jim Wayne Miller, "Anytime the Ground Is Uneven: The Outlook for Regional Studies and What to Look Out For," in *Geography and Literature: A Meeting of the Disciplines*, ed. William E. Mallory and Paul Simpson-Housley (Syracuse, N.Y.: Syracuse University Press, 1987), 11.

38. "Regional literature is generally realistic" for Karl Beckson and Arthur Ganz, authors of *Literary Terms: A Dictionary* (New York: Farrar, Straus and Giroux, 1975). From a slightly different perspective, Perosa looks at regionalism as a "danger" of realism: "Ontologically speaking, regionalism is a condition, and often a danger, of any radical realistic approach. If a writer had to write of what he knew and had experienced, more often than not he would have to rely on — and be bound by — his immediate surroundings, what he had experienced in depth rather than in geographical extension. If in realistic portraiture the use of imagination was barred and lifelikeness extolled, then all chances were rather restricted to one's own soil and one's region, to one's particular geographical and social environment. This tendency to 'narrowness' of scope was implicit — as a feature, I insist, as much as a danger — in most theories of realism and certainly in the practice of the realistic novel: from Giovanni Verga to Alphonse Daudet and Pierre Loti, from Flaubert to Galdós or Valdés." In Sergio Perosa, "Genteel Realism and Regionalism," in *American Theories of the Novel: 1793–1903* (New York: New York University Press, 1985), 158.

Take Jonathan Bate's *Wordsworth and the Environmental Tradition* as an example. Here is what Geoffrey Hartman writes on the backcover blurb:

> Bate displays the fundamentals in Wordsworth's poetry of place, including that peculiar emphasis on locality inherited by, among others, Thomas Hardy, Edward Thomas and Seamus Heaney. Honoring English poetry's turn from history to community and geography, Bate questions the claims of the new historicism; and he does so by close reading rather than polemics, and without falling back into pietistic clichés about Englishness.[39]

Foundations, inheritances, traditions — these are the terms of continuity that stubbornly resist the much celebrated "breaks" of history. New historicism, with its insistence on Wordsworth's sympathies for the French Revolution, has reduced literature to a puppet of history. Literature has lost its freedom and its identity. Whatever history has lost, however, a "peculiar emphasis on locality" will be able to recover: Walker's "resilience" of a regional identity, moderated here through the figure of a lasting "tradition," reconstructs a "sensibility" — in Mandel's terms — that grows from "place" to Wordsworth and stems from the latter to "Thomas Hardy, Edward Thomas and Seamus Heaney." It is an organic tradition, removed from history and capable of instituting a lost sense of "community."

The appeal to "community," in this skirmish against history, may be in itself historically significant, for it is when the myth of a literary community seems shattered by "polemics" that the need for a "common" understanding of literature is demanded — an idea, that is, of "literature as common place"[40] that the literature of place strives to accommodate. What

39. Jonathan Bate, *Romantic Ecology: Wordsworth and the Environmental Tradition* (London: Routledge, 1991). It might be too early to speak of a new "ecological" trend in literary studies, one whose explicit goal is that of substituting "green" politics for the "red" politics of new historicism. However, Karl Kroeber, *Ecological Literary Criticism: Romantic Imagining and the Biology of Mind* (New York: Columbia University Press, 1994), is one step forward in the establishment of such a trend. For the future, Garland Publishing of New York was planning to publish in 1997 *Literature and the Environment: An Encyclopedia* — a work justly "international and interdisciplinary in scope," given the general and ubiquitous revivals of New Age mysticisms, fantasias about the planet Earth, and sociobiological euphorias. The work, however, has not been published yet.

40. See, for instance, Rocco Ronchi, *Luogo comune. Verso un'etica della scrittura* (Milano: EGEA, 1996). Hartman himself had lamented, in the essay "Sign of the

is Beauty, what is Aesthetic, what is Culture, and what is Literature itself, today, when all such values, turned into the battlefield of politics, have been denounced by postcolonialists and new historians alike as the product of historical articulations and political negotiations? "Culture is a system of discriminations and evaluations," writes Said with Benjamin in mind, "for a particular class in the State able to identify with it." This means, among other things, that whatever has been predicated in the West as Literature, the Canon, the Great Books, or the World Classics, "represents only a fraction of the real human relationships and interactions now taking place in the world."[41] The palimpsest of Auerbach's "historism," according to which arts must be judged historically and "not by absolute rules of perfection" is still visible here.[42] Beyond this small fraction, a boundless number of other representations of human experience exist in the world and struggle against the Eurocentric assumptions of the Western world to affirm themselves. They press against the traditional borders of the discipline.

Against the anxiety thus created, and to give a positive answer to it, the *fin de siècle* notion of a "natural region" — the idea of place as a "fixed" background of human sensibility[43] — starts taking the shape of an "environmental tradition," of an "ecoliterature," or, more simply, of "regionalism." Within the boundaries of place, all the values that history has made relative and ephemeral are brought back to stable certainties. "Place," as Eudora Welty has written regarding precisely the regional novel, "has a more lasting identity";[44] and a lasting identity for literature, beyond the temporary "uses" that history has found in it, is granted by the tradition of

Times," that contemporary "[s]ociety is built up of tribes, communities and special interests. To bind them together it needs places, myths and heroes in common. The idea of a 'commonplace' is more concrete here than in the History of Ideas or Topoi." In Geoffrey H. Hartman, *The Fate of Reading and Other Essays* (Chicago: University of Chicago Press, 1985), 108.

41. Edward W. Said, *The World, the Text, and the Critic* (Cambridge: Harvard University Press, 1983), 21, 25.

42. Eric Auerbach, "Vico and Aesthetic Historism," in *Scenes from the Drama of European Literature* (Minneapolis: University of Minnesota Press, 1984), 184.

43. For the notion of "natural region," see L. Gallois, *Régions naturelles et noms de pays. Étude sur la région Parisienne* (Paris: Colin, 1908).

44. Eudora Welty, *The Eye of the Story: Selected Essays & Reviews* (New York: Vintage, 1990), 119.

place. The "turn from history to . . . geography" is therefore a true reevaluation of all values, a restoration akin to the passage from history to geography that Nietzsche had already imagined as the foundation for a hypothetical eternal return:

> History . . . is in general the doctrine of remedies (*Heilmittellehre*), but not the science of the cure itself (*Wissenschaft der Heilkunst*). . . . Through history, one can make room for [whatever was lost], and try to preserve [it]. . . . But along with this preservation of the spirit, humankind ought . . . to define . . . a medical geography (*eine medicinische Geographie*). . . . The entire earth will be, in the end, a sum of health centers (*Die ganze Erde wird endlich eine Summe von Gesundheits-Stationen sein*).[45]

In its inexorable progress, history can "make room" in its books for every lost certainty but can never return any to life. The insufficiency of history is its inflexibility, the fact that it records the past as something simply lost. An epoch and a certain understanding of literature seem, today, under attack, and the poetry of postcolonial England is exactly in the eye of the hurricane, threatened to be swept away by the winds of postcolonialism and new historicism alike. The goal posited by the literature of place is therefore an ethical one: to replace the "insufficient" historical remedy with the geographical cure — a cure that, without "pietistic clichés," will let a tradition survive and be honored, sheltered in the boundaries of place.

45. Friedrich Nietzsche, *Der Wanderer und sein Schatten* (Chemnitz, Germany: C. Stosseln, 1880), 109–10; translation mine. On the cruelty of history, see also the following: "We should wish to know, for example, how it would be possible to tolerate, and to justify, the sufferings and annihilation of so many peoples who suffer and are annihilated for the simple reason that their geographical situation sets them in the pathway of history. . . . [W]hen historical pressure no longer allows any escape, how can man tolerate the catastrophes and horrors of history — from collective deportations and massacres to atomic bombings — if behind them he can glimpse no sign, no transhistorical meaning; if they are only the blind play of economic, social, or political forces, or, even worse, only the result of the 'liberties' that a minority takes and exercises directly on the stage of universal history?" In Mircea Eliade, *The Myth of the Eternal Return: Or, Cosmos and History*, trans. Willard R. Trask (1954; Princeton, N.J.: Princeton University Press, 1974), 151. For a discussion of Eliade's opposition between history and the "place" of myth, see Furio Jesi, *Mito* (1973; reprint, Milano: Mondadori, 1980), 66–69.

In regionalism, after all, nothing is lost — all is displaced. All things have their place, and all places have their own tradition. Whereas history can accept no coexistence but only brutal selection — what, in a word, is called "hegemony" — the literature of place and region will transform the entire planet into a happy coexistence of different regional traditions, each valid in its "place." These traditions are left untouched by history. They will grow, resilient still, and still springing from the same old root. *Die ganze Erde wird endlich eine Summe von Gesundheits-Stationen sein.*

This survival of cultural identities against universal history means, first of all, that the region is a bounded space — in the etymological sense of an environment, an ambiance, a surrounding.[46] As the "boundaries of some sort" separate and shelter from the historical outside, symbols of purification, demarcation, and punishment of transgression abound in what is called the "regionalist novel." In Pagnol's *Jean de Florette*, for instance, it has become a ritual to spit at the door of whoever has left the region for the polluting "outside."[47] In Thomas Hardy's "A Tradition of Eighteen Hundred and Four" the perils represented by the historical outside are most admirably put: the arrival of the "Corsican ogre" Napoleon "Boney" Bonaparte in the regional "Wessex" threatens to annihilate a whole folk culture and supplant it with that very universal history that France was meant to embody. Luckily, Wessex, too, is a quite resilient region: "Boney's

46. See Leo Spitzer, "Milieu and Ambiance," *Philosophy and Phenomenological Research* 3 (1942–1943): 169–218.

47. " . . . les Testard, qui étaient aller piocher ailleurs une terre moins ingrate [que les Bastides], avaient ainsi diffamé le sol natal, et trahi l'honneur du village: quand on passait près des ruines de leur ferme, on crachait par terre." In Marcel Pagnol, *Jean de Florette* (Paris: Fallois, 1988), 58. On the tropology of purity and contamination, inside and outside, see Mary Douglas, *Purity and Danger: An Analysis of the Concepts of Pollution and Taboo* (New York: Routledge, 1966); and Gaston Bachelard, "The Dialectics of Outside and Inside," in *The Poetics of Space*, trans. Maria Jolas (Boston: Beacon, 1969). The new geographic imagination at work in regionalism often translates the dialectics between inside and outside in terms of rootedness versus unrootedness. The parallel notions of "existential insideness" and "existential outsideness" are developed in E. C. Relph, *Place and Placelessness* (London: Pion, 1976). An interesting "application" of Relph's terminology to the analysis of literary texts can be found in David Seamon, "Newcomers, Existential Outsiders and Insiders: Their Portrayal in Two Books by Doris Lessing," in *Humanistic Geography and Literature: Essays in the Experience of Place*, ed. Douglas C. D. Pocock (Totowa, N.J.: Barnes & Noble, 1981).

army never came, and a good job for me. . . . We coast-folk should have been cut down one and all, and I should not have sat here to tell this tale."[48]

This indifference to historical processes, this myth of resilience, and this isolation that prevents dialectics all separate regionalism, in the last analysis, from the postcolonial discourse that regionalism tries to imitate. In 1963, Fanon had justly remarked that "colonialism is separatist and regionalist," and that postcolonialism should then be "closely involved in the liquidation of regionalism."[49] Aimé Césaire's postcolonialist admonition that "We do not want to resuscitate a dead society. . . . What we do need is a new society"[50] — or Said's declared impossibility to restore an original "first map" preceding the colonial remapping — are all assertions radically different from the characteristically nostalgic tone of regionalism. What Césaire calls "new society" and Said calls "third map" entails, as Timothy Reiss suggests, the alchemy of Marxist dialectics and historical process — not the profoundly antihistorical return to a concept of identity bounded by that of place.[51]

Of course, regionalists and their sympathizers may claim that the picture I am providing of their "reading" is a rather caricatured one: no regionalist is so naive as to believe, really, in any "return"! Regionalism, says Kenneth Frampton, is not simple-minded:

> It is necessary to distinguish between Critical Regionalism and simple-minded attempts to revive the hypothetical forms of a lost vernacular. . . . Critical Regionalism . . . involves a more directly dialectical relation with nature than the more abstract, formal traditions of modern[ism].[52]

T. S. Eliot, in a similar "critical" mood, had observed that regionalism was not the attempt "to revive some language which is disappearing . . . or

48. Thomas Hardy, "A Tradition of Eighteen Hundred and Four," in *Wessex Tales* (Oxford: Oxford University Press, 1992), 38.

49. Frantz Fanon, *The Wretched of the Earth*, trans. Constance Farrington (New York: Grove, 1963), 94.

50. Aimé Césaire, *Discours sur le colonialisme* (Paris: Présence Africaine, 1989), 29; translation mine.

51. Timothy J. Reiss, "Mapping Identities: Literature, Nationalism, Colonialism," *American Literary History* 4.4 (Winter 1992).

52. Kenneth Frampton, "Towards a Critical Regionalism: Six Points for an Architecture of Resistance," in *The Anti-Aesthetic: Essays on Postmodern Culture*, ed. Hal Foster (Seattle: Bay Press, 1983), 21.

to revive customs of a bygone age which have lost all significance . . . or to obstruct the inevitable and accepted progress of mechanisation and large-scale industry." Rather, regionalism was for him the necessity "to grow a contemporary culture from the old roots."[53] What is striking, nonetheless, is the way in which in all regionalisms, critical or otherwise, dialectics is no longer the automaton of history that pits one force against another but rather a "relation with nature." If Critical Regionalism does not believe in a *revival* of "lost languages," it believes instead, in a quite uncritical way, in the *survival* of past traditions and "old roots" still available to a "contemporary culture." It believes in the possibility to return, in short, to a past idea of culture as *cultus*, of literature as the local crop of a regionalized *genius loci*. If this old root survives, it is because place is a bounded environment, and because no external, historical pressure has eradicated it. Yet, if it survives, it must be also because no *internal* challenge has ever arisen. The inside of a region is then envisioned as a homogenous whole — one that is not divided within. The dialectic of history, we are told, annihilates "marginal, subaltern," powerless cultures. Regionalism, instead, annihilates history. What is left for us to contemplate is only idyllic regions and their perfect communities.

The hankering for grounded, rooted, natural, authentic values shared by a true community is the leading motive of regionalism. Yet, where are these values "rooted"? On what can the figure we call "regionalism" ground its reading? On the region, of course! Of course, but as Raymond Williams asks, would "a novel 'set in' or 'about' the Home Counties, or 'set' in or 'about' London . . . be 'regional' in a way comparable to . . . similar novels 'set in' or 'about' the Lake District or South Devon or Wales?"[54] Would a text about the Parisian *banlieux* or the Tri-State area be "rooted" in anything we could call a "region"? Of course not! As Williams bluntly remarks, "Certain places are 'regions' . . . while certain other places are not."[55]

So, *which* places are regions? In what places do the losses of history return eternally the same? "Region" must be a peculiar place, if history does not rule within its province! How can whatever history has obliterated, in one form or another, be available to us still? The way regionalism answers

53. Thomas Stearns Eliot, "Notes Toward a Definition of Culture," *Christianity and Culture* (1948; reprint, San Diego: Harcourt Brace & Company, 1988), 125, 127.
54. Williams, "Region and Class," 60.
55. Williams, "Region and Class," 59.

this last question seems to share with Freud's *Civilization and Its Discontents* a little more than a concern for the unhappy civilization of today. In a page devoted to Rome, the "eternal city," Freud discusses the ways in which the past is preserved in some particular places:

> Historians tell us that the oldest Rome was the *Roma Quadrata*, a fenced settlement on the Palatine. Then followed the phase of the *Septimontium*, a federation of the settlements on the different hills; after that came the city bounded by the Servian wall; and later still, after all the transformations during the periods of the republic and the early Caesars, the city which the Emperor Aurelian surrounded with his walls. We will not follow the changes which the city went through any further, but we will ask ourselves how much a visitor, whom we will suppose to be equipped with the most complete historical and topographical knowledge, may still find left of these early stages in the Rome of to-day.[56]

What for the historian simply "was," and no longer is, becomes for Freud's hypothetical visitor, who supplements history with "topographical knowledge," something that one "may *still* find left" from the ruins and debris of the past. Topographical knowledge unearths what is ancient and buried, and brings it back from the soil to the life of the visitor: "Where the Coliseum now stands we could at the same time admire Nero's vanished Golden House. . . . This is the manner in which the past is preserved in historical sites like Rome." The example, for Freud, alludes to the suprahistorical horizon of psychoanalysis: what is buried in the unconscious of history can become apparent through the work of anamnesis operated by psychoanalysis. Yet, Freud's image of the psyche as a place where all historical epochs can *still* be admired, also hints for us at the place we call "region": here, in fact, a "resilient" past "is also part of our future" — as long, that is to say, as we supplement our historical loss with "topographical knowledge."

What can such "topographical knowledge" be if not a knowledge of rhetoric and its "places of memory"? As the Coliseum reminds Freud of Nero's times, so does the region remind us of life "always lived." Regions, such as Freud's "eternal city," are *loci* similar to the ones that Cicero put at

56. Sigmund Freud, *Civilization and Its Discontents*, trans. James Strachey (New York: Norton, 1961), 16–17.

the basis of his *ars memorativa*.[57] They remind of what historical memory has lost and yet continues to exist as symptom, as symbolic formation, as trace, or as metaphor. They are a supplement to memory — the "artificial" compensation, that is, of a rhetorical memory rooted in commonplaces. The region is then a topos, a place of argumentation from which the discourse of regionalism — the anamnesis of a traumatic loss — can begin.

This is a topos from where the new intellectual can reminisce the existence of a debonair sensibility that is "amazingly resilient," indeed, to all sorts of impositions. As "regionalism" is a figural reading, its *place* — the region — coincides with a rhetorical place, a locus, a τόπος, a commonplace. The region, in other words, is "the place in which arguments and demonstrations" about the existence of a cultural identity free from political impositions and from the unjust demands of history "are stored, and from which they can be retrieved" (Quintilian, *Institutio* Oratoria V.10.20). This commonplace belongs, rhetorically speaking, to the genus of the *locus amoenus*: it celebrates the beauties and blissful life of a preindustrial environment. It also fits in the variety of *laudatio temporis acti*. It argues fiercely against our unhappy civilization, against this polluted industrial present of ours, and longs for what "used to be." The postcolonialist synthesis of dialectics, in the meantime, disappears from the topography of regionalism. The art of topics has, in a Ciceronian way, replaced dialectics.[58]

Let us go back, for one moment, to Scott Walker's introduction to *Stories from the New Europe*. Here, we read of "the remarkable variety of European cultures, from the individual voices of the former Soviet Baltic states to the nuances of Croat / Serb . . . voices."[59] Of interest is that, while Walker was writing about the regionalist "nuances of Croat / Serb . . . voices," the genocide in the former Yugoslavia had already begun, and the

---

57. [Cicero], *Rhetorica ad Herennium*, trans. H. Caplan (Cambridge: Harvard University Press, 1954), III.xvii. On this topic, see also Paolo Rossi, "Che cosa abbiamo dimenticato sulla memoria?" in *Controversie nodi strumenti mappe. Percorsi di storia della scienza*, ed. Sandro Petruccioli (Napoli: Theoria, 1991), 5–18; and Bice Mortara Garavelli, *Manuale di retorica* (Milano: Bompiani, 1988), 283–285.

58. On the distinction between dialectics and topica, see Cicero, "Topica," in *De inventione; De optimo genere oratorum; topica*, trans. H. M. Hubbel (Cambridge: Harvard University Press, 1976), I.ii.6.

59. Walker, *Graywolf Annual Nine*, ix.

entire world was shocked to hear about what was already being called an ethnic cleansing. Yet, whatever could happen in Yugoslavia in those days hardly touched the rhetoric of regionalism, which sees only "nuances" and "blossomings" ("flourishing" was Ransom's term) where history might even witness blood. Historical facts are merely facts, whereas the beauties of ethnic pride and decentralization — ah!, those live and prosper quite elsewhere! They grow, in fact, in the idyllic and rhetorical soil of the region, where history has no saying, indeed. Commonplaces, after all, "because they are common [κοιναί] . . . seem to be true, since all as it were acknowledge them as such" (Aristotle, *Rhetoric*, II.xxi.11). And so the regionalist liberation of Croat and Serb voices *is* a "blossoming," since a rhetorical codification, as it were, acknowledges regionalist movements as such. Commonplaces are much more tenacious than facts. And so, all the regions felicitously blossom against political inventions, against historical repressions and national inventions, and flourish on the meanest capital, surviving stubbornly, and rebelling brilliantly: all the regions, as Shakespeare put it, do smilingly revolt, and who resist are mocked!

Against what, precisely, do all regions revolt? Against what do they claim their freedom? "Against nationalism," we are told. And yet, does regionalism differ, in any essential way, from nationalism? Thomas Crawford points out that, if one were to analyze the characteristics of nationalist discourse, one could see "that *all* its features necessarily apply to regions."[60] The same hypotheses of cultural homogeneity, and the same insistence on the unity of land and people, more often than not accompany both nationalist and regionalist claims. Gian Enrico Rusconi, too, singles out the regionalism of the Italian Lombard League, and more particularly its claim of a "Northern race," as "a mythopoietic operation in the same vein as the inventions that have forged the historical entities known as Nation-States."[61] Like nations, like the Northern Italian "region" of "Padania," says Rusconi. The League invents its own Celtic ancestry, different from an "Italian" ethnos. It invents its own anthem — Verdi's *Nabucco*, alas, once the battle cry of the Italian Risorgimento. And it also

60. Thomas Crawford, "The View from the North: Region and Nation in *The Silver Darlings* and *A Scots Quair*," in *The Literature of Region and Nation*, ed. R. P. Draper (New York: St. Martin's Press, 1989), 109.

61. Gian Enrico Rusconi, *Se cessiamo di essere una nazione. Tra etnodemocrazie regionali e cittadinanza europea* (Bologna: Il Mulino, 1993), 12.

needs its flag — the Celtic sun — its "Declaration of Independence," its "Constitution." The League launches its anathema against "the rhetoric of nationalism," but is its rhetoric of a "federation of regions" in any way different from it?[62]

The entire discussion on regionalism in the so-called "Europe of regions" does, in fact, point consistently at the difficulty of keeping the discourse of regionalism separate from that of nationalism. The INTEREG, the National Institute for Ethnic Rights and for Regionalism, explicitly proposed, in 1980, that regions be accorded not only the "right to secession" but also (or consequently) a right to constitute themselves as "nations." To the same direction were pointing the results of the seminar on minorities held at Ohrid, Yugoslavia, in the summer of 1974. Terms such as "minority" or "regional" — the seminar suggested — were vaguely discriminatory, if not at all derogatory. It was better to use a term such as "nationality"![63]

From a different perspective, Anne-Marie Thiesse, in a study of French regionalism at the turn of the century, also claims an essential relationship between the logic of region and that of nation. For Thiesse, it is at the very moment in which "France is no longer the dominant nation . . . and [can no longer] raise itself as a universal model" of modernity, that regionalism becomes increasingly fashionable as a way to repropose the classicist wonders of a premodern, true *francéité* based on the "cult of the land and its trditions."[64] Finally, the Basque region, whose "oppositional regionalism" I mentioned previously, also gave birth to a regionalist sensibility that bordered on the nationalistic claim that Vasconia was "the most 'Spanish' [region] in Spain" since it was "uncontaminated by either Jewish or Moorish blood."[65] What is, then, the difference between region and nation?

Can it be that "regionalism" is the metaphor of an old desire for authentic identity that nationalism, fallen in disrepute, can no longer repre-

62. Lega Lombarda, "A Brief History of the Northern League," http://www.geocities.com/CapitolHill/4162/ brief.htm (April 1997).

63. Commission des Communautés Européennes, *Les minorités linguistiques dans les pays de la communauté européenne* (Luxembourg: Office des publications officielles des Communautés Européennes, 1986), 31, 43.

64. Anne-Marie Thiesse, *Ecrire la France: Le mouvement littéraire régionaliste de langue française entre la Belle Epoque et la Libération* (Paris: Presses Universitaires de France, 1991), 13 ff.; translation mine.

65. Marianne Heiberg, "Urban Politics and Rural Culture: Basque Nationalism," in *The Politics of Territorial Identity*, ed. Rokkan and Urwin, 362.

sent? Can it be that regionalism is, in other words, just a nationalism without nations?[66] "Against cosmopolitan, universalizing tendencies that tend to impose the same abstract laws for all peoples," writes Chabod in *L'idea di nazione*, "'nation' means the sense of the individuality of a people, of respect for its own traditions, and a cult of its peculiarity."[67] It seems to me that regionalism answers the problems posed by a so-called "globalization" today with a return to a "sense of individuality" analogous to that used by nineteenth-century nationalism to answer the universalizing tendencies of French classicism. It might be too bad that, like nationalism, in order to justify itself, regionalism has to tend toward a sense of ethnic and cultural purity without which it could not even postulate a "region."

A "region," in fact, is the commonplace of an ethnic purity that the "nation" has lost since the times of industrial migrations. A region is, for instance, Wordsworth's Lake District, which, in the seventh book of the 1850 *Prelude* (vv. 211–229), offers an immediate alternative to the industrial city crowded by "the Italian," "the Jew," and

> The Swede, the Russian; from the genial south,
> the Frenchman and the Spaniard; from remote
> America, the Hunter-Indian; Moors,
> Malays, Lascars, the Tartar, the Chinese,
> And Negro Ladies in white muslin gowns.

Or else, a "region" is the Provence of Marcel Pagnol's *Jean de Florette*, so disdainful of the "stranger from outside"; or the Sicily of Gesualdo Bufalino, heroically resisting "the mixture of foreign bloods."[68] A "region" is, in other words, the commonplace of an organic community. It is a topos that is antithetical, from its very outset, to "the cities of the machine age," which, as Ransom had remarked, "are peculiarly debased . . . since the population is imported from any sources whatever; and therefore they are without a character."[69] In search of a shared communal identity, region is the rhetorical opposition to the modern city. It is the commonplace of what has never been debased by industry, capital, and, above all, immigra-

66. Alberto Melucci and Mario Diani, *Nazioni senza stato. I movimenti etnico-nazionali in occidente* (Milano: Feltrinelli, 1992).

67. Federico Chabod, *L'idea di nazione*, 3d ed. (1961; reprint, Bari: Laterza, 1979), 18.

68. Marcel Pagnol, *Jean de Florette* (Paris: Fallois, 1988), 33; Gesualdo Bufalino, *Saldi d'autunno* (Milano: Bompiani, 1990), 38.

69. Ransom, "The Aesthetic of Regionalism," 55.

tion — a topos that, significantly enough, can be found "in rural areas or small towns rather than [in] urban centers."[70]

One does not need to be particularly skeptical or suspicious by nature to fear that the old nationalistic dream of cultural unity, which regionalism promises to shatter, today finds in the rural areas of regionalism its sole possibility to survive. Whereas contemporary life and culture make us face the *pasticciaccio* — to use Gadda's expression[71] — of a multicultural Babel, regionalism concocts for us the pacifying, relaxing, New Age image of organic traditions and communities. Can it be that regionalism is merely the symptom of our present anxiety in facing a multicultural world? What could a rhetorical argument — regionalism — about the good old time of communal unity otherwise mean? Can it be mere chance that the "European Charter for Regional or Minority Languages," promoting its "principle of complete multilingualism," so blatantly excludes from such multilingual paradise whoever is not a "national of that [given] State"?[72]

The idea of place, I read recently, "is still a neglected and highly significant field for resistance and transformative interventions in social life. The

---

70. Beckson and Ganz, *Literary Terms*. The rural as a topos antithetical to "the strife of cities" is rhetorically at the foundation of such an epochal book as William Cobbett's 1830 *Rural Rides* (Harmondsworth: Penguin, 1983), 294. In regionalist discourse the figure of the "rural" often entails a reshaping of the countryside *to make it look like* a rustic arcadia. Industrially produced rustic furniture and wallpaper start decorating the rural summer villas of the urban bourgeoisie. Local artifacts are then supplanted by a new sense of rusticity manufactured in the city (see John Murdoch, "A Villa in Arcadia," in *Reading Landscape: Country-City-Capital*, ed. Simon Pugh [Manchester: Manchester University Press, 1990], 121–144). The indigenous artifact itself, if preserved, is reduced to pure commodity and becomes a self-referential icon, a *symbol* of the rural, a souvenir: "The indigenous human life of the countryside disappears in favor of the monument" (Simon Pugh, "Loitering with Intent: From Arcadia to the Arcades," *Reading Landscape*, 146).

71. The reference is to Carlo Emilio Gadda, *That Awful Mess in Via Merulana*, trans. William Weaver (New York: Braziller, 1965). The *pasticciaccio* — or "awful mess," in Weaver's translation — of this peculiar detective story is not so much the chain of crimes that officer Ciccio Ingravallo is called in to investigate: the real mess is the Babel of dialects within which Ingravallo has to move, while cross-examining the Roman populace (but also its bourgeoisie) of the Forties.

72. Tove Skutnabb-Kangas and Robert Phillipson, eds., "European Charter for Regional or Minority Languages," in *Linguistic Human Rights: Overcoming Linguistic Discrimination* (Berlin: Mouton de Gruyter, 1994), 383.

aim of 'resistance' is not revolution but the preservation of the potential for significant social change at a time of confused praxis and rapid restructuring" under the effects of so called "globalization."[73] Whereas the association of a literature of place with some sort of politics of resistance might not strike us as being particularly original — Edward Soja had already singled out in a reevaluation of space "the political challenge of the postmodern left"[74] — all the rest, including the peculiar mixture of a Marxist rhetoric of "praxis" with a conservative one of "preservation," should.

A few commentators have already advanced some fundamental objections to this sort of post-Marxist politics. Most notably, the Marxist geographers Neil Smith and Cindi Katz have described, in a penetrating essay entitled "Spatialized Politics," how "space" has improperly substituted "class" in a theory of postmodern agencies. As the notion of class is fragmented and questioned in the name of new "subject positions"[75] (race, gender, locality, etc.), the new intellectual, in an attempt to be organic to something, has started to see regions and localities as one last chance to be "engaged": "[t]he widespread appeal to spatial metaphors, in fact, appears to result from a radical questioning of all else, a decentering and destabilization of previously fixed realities and assumptions; space is largely exempted from such skeptical scrutiny."[76] Althusser's "regions of knowledge"; Deleuze's "marginal," "minor," and "deterritorialized" literatures; Foucault's "space of dissension";[77] and Soja's "space" have started to imag-

---

73. Rob Shields, "Spatial Stress and Resistance: Social Meanings of Spatialization," in Space & Social Theory: Interpreting Modernity and Postmodernity, ed. Georges Benko and Ulf Strohmayer (Oxford: Blackwell, 1997), 198.

74. Soja, Postmodern Geographies, 5.

75. See Ernesto Laclau and Chantal Mouffe, Hegemony and Socialist Strategy (London: Verso, 1985).

76. Neil Smith and Cindi Katz, "Grounding Metaphor: Toward a Spatialized Politics," in Place and the Politics of Identity, ed. Michael Keith and Steve Pile (London: Routledge, 1993), 80.

77. Louis Althusser, Reading Capital, trans. Ben Brewster (London: New Left Books, 1970), esp. 26; Gilles Deleuze and Felix Guattari, Kafka: Toward a Minor Literature, trans. Dana Polan (1986; reprint, Minneapolis: University of Minnesota Press, 1991); Michel Foucault, "Questions on Geography," in Power / Knowledge: Selected Interviews and Other Writings (1972–1977), ed. Colin Gordon (New York: Pantheon, 1980), esp. 69–70, 74, on the "problems of regional identity and its conflict with national identity"; Michel Foucault, The Archaeology of Knowledge, trans. A. M. Sheridan Smith (London: Tavistock, 1972), esp. 152.

ine places — some of them, at least — as "heterotopic" loci of resistance pitted against a central culture.

Although Soja has tried to describe space as a mere supplement to more traditional tools of Marxist analysis, the question remains of whether "place" and "class" can ever coexist as heuristic — let alone political — categories.[78] As T. S. Eliot once remarked:

> A man should have certain interests and sympathies in common with other men of the same local culture as against those of his own class elsewhere; and interest and sympathies in common with others of his class, irrespective of place.[79]

But can any interest of class continue to exist if the sense of locality prevails? Whereas Marxism explains difference as a dialectical relation of contrasting forces, regionalism understands difference as a metonymic contiguity of "places." "Regions," in other words, tend to solve class conflicts within their homogeneous organic identity of people and land: they suggest, if not a wholesome nation, at least a contiguity of wholesome communities, each integral in its place.

A painting such as Courbet's *Burial at Ornans* could be the proper emblem to this regional sense of community. Finished in so critical a year as 1849, just one year after the publication of the *Communist Manifesto*, the *Burial* gathers around a hole the entire social body of Ornans, a little village in the Franche-Comté region of France. It is a ritualistic communion: the justice of peace, the mayor, the priest, the villagers wearing the costumes of the veterans of 1793, the rich and the poor, are all silent symbols of a perfect community reinventing itself around an empty tomb. The Christological metaphor is unmistakable:[80] the region is the topos of a resurgent community. Outside of it, in the meantime, history rages with its strife and discords.

In fact, one does not need to revert to iconology to see how space may work against any interest of class. The Basque case, among all the historical variations on the theme of "oppositional regionalism," more clearly

78. See, for instance, Steve Pile, "Introduction: Opposition, Political Identities and Spaces of Resistance," in *Geographies of Resistance*, ed. Pile and Michael Keith (London: Routledge, 1997), 8.

79. Eliot, "Notes Toward a Definition of Culture," 133–134.

80. Robert Rosenblum and W. H. Janson, *19th-Century Art* (New York: Abrams, 1984), 223–224.

shows the irreconcilability of the two categories. The ETA (Euskadi Ta Askatasune [Basque Homeland and Freedom]), sprung from the internal divisions of the *Partido Nacionalista Vasco*, tried, in its original agenda, to couple Marxist and regionalist goals. The problem that the ETA soon faced, was that the Marxist model had necessarily to conflict with the regionalist one. Marxism divided society vertically into exploiters and exploited, whereas regionalism divided society into natives and foreigners. Indeed, the foreigners as a group coincided, at a most elementary Marxist analysis, with the very same exploited class: they were the laborers who came to the heavily industrialized center of Bilbao from the poorest and semifeudal Spanish provinces. Against them, the ETA soon dropped all pretensions of a Marxist program to concentrate instead on the regionalist questions of purity and autonomy.

Moving from Vasconia to Barcelona, we learn of an even more emblematic episode. May Day of 1892: by an instructive chronological destiny, the regionalist *fiesta catalanista*, to be held on the first Sunday of May, happens to fall on the same day as the *fiesta obrera*. As Laureano Bonet comments on it, the coincidence of two celebrations so symbolically charged did not result in a combination of the two. What happened, instead, was that the conservative press, trying to disrupt the socialist labor day, "fostered the feelings of an already strong *catalanismo*."[81] *Catalanismo*, in turn, made workers forget their *fiesta* and celebrate the ritual of regional communion *with* the local bourgeoisie.

That result goes to explain the distrust for regionalism expressed by a Marxist such as Antonio Gramsci:

> If the presupposition is to centralize what already exists, scattered and disseminated all over . . . it is obvious that an opposition in principle to such centralization is not rational. . . .[82]

Despite Soja's somehow awkward attempt to enlist Gramsci in a lineage of Marxist "geographers,"[83] Gramsci's distrust for any kind of regionalism — from that of the rustic *strapaese* to the linguistic one of the folklorists — was absolute and unbending. Had it not been a centrally pro-

---

81. Laureano Bonet, *Literatura, regionalismo y lucha de clases* (Barcelona: Publicaciones i ediciones de Universidad de Barcelona, 1983), 128.
82. Antonio Gramsci, *Grammatica e linguistica* (Roma: Editori Riuniti, 1993), 7.
83. Soja, *Postmodern Geographies*, 89–90.

duced sense of regionalist pride, after all, that once pitted the southern Sassari brigade, of fundamentally proletarian origin, against the workers on strike in northern Turin?[84]

Regionalism, for Gramsci, simply tends to bracket away the question of hegemony. As Soja reckons, "Regionalism can take on many different political and ideological forms, ranging from an acquiescent request for additional resources to an explosive attempt at secession."[85] Can it be mere chance that so many of the contemporary regionalisms — the emergence and multiplication of the *Leghe* in Italy seems to point at just that — are in fact requests for more privileges on the part of hegemonic regions? Is the notion of a hegemonic margin, after all, an unthinkable one?

The coupling of Marxism and regionalism seems, in truth, an untenable project. Yet, it is not mere chance, I believe, that the two terms are so often put together. The relation of regionalism and Marxism is not, in fact, an incidental one. Edward Soja, quoting Foucault, insists on a "nineteenth-century obsession with history" and, therefore, on a Marxist orthodoxy "dominated by a narrowed and streamlined historical materialism, stripped of its more geographically sensitive variants."[86] Against this orthodoxy, Soja proposes a "reformed" version of Marxism — what he calls the "politics of the postmodern left" — open instead to the question of space. The very basis of Soja's argument, however, is quite debatable. Along with the historicism of Marxist analysis, it could be easy to show how the nineteenth-century registers a coeval obsession with nothing else than place. Numerous similarities exist between the "boundaries of some sort" of recent regionalist theory and the return to the *genius loci* that compelled Victorian literature. And Jan Marsh's *Back to the Land* has already offered an engrossing catalogue of such similarities — from trekking and biking to all sorts of ecological anxieties.[87] Moreover, Robin Gilmour's suggestion that "the English regional novel was born in the 1840s" already points to an indisputable nineteenth-century concern with places and regions. On the nineteenth-century origin of a literature of

84. Antonio Gramsci, "Some Aspects of The Southern Question," in *Selections from Political Writings (1921–1926)*, ed. and trans. Quintin Hoare (1978; reprint, Minneapolis: University of Minnesota Press, 1990), 441–462.

85. Soja, *Postmodern Geographies*, 164.

86. Soja, *Postmodern Geographies*, 10, 31.

87. Jan Marsh, *Back to the Land: The Pastoral Impulse in England, from 1880 to 1914* (London: Quartet, 1982).

place and region, in fact, there seems to be general agreement: Raymond Williams, being "not sure when certain novels, or kind of novels, began to be called 'regional,'" is still confident enough to maintain that "the distinction began to be significant only in the late nineteenth-century." Richard Cobb, too, talks of the regional novel as of "a late nineteenth-century mode."[88] Both Cuddon's *Dictionary of Literary Terms and Literary Theory* and Beckson and Ganz's dictionary of *Literary Terms*, in the end, confidently hold on to a Victorian origin of regional literature. The obsession with places and regions — and so, also with tourism, map-making, and the like — *is* a nineteenth-century obsession, indeed.

The "region" — this peculiar topos that I have defined as both a *laudatio temporis acti* and a *locus amoenus* — is a commonplace that was originally set against a radically novel historical present that emerged with the British Industrial Revolution. What the Victorians called "the country," "the land," or simply "Merrie England" was not only the metaphor of a resistance against a nationalism often perceived as the destruction of old local privileges, or the supplement for the disappointment caused by a bleak industrialization centered on the new industrial city.[89] This commonplace was, also, a coeval alternative to a Marxist sense of history centered on the very notion of class conflict. The chronological coincidence of Marxism and regionalism — and, in a sense, also their *geographical* coincidence in the Victorian England of the Industrial Revolution — suggests only that they were both attempts to answer the same crisis of the bourgeois state. Their answers, however, were not only different: they were antithetical.

The kind of modern society inaugurated by the British Industrial Revolution is one that cannot maintain a sense of wholesome identity. England, in the 1840s, is fractured and divided. Orthodoxies fall apart. Marxism tries somehow to accelerate this historical process of decadence, and

88. Robin Gilmour, "Regional and Provincial in Victorian Literature," in *Literature of Region and Nation*, ed. Draper, 53; Raymond Williams, "Region and Class in the Novel," in *The Uses of Fiction: Essays on the Modern Novel in Honour of Arnold Kettle*, ed. Douglas Jefferson and Martin Graham (Milton Keynes, Eng.: Open University Press, 1982), 59; Richard Cobb, "Blood and Soil," in *Promenades: A Historian's Appreciation of Modern French Literature* (Oxford: Oxford University Press, 1980), 47.

89. In his "atlas" of the European novel, Franco Moretti points out that the late nineteenth-century topos of the dangerous, filthy, inhuman city refers in fact to the *English* city — notably the one of Dickens's novels — and not, say, the French city, which still preserves Balzac's connotation of "the place of desire." On this issue, see Franco Moretti, *Atlante del romanzo europeo. 1800–1900* (Torino: Einaudi, 1997), 104.

to radicalize class antagonism into the warfare of revolution. As Matthew Arnold puts it, the very idea of class tears England apart: "Well, then, what if we tried to rise above the idea of class to the idea of the whole community?"[90] The "region" of the Victorians becomes exactly the commonplace — a *locus amoenus*, indeed — in which the divisions of modern society are reconstituted into an archetypal, wholesome community. A book such as Elisabeth Gaskell's *North and South*, which is discussed in the second chapter of the present work, points out exactly this rhetorical replacement of "class" with "region" — and therefore of the reality of division with the rhetorical model of community. In this sense, the literature of place and region is not only irreconcilable with Marxism, despite Soja's more sincere efforts: it is, historically, antagonistic to it. The rhetoric of revolution, which seeks completely to destroy a society that is falling apart to make a wholly new one, is antagonized by a novel rhetorical apparatus — one of space — that aims to some sort of "resistance" that "is not revolution but . . . preservation." And whereas the discourse of revolution breaks the "old local and national seclusion and self-sufficiency" to create "from the numerous national and local literatures . . . a world literature," the discourse of place moves instead toward the regionalist restoration of localism centered on the celebration of the pastoral "idiocy of rural life."[91]

The central hypothesis of the *Capital* — that of history as the locus of irreconcilable dialectical differences that doom all social formations to their end — is therefore replaced by the understanding of space as a contiguous coexistence of differences. David Jordan's *Regionalism Reconsidered*, for instance, attributes to regionalism an "intuition" of difference "foreshadowing of Derridian deconstruction." Peculiarly enough, however, this sort of "difference" does not prevent that *within* a region Jordan singles out "a sense of identity and belonging that is shared by the region's inhabitants . . . [and which derives] from an intimate relation to the natural environment."[92] Pace Derrida, "difference" is cast by regionalism *outside* of the region's space, whereas its inside is reconstituted as an alleged whole. It is, in other words, as if difference for the regionalist were always

90. Matthew Arnold, *Culture and Anarchy*, ed. Samuel Lipman (New Haven, Conn.: Yale University Press, 1994), 64.

91. Marx and Engels, *Communist Manifesto*, 84.

92. David Jordan, Introduction, in *Regionalism Reconsidered: New Approaches to the Field*, ed. Jordan (New York: Garland Publishing, 1994), xi, xv–xvi.

somewhere else, always outside of his or her "place." In this "place," on the other hand, there is pastoral identity rather than class conflict. If history is moved by this clash of classes, identity entails, in turn, the very suspension of historical process and the return to a Golden Age of unity. Yet, one could say with Kenneth Burke in mind:

> Identification is affirmed with earnestness because there is division. Identification is compensatory to division. If men were not apart from one another, there would be no need for the rhetorician to proclaim their unity.[93]

The present work seeks to reconstruct a genealogy of the literature of place and region — the kind of literature, namely, erected on the commonplace of a perfect and communal living. This is the commonplace that occasions the figural reading we call regionalism — a reading culminating, in fact, in some sort of "pastoralization" of social divisions. I would like to insist, first of all, on the fact that regionalism is *not* a literary genre — a pastoral — but a way of reading. It is an attempt, in other words, to find an answer to the so-called "crisis of modernity" in a body of literary texts "pastoralized" exactly to offer such answers.

Beginning with an assertion of the importance of space — maps, plans, charts, geography, cartography — in the nineteenth century, the first chapter, on Thomas Hardy's *Return of the Native*, offers the emblem and archetype of such regionalist reading. Clym Yeobright, a sort of reformatory socialist himself, and a member in his own right of that "leisure class" that Thorstein Veblen describes in search of emotions and picturesqueness,[94] "reads" the map of his native village as if it were the locus of a perfect, communal coexistence. Clym is, allegorically, "blind" to the profound divide that exists, first of all, between himself and the villagers. He mistakes a terrible "region of darkness" for the felicitous topos of regional joys. The country, which he opposes to the city, is for him the commonplace of all the virtues that modern life has obliterated — just as Hardy's regional Wessex remains, in the "blind" reading of regionalism, a commonplace of all the virtues of the literature of place.

93. Kenneth Burke, *A Rhetoric of Motives* (1950; reprint, Berkeley: University of California Press, 1969), 23.

94. Thorstein Veblen, *The Theory of the Leisure Class* (1899; reprint, New York: A. M. Kelley, 1975); see also D. MacCannell, *The Tourist: A New Theory of the Leisure Class* (New York: Solouker Books, 1976).

Among all the "virtues" that Clym believes can be found in the region, one will acquire increasing relevance: this region is, in the age of chimneys and polluted cities, still propitious to art. Contrasting the fundamental ugliness and unliterariness of the modern city, the rustic region provides in fact a repository of "beautiful," classical, literary topoi — the trees, the idyllic sky, the bucolic work in the fields, the pastoral shepherd. In a way, the resilience of the region to the advance of history and progress is meant, in an allegorical way, to signify the desire for the survival of aesthetics in the epoch of pragmatic and technical reason. Following the historical rise of the cultural industry with its dailies and ephemeral entertainment, a certain humanistic culture, which Clym represents, seems to find in regionalism an outlet to an unprecedented anxiety — the fear of its cultural disappearance.

It is on the basis of this same anxiety that Elizabeth Gaskell's novel, *North and South*, is built. As I discuss in my second chapter, north and south are for Gaskell the commonplaces of, respectively, modern industrialization and "ancient" humanism. As the progressive "north" of this peculiar novel believes that commerce and industry can do well without literature, Gaskell proposes instead the indispensability of her regional south *for* the north's own sake. Only by learning the humanistic values that the south represents will the north escape the self-destruction that awaits it in the form of nothing less than class warfare. Literature — the ancient literature of a regional south — becomes a repository of rhetorical arguments for the invention, against Marxism, of a new communal identity.

In this context, my third chapter on D. H. Lawrence is the turning point in which the alleged virtues of a regional and archaic south, whose emblem Lawrence saw in Giovanni Verga's *oeuvre*, impose the necessity of translation. Lawrence's translation immediately poses the question of dialect — or of the "authenticity" of the dialect — in the regional novel. George Eliot, Thomas Hardy, and Elizabeth Gaskell had all faced this problem before, and had concluded that a "dialect in itself" was impossible to use because of the "great number of unfamiliar words" that would crop up in the text.[95] The obvious question is: unfamiliar for whom?

---

95. W. E. Axon's essay "George Eliot's Use of Dialect," quoted in *Thomas Hardy's Personal Writings: Prefaces, Literary Opinions, Reminiscences*, ed. Harold Orel (New York: St. Martin's Press, 1990), 93.

Although Lawrence devises quite a peculiar method for translating dialect — that is, he invents one anew — the fact remains that the dialect of the regional novel is *not* written (and are dialects ever *written*, or are they *translated* into writing?) for the region or for the community speaking the dialect in question. Rather, it is written for a general, "central" public — in this case, for a public of British readers. What emerges already from Gaskell, and acquires central importance with Lawrence, is the therapeutic relevance of the "region": it cures the malaise of the modern "north." This therapeutic value becomes increasingly explicit in Lawrence: the translation, so to speak, of the region, suggests only that such regions exist, after all, for the sake of a "center." As a matter of fact, can regionalism *ever* exist without translation — without the perspective of otherness that translation creates? Is translation a possibility of regionalism, or is it its inner necessity? Are not regions, quite literally, a translation of "central" desires into an imagined periphery?

With both Lawrence and Gaskell, the topos of "region" coincides with an ancient, archaic, premodern, agricultural south. Whereas the north is the topos of modernity, the south becomes the commonplace of a somewhat regressive alternative to the crisis of modernity — an origin of sorts. Inasmuch as fascism itself can be understood as a historical attempt to find an answer to such crisis,[96] it is important for me to end this book with it. In the fourth chapter, on Giovannni Gentile, we will see Italian fascism from exactly a southern perspective. Like regionalism, Italian fascism tries to find solutions to an irreducible social conflict — what was called a "European civil war" — in an alternative way to communism. Whereas the latter opts for the internationalization of the proletariat and the transcendence of social conflict into a further revolutionary conflict, fascism promotes a localism of blood and soil that pacifies social conflict through the idea of *Volkgemeinschaft*. For Gentile, the topos of such communal essence of the national spirit is, exactly, the "south" — a south, however, that becomes somehow immanent. Localism and nationalism, regionalism and Europeism, are synthesized in Gentile's philosophy of fascism. In his peculiar dialectical regionalism is not the (Hegelian) antithesis *opposed* to the given of nationalism, but the epiphany of the same totalitarian logic

96. Salvatore Natoli, "Il fascismo di Gentile e 'la guerra civile europea,'" in *Giovanni Gentile filosofo europea* (Torino: Bollati Boringhieri, 1989), 54–89.

that appears, again and again, in all particular aspects and "regions" of our experience.

The last chapter of this book returns to the questions of fascism, regionalism, and the crisis of modernity to look at them from a different angle. It is centered on Heidegger's question: "Why do we live in the province?" Heidegger's "province," like the regionalist's "region" or "place,"

> places the uniqueness of man in that dimension where any adjectival qualification, such as political, social, or economic, is the description of only one aspect of his being, leaving the depths of the vertical dimension untouched and excluded.[97]

Reduced to mere "adjectival qualifications," politics, society, and economy leave the "vertical" relation between "man" and place "untouched." Place is, in other words, the place of freedom from the contingent impositions — and crises — of what we have come to know as history. It is the transcendental value — hence its "verticality" — that defines humankind in its authentic essence, and defines a community in its organic identity. This is, after all, the reactionary trait of the literature of place: it tries to take the question of identity away from the space of politics — away from the space of negotiation. It imposes identity as a rooted absolute, and fosters what Adorno called a "jargon of authenticity"[98] — but this time against itself, and against its own passionate affirmation of multicultural peace and harmony.

97. Jean T. Wilde and William Kluback, "An Ontological Consideration of 'Place,'" in Martin Heidegger, *The Question of Being*, ed. Wilde and Kluback (New Haven, Conn.: College & University Press, 1958), 19.

98. Theodor W. Adorno, *Jargon der Eigentlichkeit: zur deutschen Ideologie / The Jargon of Authenticity*, trans. Knut Tarnowski and Frederic Will (Evanston, Ill.: Northwestern University Press, 1973).

Mapping the Country

Thomas Hardy and the Return of Topography

> The men who dwell in the city are my teachers, and not the trees
> or the country. Though I do indeed believe that you have found
> a spell with which to draw me out of the city into the country,
> like a hungry cow before whom a bough or a bunch of fruit is
> waved.
>
> — PLATO, *Phaedrus*

The year 1826 was a glorious one — or so cartographers like to think.[1] In that *annus mirabilis*, while the forces of the Bourbon restoration were clamoring the failure of the Napoleonic dream, cartographer Charles Dupin gave back a sense of hope to his colleagues around the world. On November 30, delivering a speech on the relation between literacy and economic prosperity to the *Conservatoire des Arts et des Métiers* in Paris,

---

1. For instance, François de Dainville, *La cartographie reflet de l'histoire* (Genève: Slatkine, 1986), 153 ff. Dainville dates Dupin's map to 1819, following the apparently erroneous indications of H. G. Funkhouser, "Historical Development of the Graphical Representation of Statistical Data," *Osiris* 3 (1938): 300.

Dupin pulled out, like a rabbit from a magician's hat, a rather peculiar map. Apart from presenting a generic outline of France, the map, contrary to what one would expect a map to do, carried little or no information about the environment. No rivers or lakes, no valleys or mountains, no cities or towns were visible in the "Map of Illiteracy in France," but only shades of grays dividing France into what geographers would have called, *faute de mieux* — "conceptual regions." These regions represented the result of Dupin's statistical studies on literacy and wealth: the lighter the color of the region, Dupin explained, the higher the level of education of its people; the darker, the gloomier its ignorance. The numbers indicated the wealth produced in each "region."

As Dupin stood silent and the map became the center of attention and awe, his point came across poignant and clear: the darker the region, the lower the number! As the story goes, there Dupin rested his case. And while the public, puzzled, pondered the implications of Dupin's argument — does wealth produce education, or is it the other way around? — the "Map of Illiteracy" became reason enough for — at least — cartographic optimism. To make a long chapter in the history of cartography short, Dupin lifted the art of mapmaking to its higher, more pious vocation. Ending the age in which maps were the product of prosaic minds employed to the servile representation of the "body of the king,"[2] Dupin claimed the autonomy of geography from any power but its own. Not only did the land cease to dictate the content of the map, but even the king could no longer impose on the map the signs of his control of the territory, these being counties, districts, precincts, municipalities, and boroughs. Neither mimetic of nature, nor representative of the constituted political order, Dupin's "regions" were the articulation, on a map, of nothing less than a concept: wealth rewards education, and vice versa. The goal of geography was not to represent but to *conceive* a discourse — one, for instance, about the correlation of culture and cash. The logic of the map, accordingly, was no longer mimetic but formal — like that of narrative, or of rhetorical discourse. In what ways, for instance, does the "Slave Population of the Southern States" map (Figure 1), produced by the Washington Census in 1861, "Sold to the benefit of the sick and wounded soldiers," and executed in the very light-and-dark technique of the "Map of Illiteracy,"

2. The expression, which considers mapping as the illustration of political power's extension and dominion on the territory, is Vauban's and is quoted in François de Dainville, *Le langage des géographes* (Paris: Picard, 1964), 160.

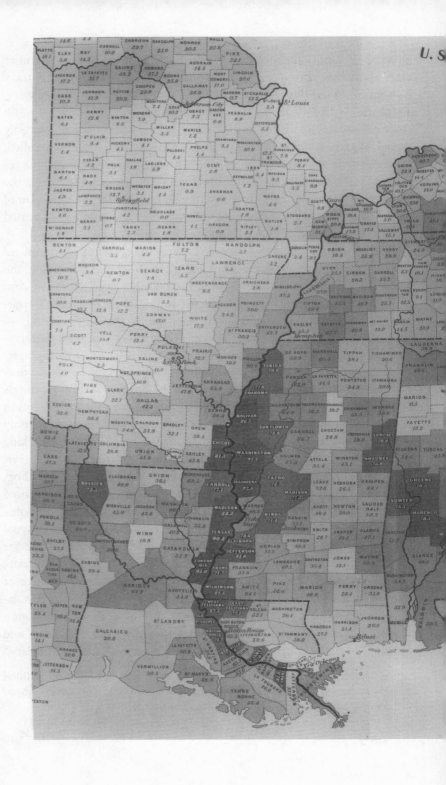

Figure 1. Census Office, Department of the Interior of the United States of America. *Map showing the distribution of the Slave Population of the Southern States of the United States.* Washington: Census Office, 1860. By permission of Duke University, The Rare Book, Manuscript, & Special Collections Library.

differ from the address that Lincoln was to pronounce at the Gettysburg National Cemetery only two years later?

"Poets make the best topographers," William Hoskins once said of Wordsworth's guide to the Lake District;[3] topographers, after Dupin, made the best rhetoricians in some cases. In 1829, with the intent of demonstrating how schooling could extinguish all delinquent tendencies from society, Balbi and Guerry drew a "comparative" map of the state of education (light, enlightened) and the state of crime (dark); Quetelet in 1831, D'Angeville in 1836, and the British Mayhew in 1862 all drew similar maps of criminality. Augustus Petermann's 1852 map of the cholera outbreak of 1831–1833 in Great Britain is a most illustrious example of this kind of rhetorical mapping based on chromatic contrasts. Britain is spotted by ominous, almost expressionist blots of dark crayon. The "black" disease of the bile (*colera* in Middle English and according to a medieval theory of humors) thus finds in Petermann's map a suggestive and moving symbol, rather than a mimetic representation, of the black shadow of death that was terrifying England. Only a few years later, Petermann's map would become the model for the cartographic topos of the "blackening of England" — representations of industries and coalmines, dirty and polluting, that were to foster the environmentalist outrage so characteristic of the Victorian age.[4] The same symbolic technique comes down to us in a rather recent United Nations map illuminating the impact of pollution in a once pastoral Attica (Figure 2). The threat to the natural marine flora (*Posidonia oceanica* and the disappearing *Cymodocea nodosa*) is the black shadow of a tourist industry expanding over the coast with hotels and other polluting agents. On the side of *Dichtung* and rhetoric rather than science and *Wahrheit*, the map's symbols affect its reader with the techniques of rhetorical persuasion. The map does not represent; it conceives arguments, and convinces well.

Modern cartography begins then, in the nineteenth century, with a "weak" scientific power to represent but also a strong rhetorical will to persuade.[5] Hills and mountains have disappeared behind the rhetorical

3. W. G. Hoskins, *The Making of the English Landscape* (London: Hodder and Stoughton, 1955), 17.

4. On the "blackening of England," see David Daiches and John Flower, *Literary Landscapes of the British Isles: A Narrative Atlas* (New York: Paddington Press Ltd., 1979), 172 ff.

5. On rhetoric as persuasion, see Kenneth Burke, *A Rhetoric of Motives* (1950; reprint, Berkeley: University of California Press, 1969), 49–54.

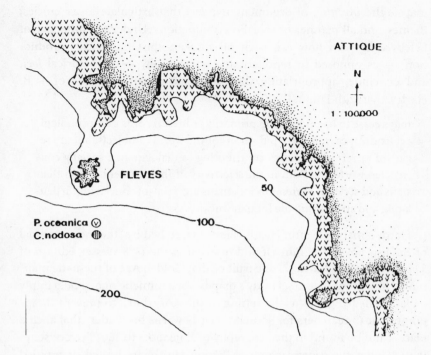

Figure 2. United Nations Environment Programme. *Study of Ecosystem Modifications in Areas Influenced by Pollutants (Activity I)*. Athens, Greece: United Nations Environment Programme, 1988.

goal of the map maker, but the lack of iconic content should not be taken as a deficiency or defect: Aristotle himself (*Nichomachean Ethics*, 1094b, 12–17) remarked that one should not expect to find factual precision in rhetorical discourse, just as it would be impossible to expect that factual precision would carry the persuasive force of rhetoric. Accordingly, one should know what to expect from a nineteenth-century map: not geographic or mimetic objectivity, but the traces of a true rhetorical discourse perfectly organized along the lines of thematic places and *topoi*. In this novel discourse, which geographers aptly call "thematic cartography,"[6] the

6. For instance, Norman J. W. Thrower, *Maps and Man: An Examination of Cartography in Relation to Culture and Civilization* (Englewood Cliffs, N.J.: Prentice-Hall, 1972), 84; a history of thematic mapping can be found in Arthur H. Robinson, *Early Thematic Mapping in the History of Cartography* (Chicago: University of Chicago Press, 1982). On the narrative quality of maps, see also J. B. Harley, "Historical Geogra-

map is the *inventio*[7] of argumentative *loci* that articulate ideas, stories, themes, and all manner of social preoccupations. Under the influence of Lefebvre, we can now call such *inventio* an epistemological "production" — as opposed to representative cartography — of rhetorical *loci*, and conclude, appropriating the post-Foucauldian language of J. B. Harley, that with Dupin

> maps cease to be understood primarily as inert records of morphological landscapes or passive reflections of the world of objects, but are regarded as refracted images contributing to dialogue in a socially constructed world. . . . Both in the selectivity of their content and in their signs and styles of representation, maps are a way of conceiving, articulating and structuring the human world. . . .[8]

Hardy's map of Egdon Heath (Figure 3), etched by "the most regional of English novelists"[9] himself and inserted in the 1878 Wessex edition of *The Return of the Native*, is one fruit of that Golden Age of thematic mapping.[10] Similar to Dupin's, Hardy's map is not a mimetic one. It *does* imply a place called "Egdon" as the setting of the story, but, "to prevent disappointment to searchers for scenery," Hardy warns his readers that such a place is not be found in the geography of England. His 1895 Preface states that: "Under the general name of 'Egdon Heath' are united or typified

---

phy and the Cartographic Illusion," *Journal of Historical Cartography* 15 (1989): 80–91.

7. I mean *inventio*, in Cicero's sense, as the first of the five traditional parts of rhetorical discourse, which includes the finding and elaboration of the argument. For both Cicero and Quintilian (the question seems slightly different for Aristotle) the *inventio* begins with an analysis (which in Dupin or Petermann is statistical) of the facts; it then goes on with the statement of the issue (what do these facts prove? That education in France could be better? That sanitary prevention in England could be necessary?); and ends with an exploration of the best means to persuade (and what is better than black smears of ink?).

8. J. B. Harley, "Maps, Knowledge, and Power," in *The Iconography of Landscape: Essays on the Symbolic Representation, Design and Use of Past Environments*, ed. Dennis Cosgrove and Stephen Daniels (Cambridge: Cambridge University Press, 1988), 278.

9. Daiches and Flower, *Literary Landscapes of the British Isles*, 158.

10. On the popularity and distribution of maps in the nineteenth century, see Arthur H. Robinson, "Mapmaking and Map Printing: The Evolution of a Working Relationship," and Elizabeth M. Harris, "Miscellaneous Map Printing Processes in the Nineteenth Century," in *Five Centuries of Map Printing*, ed. David Woodward (Chicago: University of Chicago Press, 1975), 1–24, 77–112.

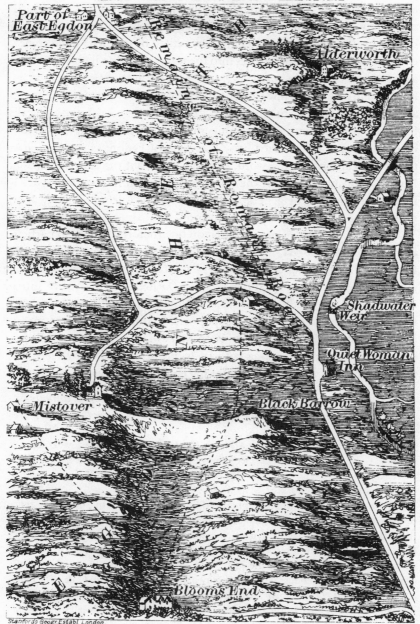

Figure 3. Thomas Hardy, "Sketch Map of the Scene of the Story." *The Return of the Native.* London: Smith, Elder & Co., 1878. By permission of Duke University, The Rare Book, Manuscript, & Special Collections Library.

heaths of various real names." Egdon Heath, then, is not the real name of a real place but rather a *conceptual* region or, in a more literal sense, a *locus communis* — a general idea, that is, where different features common to diverse heaths and their inhabitants "are united or typified." Such coalescence of disparate characteristics into the topos of Egdon happens at both a cartographic level (the map represents "general" features proper of many heaths) and a narrative one (the characters of the story perform deeds and actions of the "typical" inhabitants of various heaths). Aristotle, who calls it κοινὸς τόπος, commonplace, puts this sort of synthesis at the basis of *inventio* (Aristotle, *Rhetoric* I.ii.21). The map of Egdon, as an *inventio* in the rhetorical sense of the word, factually maps out the entire story that Hardy begun publishing in the magazine *Belgravia* in January 1878. Although met initially by general dislike, the map is celebrated today as an outstanding work of literary regionalism.[11]

Like Dupin's, Hardy's map is based on one rhetorical figure in particular: personification.[12] As "The Map of Illiteracy" was a spatial representation not of the land but of the people — or at least their degree of literacy and wealth — who inhabited that land, so *The Return of the Native*, introduced in the Wessex edition of 1912 as a "Novel of Character and Environment," begins as an extended prosopopoeia. In the initial chapter, meaningfully titled "A Face on Which Time Makes Little Impression," Egdon comes into view as a persona with its own lineaments. Conversely, humankind appears as an outgrowth of the land itself:

> Along the road walked an old man. He was white-headed *as a mountain*, bowed in the shoulders, and faded in general aspect. He wore a

11. For instance, Douglas Brown, *Thomas Hardy* (1954; reprint, Harlow: Longman, 1961); H. C. Darby, "The Regional Geography of Thomas Hardy's Wessex," *Geographical Review* 38 (1948); and George Wing, "Hardy and Regionalism," in *Thomas Hardy*, ed. Norman Page (New York: St. Martin's Press, 1980).

12. Personification is, as geographer Carl Otwin Sauer confirms, the very essence of thematic mapping: "the designation of 'personality' applied to a particular part of the earth embraces the whole dynamic relation of life and land." Personification, in other words, asserts an interdependence between humankind and its environment, culture and cultivation: one is the image and, at the same time, the product of the other. See Carl Otwin Sauer, "The Personality of Mexico," in *Land and Life: A Selection from the Writings of Carl Otwin Sauer*, ed. John Leighly (Berkeley: University of California Press, 1965), 104. For the etymological argument of culture as extension of *cultus*, see Guy Davenport, *The Geography of the Imagination* (Berkeley: North Point Press, 1981), and Dainville, *La cartographie*.

glazed hat, an ancient boat-cloak, and shoes; his brass buttons bearing an anchor *upon their face*. In his hand was a silver-headed walking-stick, which he used as *a veritable third leg. . . .*[13]

Prosopopoeia — the man "like a mountain," the button "with a face," the wooden stick "as a leg" — substantiates the allegorical contiguity between the human and the geographic. In this relation between land and life, Hardy's characters become the expression of a topography laid out in the map. The plot, created by their deeds and desires, becomes in turn a question of place.

Let us then look, briefly, at the plot. At its most elementary level, as one disapproving reviewer once pointed out, "the general plot of the story turns on the old theme of a man who is in love with two women, and a woman who is in love with two men."[14] More precisely, Eustacia Vye is the object of desire contended between Clym Yeobright (the native returning from Paris) and Damon Wildeve (who wishes to leave Egdon for a more central spot in the world). The only variation on the old theme of the love triangle lies in the fact that the object of desire coincides here with a *place* — Eustacia's house — that must be reached from Clym's and Wildeve's respective and faraway homes. For Eustacia, not altogether differently, the object of desire is not so much Clym the man but rather the *place* that Clym, "a visitant from a gay world" (III.4.240), represents for her — Paris, "the French capital, the centre and vortex of the fashionable world" (II.1.130).[15]

---

13. Thomas Hardy, *The Return of the Native* (New York: Everyman, 1992), I.1.8; emphases mine. References to *The Return of the Native* are given in the body of the text as (book) I. (chapter) 2. (page) 8. On the question of prosopopoeia in *The Return of the Native*, see J. Hillis Miller, "Prosopopoeia in Hardy and Stevens," in *Alternative Hardy*, ed. Lance St. John Butler (New York: St. Martin's Press, 1989) and, especially in reference to Hardy's recuperation of a rhetoric of commonplaces, Jonathan Wike, "The World as Text in Hardy's Fiction," *Nineteenth-Century Literature Electronic Edition* 47.4 (March 1993).

14. An anonymous review of *The Return of the Native* appeared in *The Athenaeum* (November 23, 1878), quoted in Laurence Lerner and John Holmtrom, eds., *Thomas Hardy and His Readers: A Selection of Contemporary Reviews* (New York: Barnes & Noble, 1968), 44.

15. In fact, Clym hardly strikes as a Don Juan; it is only Eustacia's expectations concerning Paris that "would, indeed, have caused her to be influenced by the most commonplace man" (II.6.166).

In Hardy's triangular plot, in short, each character is the personification of a place. To Eustacia, for instance,

> Egdon was her Hades, and since coming there she had imbibed much of what was dark in its tone, though inwardly and eternally unreconciled thereto. Her appearance accorded well with this smouldering rebelliousness, and the shady splendour of her beauty was the real surface of the sad and stifled warmth within her. A true Tartarean dignity sat upon her brow, for it had grown in her with years. (I.7.78)

Personification of a topic inferno, Eustacia is the ambiguous prosopopoeia speaking the same "wild rhetoric" (I.6.62) uttered by the ambiguously gothic place in which she presides.

Whereas Hardy extends the figure of prosopopoeia to pervasive proportions, characters end up being identified by cartographic notations:

> "I have made so bold, miss, as to step across and tell you some strange news which has come to my ears about that man."
> "Ah! what man?"
> He jerked his elbow to the southeast — the direction of the Quiet Woman.
> Eustacia turned quickly to him. "Do you mean Mr. Wildeve?" (I.10.105)

As geographic coordinates substitute for a name, and as a place — Quiet Woman — becomes the toponym for a person, so cartography orients the characters' own actions, deeds, and desires. The mutual attractions among Eustacia, Wildeve, and Clym are thus *located* on the etched map: as Wildeve "stood and looked north-east" (I.5.59) toward Eustacia's house, Eustacia's "interest lay in the southeast" (I.6.60) — until, that is, the arrival of Clym from Paris, when the axis of Eustacia's desire shifted "in the direction of Mrs. Yeobright's house at Blooms End" (II.5.156), where Clym had taken residence.

It can hardly be surprising that, in a narrative organized in such a topographic fashion, the bulk of the characters' actions consists of their *movements* from one place of the heath to another in their quest for their object of desire. A capability to move seems in fact required of all of Hardy's characters. Wildeve, for instance, was quite a young man, and of the two properties, form and motion, the latter first attracted the eye in him. The grace of his movement was singular; it was the pantomimic expression of a lady-killing career. (I.5.48)

Undoubtedly, it is this very "grace of movement" (with the initial hope that Wildeve will "move" her out of Egdon) that attracts (and kills) Eustacia — whose dream, on the other hand, is a rambling one as well: to stroll along the Parisian boulevards and the Tuileries (III.4.237).

Incidentally, the life of Hardy's characters truly depends on their ability to move along the map of Egdon. As we are informed that Mrs. Yeobright's "once elastic walk had become deadened by time" (III.3.228), we should be ready to register this piece of information as an anticipation of her coming death. Of what use is a motionless character in a novel that unfolds topographically? The basic triangular plot then multiplies the vectors of its action to form a whole, intricate network of paths to be taken and destinations to be reached: the characters go to places, meet other characters along the way ("They met in the little ditch encircling the tumulus," I.9.96), walk together (with more or less overt sexual allusions, as in Granfer Cantle's suggestion that Wildeve and Thomasin "had walked together," I.3.21), and part company ("a faint diverging path was reached, where they parted company," I.4.40).[16] In essence, their narrative mission is to reach a destination, avoiding the supreme peril of losing their path: "If we should lose the path it might be awkward" (III.7.268), says one character, quite apropos. In *The Return of the Native*, in fact, a path *is* the life of a character: "once lost it is irrecoverable" (V.8.437).

Each of the places entered by these characters, then, gives place to a narrative episode: each journey is an action, each excursion a deed, and each arrival a narrative solution. In Hardy's attempt at working a popular and commercial serialized narrative,[17] each place offers, in other words,

16. "The characters [of *The Return of the Native*] trace out the courses of their lives as they cross back and forth, transversing the heath on the paths and roads Hardy drew on his map." In J. Hillis Miller, *Topographies* (Stanford: Stanford University Press, 1995), 23.

17. Hardy's desire to write commercial and popular fiction is well documented and is admitted by Hardy himself in a letter to Stephen cited in the pseudo-biography (more probably an autobiography in disguise) signed by his wife Florence Emily: "The truth is that I am willing, and indeed anxious, to give up any points which may be desirable in a story when read as a whole, for the sake of others which shall

the setting to unfold one narrative cliché after another — a series of commonplaces of the classic love-triangle plot that, put sequentially together, form a story, a dis-*course*. Take the episode of the mummers' play in the Yeobright's living room, for instance. In this peculiar chamber — topos of *marriages à la mode* and bourgeois courting since the times of Hogart — Eustacia, like "the disguised Queen of Love [when she] appeared before Aeneas" (II.6.171), cross-dresses as a Turkish knight to conquer Clym's heart. Only a few pages prior to this gender-crossing topos, an altogether typical falling-in-love-with-moonlight scene has taken place in "an area of two feet in Rembrandt's intensest manner" (II.6.165), which the reader is asked to locate at Mistover Knap:

> Yeobright and Eustacia looked at each other for one instant, as if each had in mind those few moments during which a certain moonlight scene was common to both. (III.3.220–221)

The moonlight scene, "common to both" and certainly familiar to the reader as well, is undoubtedly a literary commonplace. And what else than commonplace is the reduction of Paris to the clichés of the Louvre and the Tuileries, Versailles, "Fontainebleau, St. Cloud, the Bois and many other familiar haunts" where "you would doubtless feel in a world of historical romance" (III.4.237)? Or, again, what, if not a *locus communis*, is the Shadwater river, "slowly born[ing]" the dead body of Eustacia "by one of the backward currents" (V.9.445), with the mannerism of Rossetti's *Death of Ophelia*?

Personifications of commonplace environments — and actors in a commonplace plot — the characters themselves become, quite expectedly, commonplace literary types: as tearful Thomasin "seemed to belong rightly to a madrigal" (I.4.43), Clym's love for Eustacia is "as that of Petrarch for his Laura" (III.4.241); Eustacia's Tennysonian dream, in which she "was dancing to wondrous music, and her partner was the man in silver armour," is, by the narrator's own blunt admission, "not far removed

---

please those who read it in numbers. Perhaps I may have higher aims some day, and be a great stickler for the proper artistic balance of the completed work, but for the present[,] circumstances lead me to wish merely to be considered a good hand at a serial." In Florence Emily Hardy, *The Life of Thomas Hardy, 1840–1928* (1928, 1930; reprint, London: Macmillan, 1975), 100. On Hardy's attempts at gaining popular success (and consequent financial retribution), see J. A. Sutherland, "Hardy: Breaking into Fiction," in *Victorian Novelists and Publishers* (Chicago: University of Chicago Press, 1976).

from commonplace" (II.3.140). Commonplace plots — no doubt! — require commonplace characters, and Hardy seems to be quite at ease with the ironic mission of peopling his commonplace environment with a handful of commonplace personifications.

In fact, Hardy's peculiar project seems to be exactly that of ordering an entire stock of commonplaces about a "general" English heath and its "typical" inhabitants into a visual catalogue (the map) that will in turn generate a narrative one (the story). The map of Egdon, in other words, is meant to function here as a rhetorical thesaurus — a repertoire of various discursive possibilities[18] in which each location is also a locution, and each place a topos. As the plot unfolds along with the spatial movements the characters take along discursive itineraries and etched paths, so does narrative materialize in a panoramic succession of settings and descriptions.

The commonplace nature of Egdon is apparent from a cursory glance at its map, which is, unmistakably, a thesaurus of topoi of an ancient and sometimes glorious British past. The eye is first caught by the Roman road, which cuts the map from north to south; at its right is Black Barrow, originally built by "one of the Celts" (I.2.13), and where "Saxon ceremonies" (I.3.16) take place annually. West of the Roman road is Mistover Knap, where "a very curious druidical stone" (III.3.224) reminds Clym of the whole mystical past of England; and descending from Mistover, on the way to Blooms End, is a little ditch — "the original excavation from which it had been thrown up by the ancient British people" (I.9.96). Blooms End itself, with its "dignified" white paling (II.1.129–130) and the decorous house "cozy and comfortable" (II.8.187), is, like Jonson's *Penshurst* ("not . . . built to envious show"), a proper emblem of British land-owning bourgeoisie that the Yeobrights personify. Quiet Woman, east of the Roman Road, is the characteristic all-British inn, where travelers eat soups and drink ales. The rest is all fields, wild slopes, ravines, and narrow paths walked in the centuries by generations of British farmers.

What one can notice, incidentally, is that in the thesaurus mapped with Egdon, regional and *national* identity do coincide. Unifying various British heaths under its "general name," Egdon, as an imaginary region of England, is the part that signifies the whole. It signifies a *general* British "regionhood," or, in the end, a general *Britishness* uncorrupted by the

18. See Mary Carruthers, *The Book of Memory: A Study of Memory in Medieval Culture* (Cambridge: Cambridge University Press, 1990).

fashions and glitters of the continental world. The agon against the continent — and, particularly, against Paris — should not be overlooked here. It is interesting, for instance, to notice how Eustacia's dislike for Egdon coincides with a form of xenomania — but also, as the following dialogue with Clym suggests, with a phobia for anything English:

> [Eustacia:] "And Versailles — the King's Gallery is some such gorgeous room, is it not? . . . When used you to go to these places?" "On Sundays."
> "Ah, yes. I dislike English Sundays." (III.4.237–238)

Against this dislike for what is English, Clym's unrelenting praise of Egdon aims instead at the recovery of the very roots of an uncontaminated, archaic Englishness,[19] emerging from the soil of Egdon with the haunting presence of Saxon and Celtic ruins. As Peter Hampson Ditchfield remarked in 1889, "In most of our large towns the old features are fast disappearing . . . whereas in the country everything remains the same, and it is not so difficult to let one's own thoughts wander into the past."[20] Egdon is, exactly, a part of this country where the origin of the country is still alive and well:

> The instincts of merry England lingered on here with exceptional vitality, and the symbolic customs which tradition has attached to each season of the year were yet a reality on Egdon. (VI.1.462–463)

In *The Return of the Native*, a recovery of the original merry England that is mapped in the chart of Egdon is then accomplished, primarily, via

19. These roots, as Hobsbawm has noticed, were being transferred in those years into the Egdon-like rustic countryside. It was the myth of the Merrie England (as the name was canonized in Robert Blatchford's 1893 treatise by that title), opposing the decadence of an industrial society in those years losing its boasted dynamism. See Eric Hobsbawm, *Industry and Empire: An Economic History of Britain since 1750* (London: Weidenfeld & Nicolson, 1968), 140 ff.

20. Peter Hampson Ditchfield, *Our English Villages: Their Story and Their Antiquities* (London, 1889), quoted in Martin J. Wiener, *English Culture and the Decline of the Industrial Spirit: 1850–1980* (Cambridge: Cambridge University Press, 1981), 47. The following may stand as evidence of the resilience of the trope: "the country reassures us that not everything these days is superficial and transitory; that some things remain stable, permanent and enduring." In Howard Newby, "Revitalizing the Countryside: The Opportunities and Pitfalls of Counter-Urban Trends," *Royal Society of Arts Journal* 138 (1990): 635.

a peripatetic metaphor: to walk in Egdon *means* to wander into the past.[21] Away from the highways, railways, and central routes of modernity, far from the boulevards of Paris, or from the geometric avenues of the modern metropolitan utopia (Figure 4), the etched paths of Egdon, following rather than transforming the natural topography of the terrain, invariably lead Clym to the various (common)places of the old England that he is longing to revive: Roman roads, Celtic burrows, Druidic stones, and Saxon urns. As desires for boulevards are certainly the fruit of "Eustacia's modern ideas" (V.2.381), a walk in Egdon makes Clym feel like he "had suddenly dived into past ages" (I.3.17). The narrative opposition between Paris and Egdon therefore engenders a further antithesis between modernity and antiquity, history and seclusion, present and past. What must be noticed, however, is that the Victorian cult of the "past" and of "antiquity" has little to do with history: led by Foucault's assumption that "the great obsession of the nineteenth century was . . . history," scholars of Victorianism have often mistaken the *religio loci* of the last *fin de siècle* for a concern with history.[22] What we are facing here, instead, is a real epistemological break — one that opens, in fact, not so much Foucault's new "epoch of space," but, undoubtedly, a new epoch of places. Places — topoi, more properly, coinciding with the *loci* of Cicero's *artificiosa memoria* (*Ad Herennium* III.xvi.29ff.) — are the concern of the new epoch, and not history. The "past" is nothing less than a place, where any Clym, like nothing, can just enter:

> [Clym] frequently walked the heath alone, when the past seized upon him with its shadowy hand, and held him there to listen to its tale. His imagination would then people the spot with its ancient inhabitants; forgotten Celtic tribes trod their tracks about him, and he could almost live among them, look in their faces, and see them standing beside the barrows which swelled around, untouched and perfect as the time of their erection. (VI.1.459)

21. See Anne D. Wallace, *Walking, Literature, and English Culture: The Origins and Uses of Peripatetic in the Nineteenth Century* (Oxford: Clarendon, 1993).

22. References to Foucault are from Michel Foucault, "Of Other Spaces," *Diacritics* 16 (1986): 22; for the scholarship on the Victorians and the "cult" of history, see Christine Crosby, *The Ends of History: Victorians and "The Woman Question"* (New York: Routledge, 1991), esp. 4–6.

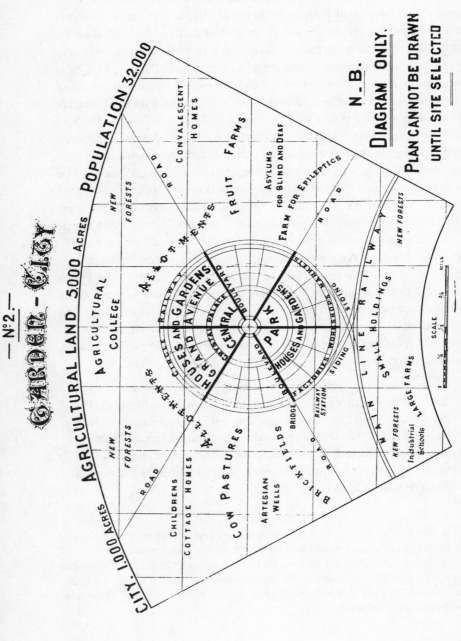

- N°2. -

GARDEN - CITY

CITY. 1,000 ACRES   AGRICULTURAL LAND 5,000 ACRES   POPULATION 32,000

NEW FORESTS

AGRICULTURAL COLLEGE

ALLOTMENTS

CONVALESCENT HOMES

FRUIT FARMS

ASYLUMS

FARM FOR EPILEPTICS

ROAD

NEW FORESTS

CHILDRENS COTTAGE HOMES

COW PASTURES

ALLOTMENTS

ROAD

ARTESIAN WELLS

BRICKFIELDS

BRIDGE

RAILWAY STATION

SIDING

WORKERS WAREHOUSES MARKETS

RAILWAY

CIRCLE RAILWAY

HOUSES AND GARDENS

GRAND AVENUE

CENTRAL PARK

BOULEVARD

CRYSTAL PALACE

BOULEVARD

HOUSES AND GARD

FACTORIES

SIDING

ROAD

NEW FORESTS

SMALL HOLDINGS

MAIN LINE RAILWAY

Industrial Schools

LARGE FARMS

NEW FORESTS

SCALE

0   ¼   ½   ¾   MILE

N.B.

DIAGRAM ONLY.

PLAN CANNOT BE DRAWN

UNTIL SITE SELECTED

Figure 4. Sir Ebenezer Howard. "Diagrammed Map of the Garden City." *Garden Cities of Tomorrow (Being the Second Edition of "To-morrow: A Peaceful Path to Real Reform")*. London: S. Sonnenschein & Co., Ltd., 1902. By permission of Duke University, The Rare Book, Manuscript, & Special Collections

What history has lost still resides in the map of Egdon. Its places are commonplaces of a past still available to Clym. Yet, what discourse do these commonplaces create? And for what purpose? To what rhetorical goal are they aimed? Remo Ceserani, observing the recurrence of verbs like "to walk," "to wander," "to ramble," and "to stroll," has suggested that Hardy's oeuvre articulates a discourse opposing, *in absentia*, modern means of locomotion, railways, and trains.[23] A likely believer in the doctrine of silence as the best revenge, Ceserani notices that all travelers in *The Return of the Native* (with the possible exception of the "mephistophelic reddleman" riding his cart) wander rigorously on foot — far from railways, and at leisure on that very account. In *The Return of the Native*, the one single reference to the "introduction of railways [in] Wessex" is made, in fact, to evoke the destruction of a "local class of artisans," with the consequent loss of any "poetry of existence" (I.9.91). An intertextual look at the rest of Hardy's oeuvre would show us how disaster, in Wessex, has often come by train: the railroad, in this peculiar locale, brings death and destruction "at a stroke."[24] If not a blatant anachronism, the absence of trains from a novel set "between 1840 and 1850" (as the preface remarks) must then be part of a general rhetorical strategy: free from the diabolical and pervasive influence of the train, Egdon organizes its space as an *antithesis* to the effects of the railroad — as the topos, therefore, where a "poetry of existence" can survive.

Ceserani's train, however, should be taken here as a synecdoche, as a part that stands for the whole of the incessant movement characteristic of the industrial era. At the frenetic tempo of this age, in Marx's expression, "all that is solid melts into the air":[25] what seemed to be reality evanesces, customs disappear, and traditions die. History speeds up and leaves nothing, not even nature, the same as before. "Railways" and "electric telegraphs" — the *Communist Manifesto* reads — eradicate "entire populations . . . out of the ground."[26] The destructive impact of the train in the

23. Remo Ceserani, "La cattedrale gotica: da Ruskin a Hardy," in *Treni di carta. L'immaginario in ferrovia: l'irruzione del treno nella letteratura moderna* (Genova: Marietti, 1993), 133–152.

24. Florence Hardy, *Life*, 25.

25. Karl Marx and Friedrich Engels, *The Communist Manifesto* (Harmondsworth, Eng.: Penguin, 1985), 83.

26. Marx and Engels, *Communist Manifesto*, 85.

reality of Wessex seems, then, to dramatize a more general fear for modern movement — a fear antagonistic, indeed, to the communist celebration of speed, seen as the nearing of revolutionary times, "thanks to the railways."[27] This fear, as Thomas Hardy voiced it, was mostly an apprehension for the way the modern movement that was generated by industrialization — tourism, commuting, and, above all, migrations — was to uproot humankind from "place." This sort of movement was dispersing from the countryside an organic "class of stationary cottagers who carried on the local traditions and humours" and was supplanting it with "a population of more or less migratory labourers." The whole of modern movement, for the settled communities of Wessex, means then "a break of continuity in local history, more fatal than any other thing to the preservation of legend, folk-lore, close inter-social relations, and eccentric individualities."[28] We can therefore say that the main argument that Egdon articulates, through a narrative that is so much about movements, is a discourse against *modern* movement.

The topos, antithetical to Egdon, that provides the ideas to discuss the dangerous effects of such mobility, is a place that, like the train, is kept outside of the narrative setting — and outside, consequently, of the map of Egdon. This place is the city, the locus where, as Georg Simmel nicely put it, the velocity of modernity "thickens."[29] It is in the city that modern movement becomes, in Clym's words, a "bustle" (III.3.224) — like that "bustle of ants" about which, later in the novel, the narrator observes: "To look down upon them was like observing a city street from the top of a tower" (IV.6.347).[30] With its crowds "out of doors in all winds and weath-

27. Marx and Engels, *Communist Manifesto*, 90. It might also be curious to notice Marx's polemic against Proudhon, articulated exactly on the discussion of "speed" and "railways," in Karl Marx, *The Poverty of Philosophy* (New York: International Publishers, 1963), 90–102.

28. The citations by Hardy are from Harold Orel, ed., *Thomas Hardy's Personal Writings: Prefaces, Literary Opinions, Reminiscences* (New York: St. Martin's Press, 1990), 10–11.

29. Georg Simmel, "Die Großstädte und das Geistesleben," *Brücke und Tür*, ed. M. Landmann and M. Susman (1903; reprint, Stuttgart: Koehler Verlag, 1957).

30. This image, too, is a cliché, and we find it again and again — for example, in Victor Considérant's coeval advice to look at the city ("a sad spectacle to see"!) from an implicitly ethical "above," by climbing "on top of the high towers of Notre-Dame." In Victor Considérant, *Déscription du Phalanstère et considérations sociales sur l'architectonique* (Paris: Librairie sociétaire, 1848), 11; translation mine.

ers" (III.1.206), the city is a frenetic come and go with no end and no goal: Baudelaire had written already, "One goes, one runs, one searches. What does one look for?"[31] For Clym, too, the movement of the city, with all its "rookery of pomp and vanity" (I.11.122), is *vanitas vanitatis*:

> [The city] was very depressing. But not so depressing as something I next perceived — that my business [there] was the idlest, vainest, most effeminate business that ever a man could be put to. That decided me — I would give it up and try to follow some rational occupation among the people I knew best, and to whom I could be of most use. I have come home. . . . (III.1.206)

The city is a place of perversion, "effeminate and mercenary"[32] like Rousseau's Paris: "Talk about men who deserve the name, can any man deserving the name waste his time in that effeminate way?" (III.2.211). Dickens had already established, for the Victorian imagination, an emblematic "city" as the center of vice and corruption. Peopled by the paupers, the unemployed, the criminals, the drunkards, and the prostitutes of the depression of 1836, the city is an unnatural place, a inhuman way of living: no "organic" communities live there, but rather a chaos of peoples and races, an "anarchy" brought about by labor migration. Dickens and Gissing, but also Fourier, Proudhon, Owen, Carlyle, Marx, Engels, Ruskin, William Morris, and the Salvation Army, had seen this modern, overcrowded city as the growing symptom of a modern malaise: "alienation."[33]

31. Charles Baudelaire, "Le peintre de la vie moderne," in *Critique d'art. Suivi de Critique Musicale*, ed. Claude Pichois (Paris: Gallimard, 1992), 355; translation mine.

32. Jean-Jacques Rousseau, *Lettre à D'Alembert* (Paris: Garnier-Flammarion, 1967), 233; translation mine. For a good inventory of Victorian commonplaces related to the city, see Asa Briggs, *Victorian Cities* (1963; reprint, Berkeley: University of California Press, 1993), esp. 59–87. More "Victorian" and certainly more regional in its (commonplace) attack against the industrial city is Lewis Mumford, *The City in History: Its Origins, Its Transformations, and Its Prospects* (San Diego: Harcourt Brace Jovanovich, 1961), esp. 446 ff. See also Françoise Choay, *L'urbanisme. Utopies et réalités* (Paris: Éditions du Seuil, 1965).

33. See chapter on Robert Owen in Choay, *L'urbanisme*, 89–96; also, Arnold Jules Levine, *Alienation in the Metropolis* (San Francisco: R & E Research Associates, 1977). For a more ambiguous relation to the city — alienating on the one hand, liberating on the other — see Friedrich Engels, *The Condition of the Working-Class in England in 1844*, trans. Florence Kelley Wischnewtzky (London: Allen and Unwin, 1850), esp. the chapter "The Big City." In the context of alienation and mixed ethnos, see Richard Sennet, "The Rhetoric of Ethnic Identity," in *The Ends of Rhetoric: History, Theory, Practice*, ed. John Bender and David E. Wellbery (Stanford: Stanford University Press, 1990), 191.

Clym still bears the traces of it: like a living dead, he is recognizable in Egdon for that "paleness of face which he had brought with him from Paris" (III.5.247).

The city, finally, is for the Victorians the topos of an imminent catastrophe. The workers' strikes, exploded in various British cities between July and August 1842, had in fact complicated an already lugubrious commonplace with the true fear of a new "Jacobean" revolution. It is significant that Clym's arrival from Paris evokes for the Victorian reader this very fear:

> "The place he's been living at is Paris," said Humphrey, "and they tell me 'tis where the king's head was cut off years ago. My poor mother used to tell me about that business. 'Hummy,' she used to say, 'I was a young maid then, and as I was at home ironing Mother's caps one afternoon the parson came in and said, "They've cut the king's head off, Jane; and what 'twill be next God knows."'" (II.1.126)

Chaotic, perverted, catastrophic — this is "the city" for Clym and his Victorian public. "Five years of a great city — says Clym — would be a perfect cure" (III.3.224) for anyone believing the contrary. And who could contradict the perfect rhetoric of the native who has returned home!

As the antithesis of the effeminate city, Egdon, "of all contrasting places in the world" (II.1.129), acquires its rhetorical status as an anti-city — a "home," an original, uncorrupted *heimat*. Daniel Pool informs us that for the Victorians the anti-city coincided with "the country," and that Hardy's Wessex, in fact, was read by them as a "country" *par excellence*.[34] Hardy's friend and editor Leslie Stephen supplements this information by telling us that, among his contemporaries,

> a love of the country is taken, I know not why, to indicate the presence of all cardinal virtues. . . . I too love the country — if such a statement can be received after such an exordium; but I confess — to be duly modest — that I love it best in books. In real life I have remarked that it is frequently damp and rheumatic and most hated by those who know it best.[35]

34. Daniel Pool, *What Jane Austen Ate and Charles Dickens Knew: From Fox Hunting to Whist — the Facts of Daily Life in 19th-Century England* (New York: Simon & Schuster, 1993), 158.

35. Leslie Stephen, *Hours in a Library* (1899), quoted in Jan Marsh, *Back to the Land: The Pastoral Impulse in England, from 1880 to 1914* (London: Quartet, 1982), 37.

The country, as Stephen correctly points out, is a Victorian common-place — or, more precisely, a whole thesaurus of "all cardinal virtues" rooted perhaps on Wordsworth's *Excursions*.[36]

Two antithetical topoi, in conclusion, produce the argument about movement that unfolds in *The Return of the Native*: the city, with its "bustle of ants," and the country, where Clym can again find the cozy joy of "walking leisurely among the turves and furze-faggots" (I.7.81). Sick and tired of the city, where everyone runs toward some mysterious goal and imagines "the areas between [point of departure and point of desti-nation] as somehow 'empty,'" Clym, like the "traveler" of a Victorian the-saurus outlined by James Buzard, goes back in the country and there "travel[s] every step of the way . . . so that everything [he] pass[es] is fully a 'place' to [him]. . . ."[37]

But who is this Clym, who flees Paris to go on foot around provincial Egdon, "walking with a will over the furze, as straight as a line, as if his life depended upon it" (III.3.218)? For Eustacia, as we saw, Clym is a *metaphor* for Paris. For the narrator, not altogether differently, he is, first of all, a *symbol*:

> The observer's eye was arrested, not by his face as a picture, but by his face as a page; not by what it was, but by what it recorded. His features were attractive in the light of symbols, as sounds intrinsically common become attractive in language, as shapes intrinsically simple become in-teresting in writing. (III.1.201–202)

After the narrator's hint, we ought to read Clym's decision to leave the modern city and return to the old native country "in the light of symbols," and interpret Clym himself, accordingly, as a model — an *exemplum*, a page in a larger rhetorical discourse. Now, what can Clym ever represent

36. See also, in a vein similar to Stephen, a thesaurus of the horrors of the country in William Hazlitt, "Country People," *Selected Writings*, ed. Ronald Blythe (Har-mondsworth, Eng.: Penguin, 1970), 463.

37. James Buzard, *The Beaten Track: European Tourism, Literature, and the Ways to 'Culture': 1800–1918* (Oxford: Clarendon, 1993), 34 ff. Narratively, *The Return of the Na-tive* is not a story like the typically Victorian detective novel, nervously moving toward the final resolution, but rather a panoramic tour of commonplaces gently yielding to the pleasures of static and contiguous descriptions. For a discussion of authorial and editorial variants of the text, see John Paterson, "The Making of *Return of the Native*," *English Studies* 19 (1960).

as a "symbol"? To begin, Eustacia recognizes in his enthusiasm for the heath the prototypical sensibility of the artist: "[Egdon] is well enough for artists; but I never would learn to draw" (III.3.224). Wildeve, in a similar vein, discerns in it the typical passion of the painter: "It seems impossible to do well here, unless one were a wild bird or a landscape-painter" (I.9.101). The narrator itself, in an early description, introduces Clym as an "artist and scholar" (III.2.203). Educated in the city to the love of the country, abreast with the newest "ethical systems popular at the time" (III.2.207), Clym emerges, slowly but surely, as the symbol of a modern generation of Victorian humanists.

And what can an "artist and scholar" like Clym find in a place like Egdon? What does the Victorian humanist, this wanderer of "a more recently learnt emotion . . . than that which responds to the sort of beauty called charming and fair" (I.1.5), look for in the countryside? Not beauty, the narrator suggests, but the trace of "a curious, interesting, and nearly perished link between obsolete forms of life and those which generally prevail" (I.2.9) will be the goal of this Victorian wanderer. What fascinates Clym about Egdon, in fact, is exactly its resilience to historical change, to modernity, and to the "effeminacy" of contemporary life — its ancientness, its Celtic burrows, its druid stones, its archaic, manly peasants. Clym, like the prototypical Victorian artist mused by William Morris (a contemporary of his, in fact), has made a cult of the past:

> How is it that though we are so interested with our life for the most part, yet when people take to writing poems or painting pictures they seldom deal with our modern life, or if they do, they take good care to make their poems or pictures unlike that life? Are we not good enough to paint ourselves? How is it that we find the dreadful times of the past so interesting to us — in pictures and poetry?[38]

A reaction against modernity was a rather familiar argument for the Victorian humanist, who could, in fact, easily sympathize with Clym's quest. Modernity, "to beauty unpropitious and to song" (as Anna Seward wrote in "The Swan of Lichfield"), had revealed itself less than inspiring. For Matthew Arnold, no artist could "succeed in [his/her] attempt freely

38. William Morris, *News from Nowhere and Other Writings* (Harmondsworth, Eng.: Penguin, 1993), 131.

to apply the modern spirit in English literature." The only solution for literature to survive modernity was to follow Wordsworth's example: he "retired (in Middle-Age phrase) into a monastery. I mean . . . he voluntarily cut himself off from the modern spirit"![39]

"Retiring" from the modern life of Paris, Clym becomes the symbol of a whole "artistic and scholarly" need to escape the unliterary spirit of modernity. The Brotherhood of the Ancients, Ruskin's League of St. George, Rossetti's Pre-Raphaelites, Graham Arnold's Ruralists, Overbeck's Nazarenes, Morris's Kelmscott — all these groups, contemporary to Clym, lived on the same Wordsworthean (and Arnoldean) assumption that preindustrial life was better for the lungs — and for the artistic genius no less. What modernity (with the city as its commonplace) had to offer was only, as Wordsworth's 1850 preface to *Lyrical Ballads* put it, an "unfit" and merely "frantic" literature:

> a multitude of causes, unknown in former times, are now acting . . . to blunt the discriminating power of the mind. . . . The most effective of these causes are the great national events which are daily taking place, and the increasing accumulation of men in cities, where the uniformity of their occupations produces a craving for extraordinary incident, which the rapid communication of intelligence [i.e., the press, not "true" literature] hourly gratifies. To this tendency of life and manners the literature and theatrical exhibitions of the country have conformed themselves. The invaluable works of our elder writers, I had almost said the works of Shakespeare and Milton, are driven into neglect by frantic novels, sickly and stupid German Tragedies, and deluges of idle and extravagant stories in verse.[40]

39. Matthew Arnold, "Wordsworth," *Selected Prose*, ed. P. J. Keating (Harmondsworth, Eng.: Penguin, 1970), 165–166.

40. William Wordsworth, Preface to *Lyrical Ballads* (1850), in *Selected Prose*, ed. John O. Hayden (Harmondsworth, Eng.: Penguin, 1988), 284. One difference between Wordsworth's and Clym's treatment of the topos of the return to the origin might be the alertness of the former, and the blindness of the latter, to the rhetorical nature of the topos at hand: "My purpose was to imitate, and, as far as possible, to adopt the very language of [country-]men; and assuredly such personifications . . . are, indeed, a figure of speech. . . ." In Wordsworth, *Lyrical Ballads*, 284–285. On the Victorians' blindness reading the rhetorical nature of Wordsworth's trope of the return to nature, see Paul de Man, "Wordsworth and the Victorians," in *The Rhetoric of Romanticism* (New York: Columbia University Press, 1984).

Clym Yeobright's goal then coincides with Wordsworth's: he needs to find a place, antithetical to the "rapid communication" (or the "bustle") of the modern city — a place to "walk" (or read) leisurely, and from where one can recuperate the "former times" of an old "poetry of existence." This artistic place, for which "civilization was its enemy" (I.1.6), is Egdon — but it is also Eustacia, personification of Egdon, and ironic personification, as well, of the literature "of our elder writers":

Eustacia Vye was the raw material of a divinity. On Olympus she would have done well with a little preparation. . . . To see her hair was to fancy that a whole winter did not contain darkness enough to form its shadow. . . . She had pagan eyes, full of nocturnal mysteries. . . . The mouth seemed formed less to speak than to quiver, less to quiver than to kiss. Her presence brought memories of such things as Bourbon roses, rubies, and tropical midnight; her moods recalled lotus-eaters and the march in *Athalie*; her motions, the ebb and flow of the sea; her voice, the viola. . . . The new moon behind her head, an old helmet upon it, a diadem of accidental dewdrops round her brow, would have been adjuncts sufficient to strike the note of Artemis, Athena, or Hera respectively, with as close an approximation to the antique as that which passes muster on many respected canvases. . . . (I.7.76–78)

In a crescendo of allusions and classicist clichés, Eustacia is Athalia, Artemis, Athena, Hera, Sappho (I.6.63), and Alcinous (I.7.79). For Clym, more simply, she is an ideal of that classicist beauty — black eyes, black hair, quivering mouth — of which the elder writers wrote.[41]

Not only does "the country" offer a merry topos sheltered — because of its very closeness to nature and its laws — from Jacobean violence and the necessities of the "idlest, vainest, most effeminate business" that cities impose; moreover, this topos represents an alternative to the modern

41. After comparing Eustacia to "a young goddess of sensuality" (p. 65), Irving Howe (*Thomas Hardy* [New York: Macmillan, 1967]) overlooks Hardy's ironic intention in putting together such a commonplace beauty, and attributes Eustacia's total lack of credibility to Hardy's faulty narrative skills. A different stand is taken by David Eggenschwiler, "Eustacia Vye, Queen of Night and Courtly Pretender," *Victorian Literary History* 25 (1971): 444–454; Eggenschwiler believes that the split between Eustacia's sublime presentation on the one hand, and her triviality on the other, is intentional on Hardy's part, and to be understood as a parody of romantic fiction.

decadence of aesthetic — namely, to Wordsworth's "frantic novels" that gratify a citified gusto for "extraordinary incident," or to Hazlitt's badly written newspapers, "the lungs of the British metropolis."[42] The country *is* a thesaurus of "beautiful" literary topoi — the trees, nature, pastoral simplicity — that are opposed to the "unliterary" figures of the modern city — chimneys, crowds, the bustle. The country is a thesaurus of artistic loci to be enjoyed "walking leisurely," and not through a "rapid communication." Yet, as the country is threatened by modernity, so is literature. The country becomes, in the end, some sort of metaphor for the humanities themselves, endangered by Arnold's "anarchy" and Wordsworth's dailies.[43]

Clym's return to Egdon, then, is symbolic of the artist's need for an "obsolete, superseded country" (I.1.6). Clym's longing for Egdon is the desire to experience the picturesqueness of an original place,

> from prehistoric times as unaltered as the stars overhead. . . . The great inviolate place had an ancient permanence which the sea cannot claim. . . . The sea changed, the fields changed, the rivers, the villages, and the people changed, yet Egdon remained. (I.1.7)

Hardy's frequent allusions to Clym's wealth as a "Manager to a diamond merchant, or some such thing" (II.1.127) seems not at all casual in this context. Already in an article of the *Longman's Magazine* of July 1883, Hardy had pointed out the relation of aesthetics and social class — and, more precisely, the dependence of an aesthetic of "the country" from an urban, bourgeois sensibility:

> That seclusion and immutability [of country life], which was so bad for their [country laborers'] pockets, was an unrivaled fosterer of their per-

---

42. William Hazlitt, "The Times Newspaper," in *Selected Writings*, ed. Blythe, 259.

43. From its very outset — from the lengthy description of the setting-place — the "novel of environment" can be read as a defense of the literary product in its time of crisis: Literature, in fact, and not the daily chronicle, possesses the powers of invention and description without which neither idyllic landscapes nor rustic places — no Egdons! — could exist for the modern, urban reader: "[L]'écriture est ici juge et partie: elle retrouve la parole sans laquelle le paysage n'existerait pas et elle en domine l'effet. . . . En effet [l'écriture] s'est constitué en simulacre autonome, ne paraissant pas suspendre le principe de réalité dont il est pourtant la negation." In Patrice Thompson, "Le paysage comme fiction," *Revue des Sciences Humaines* 1.209 (1988): 13.

sonal charm in the eyes of those whose experiences had been less limited. But the artistic merit of their old condition is scarcely a reason why they should have continued in it when other communities were marching on so vigorously towards uniformity and mental equality. It is only the old story that progress and picturesqueness do not harmonise. They are losing their individuality, but they are widening the range of their ideas, and gaining in freedom. It is too much to expect from them to remain stagnant and old-fashioned for the pleasure of romantic spectators.[44]

Hardy's suggestion that a feeling for the picturesque develops in a situation "less limited" than the one it cherishes helps explain why, in the economy of the novel, it is Clym — not Eustacia, Wildeve, or the villagers — who finds Egdon charming. Not only is he the rich bourgeois who seeks artistic merit in an "old condition of poverty"; he is, also, the "romantic spectator" returning from an urban experience different — if

---

44. Orel, ed., *Hardy's Personal Writings*, 181. So, is the countryside "good" or "bad"? My intention so far has clearly been to suggest that the beauty of secluded country life is but a Victorian commonplace. Against rhetoric, I am pitting here what I imply is the "real" country life, as "faithfully" described in the words of Thomas Hardy — a life of hunger, poverty, and strife. However, one problem arises. David Simpson, yielding to the Zeitgeist of our own epoch, articulates the fundamental question in the unmistakable tones of rhetorical undecidability: "Who is right, in terms of a fidelity to what is (or was) the case, 'really'? Readers may all too readily decide, as they often do with Crabbe against the writers he purports to satirize, that one writer is in possession of a truth which efficiently unmasks another's self-deception or purposeful mystification." By contrasting Wordsworth's love for the country with Hazlitt's hatred for country people and their "stupid and selfish" life, Simpson suggests that "Hazlitt too is 'seeing' in a motivated way, constructing a covert apologia, behind the guise of 'realism', for a system of values which it is one of Wordsworth's poetry to deny." In David Simpson, *Wordsworth and the Figurings of the Real* (Atlantic Highlands, N.J.: Humanities Press, 1982), xx–xxi. The depiction of an ugly countryside is, in other words, a rhetorical construction — a genre in its own right: realism, with its own definite political aims and agendas. Careful enough, at least, not to confer on Wordsworth's return to the rural the magic freedom of a regionalist "purity" from the world of politics, Simpson's conclusion seems to me yet another commonplace: everything is a matter of rhetoric, ergo everything falls into an undiscriminating relativism. Of course, one must read the citation from Hardy's "Dorsetshire Labourer" as a rhetorical artifact and see in that same citation a political agenda reflecting a certain "system of values." Yet, the fact remains that Hardy's rhetorical topoi can be measured against the reality he purports to describe (mortality rates, per capita incomes, sanitary conditions).

not "less limited" — than the rustic one. As the "symbol" of an urban intelligentsia, he projects onto "the country" his urban expectations, needs, and dissatisfactions. In this sense, the topos he calls "home," is not precisely an *antithesis* to the modern city but rather its *antisagoge* — the rhetorical compensation to the discontent of modernization,[45] the past that an urban present seeks to invent for its own sake and leisure.

Picturesqueness — this "sensibility" for "the country" produced by the urban bourgeoisie — is in fact the only thing that Clym finds at Egdon. Neither sublime nor beautiful, "haggard Egdon" appeals to his "more recently learnt" (I.1.5) aesthetic sensibility. "Sort of" beautiful, "wearing a sombreness distasteful to our race when it was young" (I.1.5), the heath is that "station between beauty and sublimity,"[46] that the generation of the 1840s — Clym's generation — took as the very topos of a new aesthetic.[47] Egdon is, in a way, the commonplace of a modern gusto for a picturesque past. It is, noticeably, a commonplace unlike that of the old, classical beauty with its "vineyards and myrtle gardens of South Europe" (I.1.5) — and different, also, from the sublime "infinity" for which the romantic generation had longed. This new aesthetic commonplace is a place secluded, bounded, isolated, protected from all, like a "prison" (I.1.4) from

45. Antisagoge is mostly known in Anglo-American scholarship in Roland Barthes's translation of the term as *supplément* (see Roland Barthes, *S / Z* [Paris: Éditions du Seuil, 1970]; on Balzac "supplementing" Sarrasin's antithesis, esp. 33). *Supplément* plays a decisive role in Derrida's discussion of Rousseau (Jacques Derrida, *De la grammatologie* [Paris: Éditions de minuit, 1967]), in which supplement, as the figure of antisagoge, *compensates* for the loss of the real with fantasy, that resolves into onanism. My understanding of the country as a compensation of, rather than opposition to, the city is shared, on economic grounds, by Wyn Grant, "Rural Politics in Britain," in *Rural Studies in Britain and France*, ed. Philip Lowe and Maryvonne Bodiguel (London: Belhaven Press, 1990): "the Concise Oxford Dictionary . . . defines rural as 'in, of [sic] suggesting the country (opp. Urban), pastoral, or agricultural.' My problem is that I do not see a straight opposition here between urban and rural; their social relationship is, at least in principle, a complementary one. Many smaller urban centers (and even some medium-sized ones) derive a considerable amount of prosperity from acting as service centers for the surrounding countryside" (pp. 286–287).

46. Uvedale Price, "An Essay on the Picturesque," in *The Genius of the Place: The English Landscape Garden, 1620–1820*, ed. John Dixon Hunt and Peter Willis (Cambridge: MIT Press, 1988), 354.

47. See Alexander M. Ross, *The Imprint of the Picturesque on Nineteenth-Century British Fiction* (Waterloo, Canada: Wilfrid Laurier University Press, 1916).

where "the eye could reach nothing of the world outside" (I.1.6).[48] It is a "region."

Educated in the picturesque sensibility of Ruskin, cultivated by Cobbet's abhorrence of "the stench, the noise and the strife of cities," and grown to identify with the educational zeal of Robert Owen,[49] Clym returns to Egdon to transform it into the picturesque region of his urban fantasies. The metaphor for this process of transformation is, throughout the novel, that of "education":

> He had a conviction that the want of most men was knowledge of a sort which brings wisdom rather than affluence. He wished to raise the class at the expense of individuals rather than individuals at the expense of the class. (III.2.207)

Ready to be sacrificed himself to the needs of "class," Clym returns to Egdon to enlighten[50] its people: how can a man waste time in the effeminate city, "when he sees half the world going to ruin for want of somebody to buckle to and teach them" (III.2.211)? His educational goal, however, is not to teach those people how to cope with modernity, or how to rebel to exploitation and poverty. Rather, Clym is eager to make those people learn "how to breast the misery they are born to" (III.2.211) — how to cultivate, in other words, that wretchedness that makes them picturesque in the eyes of those with a "less limited experience."

Lecturing the natives on how to become picturesque creatures idyllically content, Clym's first lesson turns, however, into a teacher's night-

---

48. "[The picturesque] is distinct from the sublime; for though there are some qualities common to them both, yet they differ in many essential points, and proceed from very different causes. In the first place, greatness of dimension is a powerful cause of the sublime; the picturesque has no connection with dimension of any kind. . . . Infinity is one of the most efficient causes of the sublime; the boundless ocean, for that reason, inspires awful sensations; to give it picturesqueness you must destroy that cause of its sublimity; for it is on the shape and disposition of its boundaries that the picturesque in great measure has to depend" (Price, "Essay on the Picturesque," 355).

49. William Cobbett, *Rural Rides*, ed. George Woodcock (1967; reprint, Harmondsworth, Eng.: Penguin, 1983), 294; Robert Owen, *Robert Owen on Education: Selections*, ed. Harold Silver (London: Cambridge University Press, 1969).

50. The Promethean irony of his last name, the "bearer of brightness," has not passed unnoticed. See Jean R. Brooks, "*The Return of the Native*: A Novel of Environment," in *Thomas Hardy*, ed. Harold Bloom (New York: Chelsea House Publishers, 1987), 62.

mare. Pupil and master — alas! — only pretend to understand each other:

> "When I first got away from home I thought this place [Egdon] was not worth troubling about. I thought our life here was contemptible. To oil your boots instead of blacking them, to dust your coat with a switch instead of a brush — was there ever anything more ridiculous? I said."
> "So 'tis; so 'tis!"
> "No, no — you are wrong; it isn't."
> "Beg your pardon, we thought that was your maning?"
> "Well, as my views changed . . . I have come home; and this is how I mean to carry out my plan. I shall keep a school as near to Egdon as possible. . . ." (III.1.205–206)

The problem is that Clym wishes country folks to see the countryside as the city sees it; to understand the past as modernity understands it; to see poverty as the wealthy imagine it — as stretches, that is, of the picturesque. His Owenite idea of man as the product of environment and education is barred by a fundamental contradiction: education *does* create the environment — or at least, as in his case, it creates a perception of the environment. Outside of Clym's education, that picturesque environment simply does not exist. Educated and wealthy Clym Yeobright finds Egdon picturesque, but what sense can picturesqueness make to its inhabitants? "What are picturesque ravines and mists to us who see nothing else?" (I.9.100–101) asks Wildeve. To which, the narrator adds:

> To many persons this Egdon was a place which had slipped out of its century generations ago. . . . The farmer, in his ride . . . bestowed upon the distant upland of heath nothing better than a frown.
> But as for Yeobright, when he looked from the heights on his way he could not help indulging in a barbarous satisfaction. . . . (III.2.209)

Behind the basic lesson in cultural relativism — where your eye sees picturesqueness, mine sees hard life and toil — all this points to the fact that, in the dialectics between Clym and the natives, relativism turns into a matter of cultural hierarchies. In fact, there is no relativism at all, but dominance of one cultural model over another. Having learned of the picturesqueness of the country during his "studious life in Paris, where he had become acquainted with ethical systems popular at the time" (III.2.207), Clym now imposes that sense of picturesqueness onto the country, which is in no position to share his vision of the heath — let alone to promote its own view of it.[51] What is "barbarous" about Clym's love for Egdon is the way in which it does not admit contradiction: Egdon has no choice to conform to what a dominant culture expects from it.

Ready, as we have seen, "to sacrifice the individual" to the general ideas of his own culture, Clym, for instance, submits the eccentric and rebellious Eustacia to his desires for a "romantic martyr" (III.2.216): she *has* to become a countrylike (and ladylike) "good matron in a boarding-school" (III.3.231). Clym, exemplary type of the cultivated citizen, is the prodigal son of Egdon who comes back from the city not to ask forgiveness but to "disturb a sequence to which humanity has been long accustomed" (III.2.208). The past to which he strives to return, like all the objects of his educated desires, is a pseudo-past, a product of his education that constructs, retroactively, what the past *is* supposed to be like — and which destroys, in the meantime, whatever the present of the place might be. Clym is a soul in constant exile, unable to live in the present (the modernity of the city *or* the present poverty of the region) *and* to accept the past as past (which he mistakes instead for the resilience of his fantasies). Wealthy and secure in his social position, Clym longs for "wild and meager living"; modern in his education, "abreast with the central town thinkers of his date," he dreams of the past; "in striving at high thinking he still cleave[s] to plain living"; his entire existence, Hardly points out, is one "local peculiarity" (III.2.207) — the local peculiarity, that is, of desiring a country that exists, and can thus be desired, only in the imagination and culture of the city.

It is because of this local peculiarity of his that Clym diverts the course of the love-triangle plot toward a story of mistaken expectations and wrong paths taken. While Clym tries to return to an innocent and picturesque past "most exhilarating, and strengthening, and soothing"

---

51. It could be interesting to see Hardy's dramatization of cultural differences in light of the discussions of those years, that accompanied the Education Act of 1870. Which "culture" to teach in public schools, when "culture" itself is a relative concept mirroring "conflicting influences and varieties of characters" between social classes and British regions? The only solution, for some, was to teach the culture of the "communities and classes that have won dominion" in the economic and political arena. (Quoted in Arnold, *Culture and Anarchy*, 82.) On the issue of education in the historical context of the Educational Act of 1870, see Philip Collins, "Hardy and Education," in *Thomas Hardy*, ed. Page.

(III.3.224), he fails to see that he is only giddily moving towards an impending tragedy.[52] The plot is simple and belongs to a subgenre of the regionalist story that I am tempted to label, as a tribute to Cervantes, "exemplary regionalism": as in Pagnol's *Jean de Florette*, we have a hero (Jean) coming from the city (Paris) and mistaking the hostility of the rustic place (where it never rains) and the envy and hatred of its inhabitants (who divert the only course of water from Jean's property and want to see him dead) for the innocence of an older and less sophisticated world. In a similar way, the simplicity that Clym expects to see in Egdon is simply not there but exists only in the presumptions of his culture. The difference between Pagnol and Hardy is that the mistake and blindness of the ironic hero becomes, in *The Return of the Native*, an almost metafictional issue. Jean de Florette, that is to say, simply mistakes the reality of Provence — its present corruption, its fall in the inferno of capitalist cravings and speculations, its idolatry of property and capital — for the fantasy of an innocent and uncorrupted countryside. Yet, Provence exists, for Pagnol and his reader, as a reality — witnessed by any map of France — and Pagnol's narrative becomes a denunciation of the *real* Provence, whose innocence has been ultimately corrupted by capital.

Clym's mistake, in a way, is not simply a mistake at the level of reality — he does not mistake, in other words, a fantasy for something real. His mistake is, I suspect, a readerly one — a hermeneutic error. Clym is a misreader, unable to create any new map, and relying only on the misleading cultural maps provided by his culture and unfolded by his expectations. Clym's fundamental problem is that, as soon as he enters the setting of Hardy's story (in book II), he immediately mistakes the *rhetorical* reality of Egdon for another rhetorical commonplace that belongs not to the story but to the dominant culture that he represents — the commonplace of "the country." He then enters an ominous *locus suspectus* — the

---

52. Peter Casagrande, *Unity in Hardy's Novels: 'Repetitive Symmetries'* (Lawrence: Regents Press of Kansas, 1982), divides Hardy's major novels into "novels of return" and "novels of restoration." The former show "the attempt — always painful — to return to one's native place after long absence"; the latter, the "struggle — always futile — to atone for error or mend defect" (p. 2). On the tragic element in Hardy, see Dale Kramer, *Thomas Hardy: The Forms of Tragedy* (Detroit: Wayne State University Press, 1975); and Jeannette King, *Tragedy in the Victorian Novel: Theory and Practice in the Novels of George Eliot, Thomas Hardy, and Henry James* (Cambridge: Cambridge University Press, 1978).

"original of those wild regions of obscurity which are vaguely felt to be compassing us about in midnight dreams of flight and disaster" (I.1.5–6) — misreading it as if it were an idyllic space: "every bird within eyeshot, every reptile not yet asleep, and . . . the surrounding rabbits" wait for him, "curiously watching from hillocks at a safe distance" (II.1.123). It is all as beautiful as in a fairy tale! But — alas! — it is all Clym's misunderstanding.

The misunderstanding, to be fair, should not be blamed entirely on him. Hardy *does* write a "novel of environment"; he *does* begin with an initial "highly wrought description" of the place that is, properly speaking, an idyll,[53] and *does* set the story in a secluded rustic place. The evocations of the picturesque are also there. Yet, frustrating all these expectations, and even betraying the title's anticipation of yet another regenerative return to the origin, Hardy throws Clym in a stretch of unredeemed

> tract of country unaltered from that sinister condition which made Caesar anxious every year to get clear of its glooms before the autumnal equinox, a kind of landscape and weather which leads travelers from the South to describe our island as Homer's Cimmerian land. . . . (I.6.61)

Egdon *is* a gloomy region, a dreary "home of strange phantoms" (I.1.5). All paratextual elements — the title, the regional map, the 1895 preface evoking the "Georgian gaiety and prestige" of the place — are but a travesty hiding the true hideousness of the place.

Unaware, Clym is swindled into his debonair entry into a quite sinister story. The place can hardly accommodate his expectations for picturesqueness. In fact, had we no expectations of our own, it should not have taken us long to realize that "the country" of Hardy's etched map, with its Dürer-like *chiaroscuro*, is one "suggesting tragical possibilities" (I.1.6) rather than picturesque unfoldings. The narrative perspective had taken us, suggestively, to the viewpoint of the tomb "where the eye could reach nothing of the world outside" (I.1.6): how did we mistake that sepulchre for the seclusion of the rustic region? The place is a system of metaphors referring to a hyperbolic Hades, a Tartarean pit "exhaling dark-

---

53. Henry George Liddell and Robert Scott, *A Greek-English Lexicon*, 9th ed. (Oxford: Clarendon Press, 1968), defines the idyll as a "short, highly wrought descriptive poem, mostly on pastoral subjects."

ness" (I.1.4), an inferno presided by Eustacia (I.7.78), and swarming with biblical serpents:

"Look at that," murmured Christian Cantle. "Neighbours, how do we know but that something of the old serpent in God's garden, that gied the apple to the young woman with no clothes, lives on in adders and snakes still? . . ." (IV.7.355)

Even the beauty of Eustacia, "nocturnal" and "flame-like" at the same time, should have raised in us a sincere fear for the fires of hell, which, like Eustacia's gaze, is said to be flamelike and consuming:

She had Pagan eyes, full of nocturnal mysteries, and their light, as it came and went, and came again, was partially hampered by their oppressive lids and lashes; and of these the under lid was much fuller than it usually is with English women. . . . Assuming that the souls of men and women were visible essences, you could fancy the colour of Eustacia's soul to be flame-like. The sparks from it that rose from her dark pupils gave the same impression. (I.7.76–78)

We should have recognized, at the very first appearance of Eustacia moving in "the direction of the small undying fire" with a "glow upon her face" (I.6.65), the appearance of a literal Lucifer. (Latin etymology says Lucifer is a "bearer of light" — another Yeobright.) We *should* have recognized all that; yet, Eustacia's demonic light blinded us — or was it our expectations about "the country" and the "novel of environment"? "You are blinded, Clym," correctly warns Ms. Yeobright: "It was a bad day when you first set eyes on her" (III.3.232)!

Thus, Clym takes the role of the *lector in fabula* in *The Return of the Native*, and becomes, in de Man's terms, his own allegory of reading. He is the bad reader who, unable to suspend his expectations regarding a commonplace "country," becomes ensnared in an almost gothic plot. His blindness becomes the ironic nemesis of this inadequate and prejudiced reader who, despite the incessant reading, ultimately fails to "see":

he read far into the small hours during many nights.

One morning, after a severer strain than usual, he awoke with a strange sensation in his eyes. The sun was shining directly upon the window-blind, and at his first glance thitherward a sharp pain obliged him to close his eyelids quickly. At every new attempt to look about him the same morbid sensibility to light was manifested, and excoriating tears ran down his cheeks. (IV.2.298)

Through Clym, it is as if Hardy has denounced the blindness of a whole generation of "artists and scholars" represented by Clym. Harold Bloom could read it as an instance of what he called the "anxiety of influence" — the agon that each writer engages against the literary tradition that immediately precedes him or her.[54] Yet, is not Hardy denouncing his own generation as well — one that has invented a "country" that is the repository and thesaurus "of all cardinal virtues"? And one, moreover, incapable of reading any other "country"? It is, after all, a contemporary of Hardy who, in the anonymous compilation written for the *British Quarterly Review*, mistakes, like a belated Clym, Egdon's Tartarean pits for lost heavens and hopes that a reading of Hardy will bring more people to "steep themselves in the fresh healthy air of Dorset, and come into contact with the kindly folk who dwell there."[55]

In an early preface to *Far from the Madding Crowd*, Hardy had asked "all good and idealistic readers to . . . refuse steadfastly to believe that there are any inhabitants of Victorian Wessex outside these volumes." Despite such warning, in a 1912 rewriting of the same preface, Hardy had to surrender to the fact that Wessex "has, by degrees, solidified into a utilitarian region which people can go to, take a house in, and write to the papers from." The Dorset region of southern England had been "reconceived" — to use Michael Millgate's term — to fit the stereotype of a Merrie England that Wessex was meant to signify. With little attention to either its present *or* its past, the identity of an entire region was altered to accomodate the fictional image of an unaltered past:

> The pilgrims manifested themselves in the streets of a Dorchester they confusingly insisted on referring to as Casterbridge, and it was not long before the indigenous inhabitants began to reconceive themselves, individually and even corporately, under such now familiar names as Wes-

54. Harold Bloom, *The Anxiety of Influence: A Theory of Poetry* (New York: Oxford University Press, 1977).

55. In R. G. Cox, ed., *Thomas Hardy: The Critical Heritage* (London: Routledge & Kegan Paul, 1970), 78–79.

sex Motors, the Wessex Water Board, The Wessex Saddleback Pig Society, the Casterbridge Hotel, the Mellstock Tea Rooms, and so on.[56]

As *The Life of Thomas Hardy* attests, Hardy was truly concerned that anyone could mistake fictions for facts, and commonplaces for actual geographies.[57] Mistaking fictional Wessex for a real Dorset had meant, after all, the destruction of the very "eccentricity" of a peripheral region, and its transformation into yet another "particular" resort in the great circus of tourism. However, what should be more worrisome for us, "artists and scholars," is the way certain cultural commonplaces manage not only to alter reality but to replicate themselves in the reading of a story by misreading, in the end, the story itself. As Clym misreads Egdon, and remaps its territory according to the commonplace of "the country," so, it seems to me, do regionalist readings. These sorts of readings, which are perhaps dominant today in the scholarship on Hardy, manage not only to rewrite *The Return of the Native* as a novel of regional Dorset[58] but also to rewrite its story to make it fit to the commonplace of a picturesque region "most exhilarating, and strengthening, and soothing." The regionalist's "region," like Clym's "country," is a picturesque place, a lost paradise, "the world we have lost"[59] — a topos, in short, where all the values that have disappeared

56. Michael Millgate, "Unreal Estate: Reflections on Wessex and Yoknapatawpha," in *The Literature of Region and Nation*, ed. R. P. Draper (New York: St. Martin's Press, 1988), 67.

57. "A curious question arose in Hardy's mind . . . whether a romancer was morally justified in going to extreme lengths of assurance . . . in respect of a tale he knew to be absolutely false" (Florence Hardy, *Life*, 61); also: "Had he not discontinued the writing of romances he would, he said, have put at the beginning of each new one: 'Understand that however true this book may be in essence, in fact it is utterly untrue'" (Hardy, *Life*, 391–392).

58. Like Millgate's "pilgrims," Hardy's scholars often try to find Wessex in Dorsetshire. One very selected bibliography exemplifying this tendency might include, in chronological order: Charles George Harper, *The Hardy Country: Literary Landmarks of the Wessex Novels* (London: A. and C. Black, 1904); Hermann Lea, *Thomas Hardy's Wessex* (1913; reprint, Mount Durand: Toucan Press, 1969); Clive Holland, *Thomas Hardy, O.M.: The Man, His Works, and the Land of Wessex* (London: H. Jenkins, 1933); W. Parker, *On the Track of the Wessex Novels: A Guide to the Hardy Country* (Folcroft, Pa.: Folcroft Press, 1969); Denys Kay-Robinson, *Hardy's Wessex Reappraised* (New York: St. Martin's Press, 1971); Desmond Hawkins, *Hardy's Wessex* (London: Macmillan, 1983); and F. P. Pitfield, *Hardy's Wessex Locations* (Wincanton, Eng.: Dorset Publishing, 1992).

59. Peter Laslett, *The World We Have Lost* (New York: Scribner's, 1971).

from our sad world still survive. This region, as Harold Williams puts it in "The Wessex Novels of Thomas Hardy," is

> a secluded agricultural country where the noise of the great industrial centres hardly comes as a distant murmur[;] the characters belong to the simplicity of an older and less sophisticated world than most of us are condemned to live in. . . .[60]

Written in 1914, while, like a distant murmur, the cannons preparing World War II could already be heard, Harold Williams's "secluded agricultural country," pitted against "the noise of the great industrial centres," is from its very outset a topos of the same nature as Clym's Egdon — the pure and uncontaminated arché where the eye can see "nothing of the world outside." The same "bounding" vision of the picturesque imagines here a place isolated from trains and all the other evils of history — a "region."

As Clym remaps Egdon, so does regionalism rewrite Hardy's tragic inferno into the idyllic simplicity of the "region." John Paterson's study of textual variants in *The Return to the Native* is clear in its thesis:[61] Hardy's original gloomy vision of Egdon had to be radically altered, already in a second draft, under the pressure of editors and readers alike. In the "Ur-novel," the heath is depicted in the unmistakable colors of a Miltonian hell, and its human counterpart, Eustacia, figures as a literal demon, a witch. The return of the native had to be, for Hardy, a descent into the hell of an original trauma, or a return, to say it with Freud, of the repressed. Everything had to finish with a catastrophe: Clym, hopelessly blind, his mother and his wife both dead; Thomasin a widow; Diggory Venn lost to Egdon Heath. But the sixth chapter — required by the editors, as Hardy resentfully reminds us in a note[62] — almost "rewrites" the "moral" of the

60. Harold Williams, "The Wessex Novels of Thomas Hardy," in Cox, *The Critical Heritage*, 433. What is this secluded "inside," after all, this "old place," if not the humanistic realm of literature and rhetoric that desperately resists the siege of technology and daily news?

61. John Paterson, "The Making of *Return of the Native*," 8–10.

62. Hardy footnotes book six as follows: "The writer may state here that the original conception of the story did not design a marriage between Thomasin and Venn. He was to have retained his isolated and weird character to the last, and to have disappeared mysteriously from the heath, nobody knowing whither — Thomasin remaining a widow. But certain circumstances of serial publication led to a change of intent. Readers can therefore choose between the endings, and those with an austere artistic code can assume the more consistent conclusion to be the true one."

entire story: with a rather inconsequential happy ending, Diggory returns to Egdon, against all odds, as a wealthy man, and marries Thomasin. Clym, for his part, crowns a new dream of his and, blind like Tiresias, becomes a preacher on the heath. They all live happily ever after!

Nonetheless, Hardy still retained some of the original gloomy moods in the later editions. It is probably this resilient element of a sinister heath that, rather than simply belying regionalist expectations of a blissful seclusion, imposes again the critical necessity to "rewrite" *The Return of the Native* and hide the dismal region behind — for instance — Frederic Manning's certainty that "[Hardy's] pessimism, after all, is only a habit of thought."[63] Pessimism is just an eccentricity of the author, a habit — something, in other words, that can be bracketed away in the reading of a fundamentally idyllic story. It does not take long before this pessimism becomes a "defect" of the author, an attempt to contaminate regionalism with the moods of tragedy. George Wing, in a seminal essay on "Hardy and Regionalism," puts Hardy in his place, so to speak:

> To adopt an Aristotelian proposal, Hardy reaches his greatest intensity, his greatest impact as novelist, when he achieves total felicity of relationship among action, person and place; and these three are all constituents of what is generally defined as the regional novel. . . . And when, as very infrequently happens, the action moves outside fixed regional limits, it often becomes melodramatic, caricatural, uncertain, at times reading like a guide book.[64]

63. Frederic Manning, quoted in Peter Widdowson, *Hardy in History: A Study in Literary Sociology* (London: Routledge, 1989), 24. What is "pessimism" for his critic is "truth" for Hardy. In "General Preface to the Novels and Poems," which he wrote for the 1912 Wessex edition of his texts, Hardy protests that "these impressions have been condemned as 'pessimistic' — as if that were a very wicked adjective. . . . It must be obvious that there is a higher characteristic of philosophy than pessimism, or meliorism, or even than the optimism of these critics — which is truth." In a chapter titled "Pessimistic Meliorist," Michael Millgate observes: "Reviewers of *Wessex Poems*, like those of Hardy's later novels, had repeatedly invoked the term 'pessimism', as if in so doing they were simultaneously defining a distinctive philosophical position and making an adverse critical judgment. Hardy's exasperation at being so crudely categorized was exceeded only by his overwhelming sense of the inconceivability of 'optimism' in a world of such radical imperfection." In Michael Millgate, *Thomas Hardy: A Biography* (New York: Random House, 1982), 409.

64. George Wing, "Hardy and Regionalism," 98.

Hardy's tragic mood is a "melodrama," a failure — not even a tragedy. What can a "relationship among action, person and place" — namely, regionalism — generate but a felicitously happy story? The rest, regionalism *dixit*, is just tourism.

With his novel altered by editors, reinterpreted by readers, conditioned by reviewers, and limited to "fixed regional limits" by its critics, Hardy, in the end, disappears behind a thesaurus of regionalist expectations.[65] Not only is Hardy *de facto* "defaced," his very text is defaced and finally obliterated by the "general name" of the "regional novel" that has taken its place. "The region" of regionalism is the product of a reading that transforms a fiction — Egdon — into a metaphor. Metaphor, this "most beautiful of all tropes," accomplishes "the supremely difficult task of providing a name for everything" (Quintilian, *Institutio Oratoria*, VIII.vi.5): it provides a name, a map, and a story, to a literature of place always in search for a place from which to originate. The region of regional literature is expressed, therefore, as a simile and a map: the alternative to modernization is *like* Egdon; the rustic paradise is *like* its etched map.

The metaphor of regionalism operates a further step, which we again learn from Quintilian (*Institutio Oratoria*, VIII.vi.9). In the simile, we compare an object to the thing we wish to describe; in the metaphor, instead, the object is actually *replaced* by the name (*pro ipsa re dicitur*). The region is not "like" Egdon — more radically, the region *is* Egdon, while Hardy's Egdon, with its ominous *chiaroscuro* and its "tragic possibilities," simply disappears behind the "region" that has taken its place.

One should be careful in giving credence to the rumors that portray regionalism as a recuperation of "minor literatures" and "marginal" voices. As Clym replaces Egdon with the undifferentiated category of "the country," so does regionalism replace Hardy's story with the dominant expectations of a beautiful region. Regionalism, in a sense, is the erasure of the other, which is rewritten to fit all the expectations of a dominant culture — rewritten, namely, as "the other." What remains of an original otherness, of what Hardy calls "eccentricity," is a trope, a metaphor good only insofar as it fits our interests, needs, dreams, and rhetorical horizons. The rest disappears. The etched map "suggesting tragic possibilities" be-

65. Contra, Miller, *Topographies*, 27 ff.

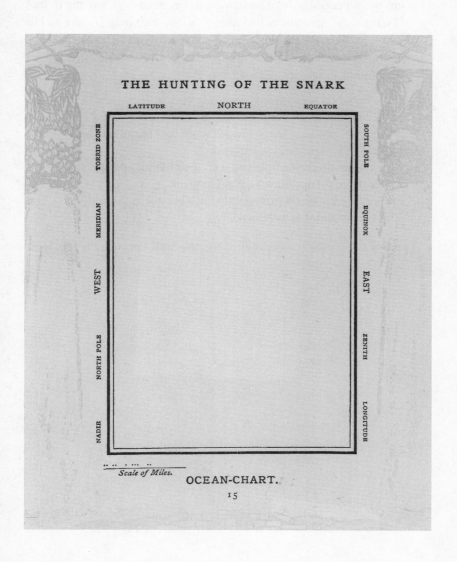

THE HUNTING OF THE SNARK

LATITUDE   NORTH   EQUATOR

TORRID ZONE   MERIDIAN   WEST   NORTH POLE   NADIR

SOUTH POLE   EQUINOX   EAST   ZENITH   LONGITUDE

Scale of Miles.

OCEAN-CHART.

15

Figure 5. Lewis Carroll. "The Captain's Blank Map." *The Hunting of the Snark and Other Poems*. New York: Harper and Brothers, 1903.

comes a blank, a void that we can fill with the topoi of origins and happiness and the tones of the idyll and pastoral. Lewis Carroll, writing in that age of cartographic optimism, had imagined one such map (Figure 5). His good Captain, like our regionalist, has steered the wheel away from the "sophisticated world most of us are condemned to live in," directed toward the land of simplicity and joy:

> He bought a large map representing the sea,
> Without the least vestige of land:
> And the crew were much pleased when they found it to be
> A map they could all understand.
> "Other maps are such shapes, with their islands and capes!
> But we've got our brave Captain to thank"
> (So the crew would protest) "that he's bought *us* the best —
> A perfect and absolute blank!"[66]

66. Lewis Carroll, *The Hunting of the Snark* (New York: Harper & Brothers, 1903), 14.

Lost in an Ancient South

Elizabeth Gaskell and the Rhetoric of Latitudes

Wandering lost upon the mountains of our choice,
Again and again we sigh for an ancient south.
                    — W. H. AUDEN, "In Time of War"

When she grew up, Elizabeth always found stories of travel spell-
binding — but she never could cope with geography.
                    — JENNY UGLOW, *Elizabeth Gaskell: A Habit of Stories*

On September 2, 1854, the first installment of *North and South* was published in Charles Dickens's London-based *Household Words*. Elizabeth Gaskell's work, a splendid allegory of the ways in which the manners of the old southern landed order made their way into the modern indus-trialized north, gave valuable lessons in survival and politics, economy and ethics, sociology and literature, history and geography. Coeval with the strike at Preston,[1] which gripped the nation for eight months with the

1. As the form that this strike took will be relevant for the following reading of *North and South*, let me quote here the summary that *The London Illustrated News*

fear of a Jacobin revolution on British soil, and similar to *Hard Times*, which had preceded it in the same magazine, *North and South* is a kind of apocalyptic journey into the inferno of the changing times — modern poverty, rage, desperation, militant trade unionism, and class antagonism.

In an era in which national attention seemed to move along the longitudinal lines of the Eastern Question raised by the Crimean War, *North and South* stood as a memento to remind public opinion that while thirty thousand British soldiers were perishing between Scutari and Balaclava, a comparable number of Her Majesty's subjects, like poor Bessy Higgins, were silently dying at home "coughing and spitting blood . . . poisoned by the fluff [from carding cotton],"[2] victims of the insalubrious working conditions of the manufacturing trade. A war was fought across the sea, but a domestic warfare, with its casualties, too, had been waged — between capital and labor, "between the employer and the employed" (NS 166). "Society as a whole is more and more splitting up into two great hostile camps" — recorded the *Communist Manifesto* of 1848 — "two great classes directly facing each other: Bourgeoisie and Proletariat."[3] So life in 1854, as Gaskell's fictionalized proletariat sees it, looks "like th' great battle o' Armageddon" (NS 202). While the world splits into East and West, England herself breaks into a "totalest separation"[4] — "God help 'em! north

---

provided of the disorders that originated at Preston: "The facts of the case seem to be that in 1847, when a general 10 percent reduction took place, the millowners either promised their operatives — or they believed so — a general 10 percent advance on the rates of piecework as soon as prosperity returned. Prosperity came, but with it no general rise — or at least none to the extent looked for. Dissatisfaction began to prevail . . . the time had come for insisting on a general rise of payments in their respective trades . . . the associated masters, feeling that the intention was to take them in detail, closed their mills." In "The Preston Wages dispute," *London Illustrated News*, November 12, 1853.

2. Elizabeth Gaskell, *North and South* (Harmondsworth, Eng.: Penguin, 1970), 146. References to *North and South* are given in the body of the text as "NS 146," for example.

3. Karl Marx and Friedrich Engels, *The Communist Manifesto* (Harmondsworth, Eng.: Penguin, 1985), 80.

4. Carlyle, in 1843, on industrial society: "We call it Society; and go about professing openly the totalest separation, isolation. Our life is not a mutual helpfulness; but rather, cloacked under due laws-of-war, named 'fair competition' and so forth, it is a mutual hostility. We have profoundly forgotten everywhere that Cash-payment is not the sole relation of human beings. . . . " In Thomas Carlyle, *Past and Present* (New York: New York University Press, 1965), 148.

an' south have each getten their own troubles" (NS 382)! And while longitude compels the imagination of British foreign policy and the imperialist adventures of Kipling's literary orientalism, it is *North and South* that posits, "with a strong Darkshire accent" (NS 288), the questions of domestic policy and regionalism.

England is divided twice: first by an underlying tension between the classes that, organized by trade unionism and the newly constituted Communist Party, threatens to climax in a civil war; and second, by the uneven development of industrialization, which increases progressively the differences between an industrialized north and the southern regions, still managed by their landowning aristocracies. *North and South* is, from its very outset, the dramatization of such divisions. It hardly makes any sense to talk now of a homogeneous nation when the latter is fragmented into classes and regions. Yet, accustomed to despair, reassured only by her Unitarian faith, Gaskell relentlessly tries, page after page, chapter after chapter, to provide a model for the synthesis of such differences into a new kind of unity. The attempt, to many, might have looked like a concession to the synthetic logic of Marxist dialectics. Karl Marx himself had cheered, in a leader published in the *New York Daily Tribune* on August 1, 1854, at Gaskell's depiction of a capitalist class "full of presumption, affectation, petty tyranny and ignorance."[5] The very heroine she has conceived for *North and South* looks like "a democrat, a red republican, a member of the Peace Society, a socialist" (NS 409) to some other characters. In truth, however, such portraits of Gaskell and her heroines are imprecise at best: "no one can feel more deeply than I — Gaskell wrote to a friend in 1848 — how wicked it is to do anything to excite class against class."[6] The protagonist of the adventures unfolding in *North and South*, for instance, acts on a conviction that has little to do with Marxist dialectics and is indebted instead to the rhetorical dialectics of catechism. Her method is, as Jauss would have defined it, the method of "question and answer":

> "A strike!" asked Margaret. "What for? What are they going to strike for?" . . .
> "They are wanting higher wages, I suppose?" asked Mr. Hale . . .

5. Angus Easson, ed., *Elizabeth Gaskell: The Critical Heritage* (London: Routledge, 1991), 487.
6. Elizabeth Gaskell, *The Letters of Mrs Gaskell*, ed. J. A. V. Chapple and Arthur Pollard (Manchester, Eng.: Manchester University Press, 1966), 67.

"Does it not make the town very rough?" asked Margaret. . . . (NS 162)[7]

Addressing a society she felt had reverted into a Hobbesian *homo homini lupus*, Gaskell orders her story in the dialogic form of a catechism. The subjects treated are well synthesized by the Baconian titles: "Masters and Men," "Men and Gentlemen," and so forth. As the final goal of each chapter is to turn the disjunctive "and" into a conjunctive one, so is Gaskell's ultimate goal, as has been correctly noted,[8] that of reconstituting the Armageddon of social divisions into a new peaceful community. Dialogue is the way to unity.

The plot, a syllabus of fifty-two discussions on various momentous topics, is centered on the *Bildung* of Margaret Hale. Representative of an "aristocratic society down in the south, with their slow days of careless ease" (NS 122), Margaret is forced to move, despite her initial "repugnance to the idea of a manufacturing town" (NS 96), to the industrial north. Here, she finds out that the new life of industry and commerce has pitted, in the allegorical figures of Mr. Thornton and Nicholas Higgins, master against man, boss against workman. The situation is, in fact, all too reminiscent of the real one at Preston: Gaskell's symbolic workers, like their historical counterparts, have sworn to fight "five or six masters who have set themselves against paying the wages they've been paying these two years past" (NS 182–183). Gaskell's contemporary reader, moving her eyes, week after week, from the newspaper to a new episode of *North and South*, must not have taken long to recognize, in the north reached by Margaret, a not so veiled allegory of the changing times. And it should not have

7. On catechism as a form of dialogism, see Hans Robert Jauss, *Question and Answer: Forms of Dialogic Understanding*, ed. Michael Hayes (Minneapolis: University of Minnesota Press, 1989).

8. The French diplomat Charles de Moüy, in an article published in 1861 for the *Revue Européenne*, synthesizes: "There are two actors in this real-life drama, and unhappily they are two opposed groups: the masters and the workers. Mrs Gaskell's purpose is to end this conflict and to turn these fierce antagonists into allies and brothers. . . . Such is the task that Mrs Gaskell has undertaken: to call men back to their duty." In Easson, *Elizabeth Gaskell*, 493. See also Catherine Gallagher, "North and South: The Paradoxes of Metonimy," in *The Industrial Reformation of English Fiction: 1832–1867* (Chicago: University of Chicago Press, 1985), on Gaskell's "metonymic" arrangement (north and south) of class divisions. Finally, on the attempt to establish a "community," see Raymond Williams, *Culture and Society, 1780–1950* (1958; reprint, Harmondsworth, Eng.: Penguin, 1963), 103.

taken her long, either, to grasp the messianic role cast by Gaskell on the heroine of her parable: as a woman *and* as a southerner, Margaret's calling is to teach northerners nothing less than the way to peace and reunification. "I am not fond of being catechised" (NS 165), she remarks. Yet, ready to quote "the clearer parts of the Bible" herself (NS 187), she eagerly dispenses instructions to Thornton on the one hand and Higgins on the other: "we have all of us one human heart" (NS 511).

This "oneness," in fact, is the ultimate goal of Margaret's *Bildung*. As class divisions are echoed by the allegorical split between north and south, Margaret's *Bildung* coincides with the realization that divisions are, after all, the fruit of mere prejudices. It is the prejudice and insolence of northern capitalism to think that "commerce were everything and humanity nothing" (NS 204); and it is the prejudice and haughtiness of southern aristocracy to want a humanistic world "still at exchanging wild-beast skins for acorns" (NS 409). Similarly, it is prejudice that keeps masters and workers inimically far from each other: "workpeople speak as though it were the interest of the employers to keep them from acquiring money" (NS 165), Margaret notices; but also masters are prejudiced if they think that workers are merely "a rough, heathenish set of fellows" (NS 171). In an Augustinian *tolle lege*,[9] Margaret learns that peace and unity begin only with an act of "humility" (NS 426): no latitude and no class, no region and no rank can live without the other. In this sense, Margaret believes, we are all one. By her example and journey, Margaret Hale therefore instructs a generation of southerners on how to participate responsibly — not simply by denial — in the new industrial order advancing from the north. They ought to participate without relinquishing their demeanor, but

9. "In her nervous agitation, [Margaret] unconsciously opened a book of her father's that lay upon the table, — the words that caught her eye in it, seemed almost made for her present state of acute self-abasement: —

'Je ne voudrois pas reprendre mon coeur en ceste sorte: meurs de honte, aveugle, impudent, traistre et desloyal a ton Dieu, et sembables choses; mais je voudrois le corriger par voye de compassion. Or sus, mon pauvre coeur, nous voila tombez dans la fosse, laquelle nous avions tant resolu d'eschapper. Ah! relevons-nous, et quittons-la pour jamais, reclamons la misericorde de Dieu, et esperons en elle qu'elle nous assistera pour desormais estre plus fermes; et remettons-nous au chemin de l'humilite. Courage, soyons meshuy sur nos gardes, Dieu nous aydera.'

'The way of humility. Ah,' thought Margaret, 'that is what I have missed! But courage, little heart. We will turn back, and by God's help we may find the lost path.' (NS 426)

rather by extending it into the safeguarding of the nation's morality and spiritual oneness. It is the woman from the southern province who will come, as a messiah, to patch together the broken vessel of the modern society of the north.

The story thus becomes, at an almost explicit level, an allegorical marriage of north and south realized, at a symbolic level, by the wedding between southern Margaret and northern Thornton.[10] At the beginning of the story, the two seem "not [to] get on particularly well" (NS 115). Following the clichés of the love war,[11] and overcoming prejudice, the symbolic marriage of north and south becomes in turn anagogic of a more compelling need to reunite the whole of society. In a game of allegorical concordances, Margaret and Thornton are united by matrimony just as south and north are to be united by the sacred vows of nationhood — and, in turn, as labor and capital should cooperate in the name of commonwealth. As the *Bildung* progresses toward the final conquest of all prejudices, Margaret's wedding reconciles, in fact, a northern interest in "the progress of commerce" (NS 409) with a southern humanism allegedly capable of handling "workmen as if they were human beings" (NS 232). The final goal of this entire catechism, then, is quite a peculiar Eucharist: in one body, north and south, capitalism and humanism, region and nation will melt. "It won't be division enough, in that awful day" (NS 202)!

Let us begin, then, from where the plot itself begins — from Margaret's loss of her beloved south, and from her fall into the northern inferno of her dividing prejudices. Departed from the south with her mother, Margaret arrives on one curious, sulfurous morning, at Milton-North station — a name, needless to say, which is all an expectation:

> For several miles before they reached Milton, they saw a deep lead-coloured cloud hanging over the horizon in the direction in which it lay. . . . Nearer to the town, the air had a faint taste and smell of smoke; perhaps, after all, more a loss of the fragrance of grass and herbage than

10. Williams, *Culture and Society*, 99; Catherine Gallagher, *The Industrial Reformation of English Fiction: 1832–1867* (Chicago: University of Chicago Press, 1985), 177–178.

11. Helen Cooper, Adrienne Auslander Munich, and Susan Merrill Squier, "Arms and the Woman: The Con[tra]ception of the War Text," in *Arms and the Woman: War, Gender, and Literary Representation*, ed. Cooper, Munich, and Squier (Chapel Hill: University of North Carolina Press, 1989), 10.

any positive taste or smell. Quick they were whirled over long, straight, hopeless streets . . . every van, every waggon and truck, bore cotton, either in the raw shape in bags, or the woven shape in bales of calico. People thronged the footpaths. . . . (NS 96–97)

The northern city, busy with traffic and industry, where all is the same and condemned to eternal darkness, deprived of fragrance and color, "smoky, dirty" (NS 123), is, like the "Paris" of Clym Yeobright, the term of opposition to a complementary place — the south. Representative of the south is, in the economy of the novel, Margaret's lost Helstone: "The life in Milton was so different" from Helstone, she remarks, "the air itself was so different" (NS 130). Yet, *what* is so different about the south? "Tell me about Helstone," Mr. Lennox asks Margaret:

> "Oh. . . . There is the church and a few houses near it on the green — cottages, rather — with roses growing all over them."
>
> "And flowering all the year round, especially at Christmas — make your picture complete," said he.
>
> "No," replied Margaret, somewhat annoyed, "I am not making a picture. I am trying to describe Helstone as it really is. . . ."
>
> "I am penitent," he answered. "Only it really sounded like a village in a tale rather than in real life."
>
> "And so it is," replied Margaret, eagerly. . . . "Helstone is like a village in a poem — in one of Tennyson's poems. But I won't try and describe it any more. You would only laugh at me if I told you what I think of it — what it really is." (NS 42–43)

Mr. Lennox, a contemptuously inconsequential character from a narrative point of view (he does not succeed in marrying Margaret, he cannot defend her brother in a court martial . . .) is useful inasmuch as he can warn the reader, with his pseudo-Socratic irony, about the fundamentally fictional and literary nature of Margaret's prejudices — of her picturesquely Tennysonian "south," but of her Miltonian "north" as well.

Margaret's north and south are latitudes of the imagination — what she "thinks of it" — stronger, in a way, than any reality principle: where her mother suffers the "damp, unhealthy air" of the south, for instance, Margaret smells "the freshest, purest fragrance" of its "delicious air" (NS 75–76). And where Mr. Thornton sees a lazy, unproductive, and reactionary south, Margaret angrily replies:

"You do not know anything about the south. If there is less adventure and less progress — I suppose I must not say less excitement — from the gambling spirit of trade . . . there is less suffering also. I see men here going about in the streets who look ground down by some pinching sorrow or care — who are not only sufferers but haters. Now, in the south we have our poor, but there is not that terrible expression in their countenances of a sullen sense of injustice which I see here. You do not know the south Mr Thornton." (NS 122–123)

Mr. Thornton, in truth, knows nothing of the south. Yet, how does Margaret know so much about "what it really is"? And how does she know so much about the north, as well?[12] She has been in Milton for only a few days, and she can already talk about its modern "progress"; she can hardly remember the south, which she left for London as a child — but she knows that an air of idyllic serenity lingers there. Sure enough, north and south are, as David Horne suggests, well-known Victorian metaphors:

In the *Northern Metaphor* Britain is pragmatic, empirical, calculating, Puritan, bourgeois, enterprising, adventurous, scientific, serious, and believes in struggle. Its sinful excess is a ruthless avarice, rationalized in the belief that the prime impulse in all human beings is a rational, calculating, economic self-interest.

In the *Southern Metaphor* Britain is romantic, illogical, muddled, divinely lucky, Anglican, aristocratic, traditional, frivolous, and believes in order and tradition.[13]

Epochal commonplaces more than simple metaphors, north and south are expectations in Margaret's mind. That is why, before she has even set foot in the north, she can already feel "detestation for all she had ever *heard* of the north of England, the manufacturers, the people, the wild and bleak country" (NS 72; emphasis mine).

Not at all differently, Margaret's south, too, is a place of the same kind — and this is what Margaret has to acknowledge at the end of her

12. Charlotte Brontë, in a letter to Elizabeth Gaskell of September 30, 1854, remarks on her reading of *North and South*: "It seems to me that you understand well the Genius of the north. Where the southern Lady and the northern Mechanic are brought into contest and contact — I think Nature is well respected." In Easson, *Elizabeth Gaskell*, 330.

13. Donald Horne, *God Is an Englishman* (Sydney: Angus and Robertson, 1969), 22–23.

Bildung. The moment of crisis, when she is forced to come to terms with the rhetorical construction of her south, occurs when her fantasies about a Utopic place where "unity may be brought into practice" (NS 167) start convincing poor Nicholas Higgins to leave the north for the mythical prospects of a sylvan land of oneness: "Now I dunnot know how far off it is, but I've been thinking if I could get 'em down theer, where food is cheap and wages good, and all the folk, rich and poor, master and man, friendly like; yo' could, may be, help me to work" (NS 381).

Is not Higgins's an understandable determination? We can hardly be surprised if he is so eager to go, no matter "how far off" this "south" may be! Southern is for him the promise of a lost paradise where "all the folk" are one and unity is total — as in the golden age of humankind, before inequality was instituted by an evil society. Nothing can stop Higgins, who is wearied by all the misadventures and injustices that make the life of a poor worker in the north ("It's a withstanding of injustice, past, present, or to come" [NS 296]). And so, in the face of Higgins's determination, Margaret feels the moral obligation to lay bare the literariness of her "south," and dissuade gullible Higgins with a different picture of it — a "more realistic" one, we could say, but keeping in mind that this "real" south, where Margaret has truly never lived either, is just another rhetorical construction. It looks like the commonplace preindustrial south, in fact, that a northerner like Mr. Thornton could have well imagined:

> for anything you could do [in the south], Higgins, with the best will in the world, you would, may be, get nine shillings a week; may be ten, at the outside. . . . You must not go to the south. . . . You could not stand it. You would have to be out all weathers. It would kill you with rheumatism. The mere bodily work at your time of life would break you down. The fare is different to what you have been accustomed to. (NS 381–382)

The old, picturesque south, is, for a moment, suspended: the place no longer is a Tennysonian poem, and its air has ceased to be fragrant. Rheumatic and somber, like the "country" unveiled by Hardy in the "Dorsetshire Labourer," the picture of a new, terrible south is evoked. Life in the modern north is the best possible life on earth! Progress and industry are the only salvation from a damp nature.

All this, of course, does not mean that Margaret will put aside the desire for cheap food, good wages, and all the folk — rich and poor, master and man, friendly alike. For her, living in the cold and warlike north, the fantasy of an elsewhere remains the only possible way to preserve, against the collapse of all the symbols of social unity, a model of justice and peaceful wholesomeness, an ethical *exemplum*.[14] As the real south is unveiled as being a rheumatic hell, the ideal one remains a topos offering a perspective of justice to be realized — "the equality of friendship between the adviser and advised classes" (NS 169). The south is, therefore, an ethical model still to be predicated, with all of Margaret's missionary zeal, in order to give the society of the north at least an idea of what is good. This ethical elsewhere, surely, is a *raisonnement hypothétique et conditionnel* — as Rousseau would have called it — a "hypothetical reasoning" whose goal is not to paint facts but to mitigate inequality, injustice, and strife amidst humankind. It is no mere chance that Victorian Elizabeth Gaskell had placed this ethical space in a "far off," hypothetical "south." A long and old rhetorical tradition of topical "norths" and commonplace "souths" was already before her and her public — a boundless thesaurus of latitudinal expectations in which many Higginses had already been lost.

> Ne sommes-nous pas convenus que les passions varient toutes les fois qu'on avance de cent lieues vers le Nord? L'amour est-il le même à Marseille et à Paris? Tout au plus peut-on dire que les pays soumis depuis longtemps au même genre de gouvernement offrent dans les habitudes sociales une sorte de ressemblance extérieure.
>
> Les paysages, comme les passions, comme la musique, changent aussi dès qu'on s'avance de trois ou quatre degrés vers le Nord.
>
> — STENDHAL, "La Duchesse de Palliano"

Around the year 1520 B.C., the Pharaoh Tutmosi I reached the source of the Euphrates with a military expedition. He was very shaken to see the water going from north to south, and had the following words written on a stele nearby as a memento of the ominous sight: "Here I have seen the water turned upside down, falling by moving upward."[15] The Pharaoh had his firm convictions of what north and south had to be, and, before the ge-

---

14. For the relevance of the *exemplum* in the rhetoric of catechism, see Carlo Del Corno, "Nuovi studi sull'exemplum," *Lettere italiane* 36.1 (1984).

15. Quoted in Giuseppe Dematteis, *Le metafore della terra. La geografia umana tra mito e scienza* (Milano: Feltrinelli, 1996), 30.

ographers of Western Europe could turn his map of the world "upside down," the idea that the water could go from bottom (north) to the top (south) was for him frankly disturbing.[16] Like the Pharaoh, many others after him held similarly clear convictions regarding the essence of north and south, and one might reasonably suppose that the geographic relevance of latitude has hardly equalled the rhetorical expectations one has of commonplaces such as north and south.

The theory of latitudinal differences is so closely associated with the name of Montesquieu that no apology should be necessary to choose *De l'esprit des lois* — instead of, say, Bodin, or Tutmosi's stele — as a point of departure to discuss the formation of a rhetoric of latitudes.[17] It is in the third part of *De l'esprit des lois* that Montesquieu deals systematically with the relationship between climate (books XIV–XVII) and land (book XVIII) to the "general spirit" of humankind (book XIX). The first chapter illustrates the general theory:

> If it is true [*S'il est vrai*] that the character of the spirit and the passions of the heart are extremely different in diverse climate, then the laws must be relative both to the difference of these passions, and to the difference of these characters.[18]

Climate is productive of differences in passion and character. Humankind, to be sure, is one, but heat and cold have different effects on the body. Cold tightens the pores and conserves "more vigor"; heat, on the contrary, dilates the pores, through which vigor escapes.

All this would not sound like a dramatic difference, were it not for the

16. David Turnbull writes: "Of course, orientation is an arbitrary convention. Indeed, the very word *orient*-ation comes from 'East' being the direction of the rising sun and hence it was common practice [until more or less the eighteenth century] to put it at the top of the map. North, whilst being one end of the Earth's axis of rotation, is not a privileged direction in space, which after all has no 'up' or 'down'. That north is traditionally 'up' on [modern] maps is the result of a historical process, closely connected with the global rise and economic dominance of northern Europe." In David Turnbull, *Maps Are Territories: Science Is an Atlas* (1989; reprint, Chicago: University of Chicago Press, 1993), 8.

17. On other alleged "origins" of the theories of north and south, see Robert Shackleton, "The Evolution of Montesquieu's Theory of Climate," *Revue Internationale de Philosophie* 33–34 (1955).

18. Charles-Louis de Montesquieu, *De l'esprit des lois*, vol. 1, ed. Victor Goldschmidt (Paris: Garnier Flammarion, 1979), XIV.1; all translations mine, unless otherwise noted.

fact that such variation in vigor translates immediately into further psychological distinctions:

> This greater force must certainly produce [*doit produire bien*] some effects: for example, more confidence on oneself, that is to say, more courage; a greater awareness of one's superiority, that is, a minor desire for vengeance . . .[19]

In the rhetorical language of syllogism ("if it is true," then "it must produce," and so on), Montesquieu manages to transfer "difference" — of habits, of laws, of culture — from humankind to nature, and from history to place. It is the place, the boundary, the environment that produces different sensibilities — facts, that is, stronger than anything that human history could modify.

From this rediscovered sense of objectivity, a new concept is born of "nation" as unity of land, people, and law. The validity of the law that presides to a particular nation is founded on the laws that are proper to its locale. Objectivity, therefore, opens up to relativism: each nation presents different versions of the universal law, because places are different, climate produces dissimilar needs, and latitude diverse races. And of all different places on earth, two of them — north and south — illustrate the most radical differences ever possible. They signify the two furthest poles within which human variations can oscillate:

> You will find, in the climates of the north, peoples who have a few vices, many virtues, a lot of sincerity and earnestness. Approach the countries of the south [*pays du midi*], and you will think you are getting further and further from morality itself; more lively passions multiply crimes; everyone will try to take from the others all advantages which may help to appease those passions.[20]

From Montesquieu's fundamentally Hobbesian point of view, humankind is driven by egotistic impulses, and therefore needs law and society to be restrained. But the only reason why humans would gather into a society is if they feel pressed by a harsh environment, an impious cold, a meager crop, and put their efforts together in order to "win" nature. As long as Cybele, under the halcyon sky of the south, provides nourishment and sun to her children, society simply will not exist. In the north, instead,

19. Montesquieu, *l'Esprit des lois*, XIV.2.
20. Montesquieu, *l'Esprit des lois*, XIV.2.

people need to gather into cooperative societies and so defend themselves against the harsh climate. Their unity is a contract: individual passions are sacrificed in order to cohere into a whole. The group will prepare a defense against an otherwise overpowering nature.

Montesquieu's north, then, is the overcoming of a state of nature and the establishment of a supraindividual spirit (*Esprit*) that unites: it is the cradle of *society*, the place where humankind first separated from nature. The south, instead, is the topos of an original state of nature, lawless and barbaric, egotistic — the locus, in fact, of an original "latent passion," resilient still, as Margaret Hale remembers it, in the "instantaneous ferocity of expression that comes over the countenances of all natives of wild or southern countries" (NS 313).

The same paradigmatic contrast between southern "passion" and northern "spirit" was popularized, at the turn of the eighteenth century, by Madame de Staël. The novelty of a work such as *De l'influence des passions sur le bonheur des individus et des nations*, 1796, lay in its attempt to develop a more precise concept of "nation" from Montesquieu's vague notion of northern "society." For the rest, de Staël had just relied on Montesquieu's teleology of progress from an original south — where people lay idle under a bluer sky, developing nothing but insane passions — to a modern north, where a harsh environment imposed the necessity, and the institution, of cooperation, industry, and "society."

From this spatialization of history and progress, de Staël could then advance the existence of "two very distinct literatures: the one that comes from the south [*celle qui vient du midi*], and the one which descends from the north."[21] This is the thesis, notably, advanced in *De la littérature considérée dans ses rapports avec les institutions sociales*. The new Romantic age then opens by bringing Montesquieu's syllogism to its ultimate conclusion: if it is true that climates have consequences on humankind, literature, among all other institutions, must also differ along latitudinal lines. The lack of a unifying *Esprit*, which causes the fragmentation of the south into a "multitude of provinces," nourishes in turn a peculiar provincialism [*les haines particulières*] from which a minor literature only can be born. Galvanized by "l'amour de patrie,"[22] instead, the literature of the north —

21. Madame de Staël, *De la littérature considérée dans ses rapports avec les institutions sociales*, ed. Paul Van Tieghem (Genève: Droz, 1959), 178, 181.
22. Mme de Staël, *De la littérature*, 160–161.

a new, *national* literature — points already at the luminous future of the Romantic sensibility.

De Staël's attempt to make of nationalism a fundamental aesthetic category has been noticed already.[23] In fact, with *De la littérature*, the existence of two different poetics is established: a poetic of national values on the one hand, and one of "marginal," "minor," and "provincial" purpose on the other. Both kinds of literatures, incidentally, connect poetic sensibility to place. The difference is that a "national" literature is progressive, modern, and, so to speak, *against nature*. A "provincial" literature, instead, is traditional, ancient, and at one with nature. As Montesquieu's "society" of cooperation created by the northern peoples is a means to insulate humankind from a hostile nature, so does de Staël's national "literature of the north" separate nature from writing via a modern "philosophical" attitude. Schiller's dialectic of "naive" and "sentimental" is translated, in other words, into de Staël's dichotomy between a naive and "ancient" south and a sentimental, "modern" north, in which, to use Schiller's own words, "nature begins to disappear from human life as an experience."[24] Montesquieu's theodicy of humankind is then recapitulated in de Staël's literary vision, as her genius of the human letters progresses from the ancient south of the Greeks — "able, under the serendipitous sky, to live with nature"[25] — to the north, where "nature" is reduced to an *idea* pondered "with the fervor, sensitivity, and sweet melancholy that we moderns do."[26]

The problem is that once a naive and immediate contact with nature, characteristic of the poetry of the ancients, is superseded by the institution of modern society, a "sentiment" supplements for the loss: melancholia. That is why, de Staël observes, "melancholia, this sentiment fecund of works of genius, belongs almost exclusively to the northern climates."[27] The observation, in fact, becomes a truth — or a commonplace — as the century progresses. Hyppolite Taine, for instance, insists, in the year 1863,

23. See Timothy J. Reiss, *The Meaning of Literature* (Ithaca, N.Y.: Cornell University Press, 1992), 160–191.

24. Friedrich Schiller, "On Naive and Sentimental Poetry," in *Essays*, ed. Walter Hinderer and Daniel Dahlstrom, The German Library 17 (New York: Continuum, 1993), 196.

25. Schiller, "Naive and Sentimental," 193.

26. Schiller, "Naive and Sentimental," 194.

27. Mme de Staël, *De la littérature*, 177.

on the "grave melancholic eloquence" of northern literature.[28] Only a few years earlier (1857), Baudelaire had reproposed Montesquieu's distinction between "the south, brutal and positive" and "the north, suffering and restless."[29] He had thus erected a funereal monument to the melancholia of the northern nations (*"nations corrompues"*)[30] while reminiscing — like de Staël herself in *Corinne* — a dream of lost naivety and *"natives grandeurs"* in the unmistakable tropology of a south *"fertile en produits généreux."*

It is then not surprising that, for Elizabeth Gaskell, melancholia should remain unknown to the Hales while in the south and should appear only, first in an epigraph from Coleridge (NS 298), when the Hales are well established in the north. And it should not be surprising, either, that suicide is conceptually connected with the north and its way of living. As they arrive in the north, the Hales will be shocked to hear the story of Thornton's father, who "speculated wildly, failed, and then killed himself" (NS 129); later on, they also hear — to cover the possible range of social classes — about the suicide of poor Mr. Boucher, who killed himself hoping that "God could na be harder than men" (NS 372). Suicide, as Montesquieu himself had to admit, is a thing of the north: "Englishmen kill themselves, without any foreseeable reason." Having proudly conquered southern "nature," driven by a passion that invariably leads to homicide, Montesquieu's north surrenders to the mysterious "illness" that "makes us [northerners] desire to see an end to this life."[31] Madame de Staël, in *Réflexions sur le sui-*

---

28. Hippolyte Taine, *Histoire de la littérature anglaise* (Paris: Hachette, 1921), 47.

29. Charles Baudelaire, "Le peintre de la vie moderne," in *Critique d'art. Suivi de Critique Musicale*, ed. Claude Pichois (Paris: Gallimard, 1992), 375.

30. Both Jean Starobinski, in his study of Baudelaire (*La mélancolie au miroir* [Paris: Julliard, 1989]), and Giorgio Agamben, in *Stanze. La parola e il fantasma nella cultura occidentale* (Torino: Einaudi, 1977), begin their studies with chapters alluding to the relation of melancholia to metaphors concerning both the sun and the south (respectively "La mélancolie, à midi" and "Il demone meridiano"). They never seem to realize, however (and this seems particularly important in the case of Baudelaire), that in the course of the nineteenth century the scholastic association of melancholia with the "meridian" is actually inverted. It is not the sun but its loss in the cold stretches of the north that generates Baudelaire's "languid" monsters. The quotations are from the poem "J'aime le souvenir de ces époques nues," collected in Charles Baudelaire, *The Flowers of Evil and Paris Spleen: Poems*, trans. William H. Crosby (Brockport, N.Y.: BOA Editions, 1991).

31. Montesquieu, *l'Esprit des lois*, III.22.

cide of 1812, echoed Montesquieu's preoccupations while expanding on her theory of northern melancholia; and Charles Victor de Bonstetten, in a book beautifully titled *L'homme du Midi et l'homme du Nord* (1824), sadly remarked that "Montesquieu is right when he says that the inhabitants of the north kill themselves without a reason."[32] The north that awaits the Victorian imagination — a north so modern, progressive, and pragmatic — is haunted by a melancholic longing for suicide.[33] While all that is natural has been bracketed away, the rational utopia of "society" and "nation" brings within itself the seeds for its self-annihilation.

Against this utopia, the Romantic Age conceives another one. Opposing Montesquieu's idea of reason as progress, the Romantics predicate a Christian acceptance of history as decline, and the consequent refusal of history for a return to the origin: all that is good is nature, which is God's work; all that is corruption is society, which is man's doing. The prophet of this inexorable journey from perfection to corruption, from the grandness of God's nature to the mediocrity of man's society, is Jean-Jacques Rousseau. In what is probably the most famous discourse on origins ever, Rousseau seems relentlessly determined to undo Montesquieu's theorem from its very basis. Rationality, to begin with, is not the only instrument for preventing violence between men: self-preservation (*notre bien-être*) and piety (*répugnance naturelle à voir périr ou souffrir tout être sensible*) are natural instincts that avoid conflict before any rational principle might intervene. It follows that the kind of society that practical reason institutes (*sociabilité*) is not the only possible human model of coexistence: there must be something else, preceding rationality, that also precedes society in the theodicy of human experience.[34]

If history fails to show the existence of this "something," a different science, capable of transcending facts to formulate hypotheses as rhetorical *exempla*, should then be engaged. In yet another discourse on origin, the *Essai sur l'origine des langues*, this supplement to history is more clearly

32. Charles Victor de Bonstetten, *L'Homme du Midi et l'homme du Nord* (Lausanne: Éditions de l'Aire, 1992), 51.

33. See Barbara T. Gates, *Victorian Suicide: Mad Crimes and Sad Histories* (Princeton, N.J.: Princeton University Press, 1988).

34. Jean-Jacques Rousseau, "Discours sur l'origine et les fondements de l'inégalité parmi les hommes," in *Discours sur l'origine et les fondements de l'inégalité parmi les hommes. Discours sur les sciences et les arts*, ed. Jacques Roger (Paris: Flammarion, 1971), 153.

defined in terms of a topical science. Discussing the formation of southern languages (*langues du midi*), Rousseau starts his syllogism by the reasoning that (northern) society must have needed a language in order to be formed, agreed on, and organized. The syllogism concludes, then, by hypothesizing the preexistence of language to society. But how (and why) could language be formed, if humans were not first together in one form or another? The hypothesis that Rousseau tries to raise, therefore, is one concerning a *different* form of living together — one that precedes society, and from which a presocial language could have originated. As Montesquieu had placed the origin of society in the north, so it is in the south, warmed up by a halcyon sun, that Rousseau imagined people coming out of their shelters and mingling with each other — not out of necessity but for love and the sheer passion of being together:

> There [in the south] the first familial ties were formed; there the first rendez-vous between the two sexes occurred . . . an unknown attraction made [the heart] less savage, and capable to feel the pleasure of not being alone. . . . There were the first festivals, the feet were restless with joy, simple gestures did not suffice anymore [to express the joy], the voice accompanied that joy with passionate accents, pleasure and desire, melted together, made themselves audible. There was, in the end, the true cradle of humankind. . . .[35]

In a prose that seems itself "restless with joy," Rousseau offers the hypothesis of an original and more beautiful form of communal life: this origin is a "south" — the same "south," namely, as that of Margaret's little "towns in the south of England," in which people live, as in a Rousseauvian time, debonair and happy, "lounging . . . at their doors, enjoying the fresh air" (NS 95). A mixture of passion and desire, not the calculus of practical reason, has brought these people together.

Like Montesquieu and de Staël, Rousseau imagines the south as the topos of an original, "natural" humankind. Like them, also, he envisions the north as a belated *locus* in the theodicy of humankind, where "the needs which generate society" were born.[36] Differently from Montesquieu, however, Rousseau considers the Biblical movement toward the "most sorrowful of the climates in the world . . . which was called [by Mon-

---

35. Jean-Jacques Rousseau, *Essai sur l'origine des langues où il est parlé de la mélodie et de l'imitation musicale*, ed. Jean Starobinski (Paris: Gallimard, 1990), 107.

36. Rousseau, *Essai*, 99.

tesquieu, in fact] the industry of humankind [*la fabrique du genre humain*]"[37] as the mere beginning of a fall. And, differently from de Staël, his aesthetic sensibility is fed up with philosophical and melancholic attitudes. In the search of more "natural" modes of expression, in which he believes a fundamental equality between "men" can be found, he recovers the naive poetry of "marginal" arts — like those "spontaneous" festivals of his native Geneva that he pits, in a famous letter to D'Alembert, against the "established" theater of central Paris.[38] These marginal arts are not "philosophical" or speculative, nor are they the social coterie typical of the Parisian stage. Rather, they are the natural expression of one organic community — organic, first of all, to place and nature. A reevaluation of all values has begun.

In the last analysis, it is true, Rousseau concedes, that society is formed only when reason starts taking care of the needs (*les besoins*) that a northern climate imposes. Yet, how sad, how impious and corrupted is this instrumental union of busy men, created for the satisfaction of material needs, when confronted with the pure possibility of a happy community, down there in the south — of a bond that, in Starobinski's terms, remains "transparent" and "immediate":

> Rousseau . . . contrasts two types of social relation, antithetical in the same way as transparency and opacity. Esteem and benevolence constitute a social bond in which men relate to one another immediately: nothing comes between one mind and another, and each individual is fully and spontaneously open to the other. By contrast the bonds created by private interest have lost this characteristic immediacy. No longer is there a direct connection of mind to mind: the relationship now involves the mediation of things . . . Mankind as a whole becomes a thing, or the slave of things.[39]

To amend Starobinski a bit, Rousseau does not contrast two types of *social* relationships and bonds but rather society with *another form* of

37. Rousseau, *Essai*, 101. The parodic reference is to Montesquieu, *l'Esprit des lois*, XVII.5: "Le Goth Jornandez a appellé le nord de l'Europe la fabrique du genre humain. Je l'appellerai plutôt la fabrique des instruments qui brisent les fers [de la tirannie] forgés au midi."

38. The reference is to Jean-Jacques Rousseau, *Lettre à D'Alembert* (Paris: Garnier-Flammarion, 1967), 232–234.

39. Jean Starobinski, *Jean-Jacques Rousseau: Transparency and Obstruction*, trans. Arthur Goldhammer (Chicago: University of Chicago Press, 1988), 23.

human communion that is more indebted to mysticism than to anything else. Society is *always* mediacy and obstacle. It divides when it pretends to unite. It does so at any moment. It separates individuals to bond them at its "rationalized," reasonable conditions. In the incestuous situation of the *Confessions,* Rousseau understands that the greatest obstacle among individuals *is* their social bond. The abysmal relationship between himself and *maman* points to the danger of all social relationships: they are divided just because they are, in the eyes of society, "mother and son." For Rousseau the mystic, there are no doubts: they are "one." But the *unio mystica* is quite the antithesis of social bonding.

What separates Jean-Jacques from *maman*? Only an image: "mother and son," their respective position in a social order. It might seem paradoxical, but images of bonding are those that separate — not in nature, that is to say, but in the social order. It is enough, for Rousseau, to regret the loss of the golden age: "Those barbarous times where the golden age; not because men were united, but because they were separated."[40] In that age, the absence of *social* bonds was what brought people together: "one became husband and wife without having ceased to be brother and sister."[41]

Nothing separates individuals more then Montesquieu's ideal of the rational society of the north. Here, humankind is divided into functions: the one that builds the house, the one that harvests the crop, and, in Gaskell's lexicon, the boss and the "hand," master and man, employer and employed. Personality, the real essence of the individual with its desires and passions, is also transformed into social function: people become "machines, no more, no less" (NS 291). Who will ever separate the master from the laborer as social functions? But what will keep them together as "men"? So-called social relations are dividing ones: they associate functions and separate "men" so that "every man has . . . to stand in an unchristian and isolated position" (NS 169). From this solitude, melancholia and a suicidal impulse — let alone all the less Romantic fury of strikes — can only grow.

That is why the hypothesis of another form of living together has to be entertained. And it is, ultimately, in Rousseau — or in a Rousseauism by now well digested — that Gaskell finds the hypothesis of a perfect "equal-

40. Rousseau, *Essai,* 93.
41. Rousseau, *Essai,* 107.

ity of friendship" (NS 169). It is in this rhetorical south that she finds, at once, an alternative to a northern society torn by strikes and tensions, and the *exemplum* of a perfect community and a beautiful *Gemeinschaft*.

> Well, then, what if we tried to rise above the idea of class to the idea of the whole community?
>
> — MATTHEW ARNOLD, *Culture and Anarchy*

"The theory of *Gemeinschaft*," Ferdinand Tönnies wrote in 1887, "starts from the assumption of perfect unity of human wills as an original or natural condition."[42] *Gemeinschaft*, a hypothesis akin to Rousseau's south, is the original state of humankind, a perfect and spontaneous association of wills — a community. Opposed to it, *Gesellschaft* is the belated advancement of society, which creates relations between individuals on the basis of their social functions. Human relationships, in *Gesellschaft*, are only a means to an end: "Accordingly, *Gemeinschaft* should be understood as a living organism, *Gesellschaft* as a mechanical aggregate and artifact."[43] Rousseau's paradox of the separating bonds and bonding separations is also here: "In the *Gemeinschaft* [people] remain essentially united in spite of all separating factors, whereas in the *Gesellschaft* they are essentially separated in spite of all unifying factors. . . . Their spheres of activity and power are sharply separated, so that everybody refuses to everyone else contact with and admittance to his sphere. . . . "[44]

It is not difficult to see, in this opposition of "organic" *Gemeinschaft* and "mechanic" *Gesellschaft*, the persistence of a rhetorical tension between two models of sociability. Rhetoric, in a way, lasts longer than history. By 1887, Tönnies might have thought the climatic hypothesis as being patently absurd and unscientific. What he probably never realized was that his entire conception of a scientific sociology was founded on the translation of the old latitudinal antithesis into a new dichotomy and a novel terminology. The rhetorical contrast that Montesquieu had articulated as an opposition between the topos of "north" and that of "south"

42. [Ferdinand] Tönnies, *Community and Society (Gemeinschaft und Gesellschaft)*, ed. and trans. Charles P. Loomis (East Lansing: Michigan State University Press, 1957), 37.
43. Tönnies, *Community and Society*, 34–35.
44. Tönnies, *Community and Society*, 65.

survived in the new lexicon as an endless rhetorical battle between civilization and culture, industry and nature, mechanicism and organicism, invented society and immediate community, historical progress and origin, city and country, organization and kinship. A few years later, after Nazism had appropriated Tönnies's terminology to pit a myth of *Volkgemeinschaft* against the mechanized style of bourgeois society, *Gemeinschaft*, in turn, starts losing its candor. The antithesis, however, persists: along with the occasional return to an explicit rhetoric of latitudes — the alleged "dignity of the south" as an alternative to industrialization[45] — "critical regionalism," written on the palimpsest of Tönnies's "opposition between these two terms,"[46] makes sure that a commonplace "south," now referred to with the more vague term of "region," will keep offering alternatives to the present.

This resilience of topoi to history, however, does not mean that the use that rhetoric makes of them will also remain the same throughout time. In Rousseau's reevaluation of all values, for instance, Montesquieu's commonplaces of north and south had been turned upside down to occasion a peculiarly revolutionary discourse against society, reason, and Montesquieu's rhetoric of northern supremacy itself. Gaskell's *North and South*, on the other hand, hardly shares Rousseau's preoccupations regarding the unethical foundations of a (northern) society based on inequality and private property. More pragmatically, the old latitudinal topos of the south is engaged as a way to cope both with the changing times brought about by the Industrial Revolution, and with the novel society — a quite "strange" society, indeed — created by the needs of commerce and production:

"You think it strange. Why?"

"I don't know — I suppose because, on the very face of it, I see two classes dependent on each other in every possible way, yet each evi-

45. See, for instance, Franco Cassano, *Il pensiero meridiano* (Bari: Laterza, 1996), which has had so much fortune in Italy by reproposing Camus's and Pasolini's paradigm of a *pensiero meridiano* — a "southern thought" as panacea to the evils of industrial society.

46. Kenneth Frampton, "Towards a Critical Regionalism: Six Points for an Architecture of Resistance," in *The Anti-Aesthetic: Essays on Postmodern Culture*, ed. Hal Foster (Seattle: Bay Press, 1983), 30, note 4. The reference to Weber is to Max Weber, *The Theory of Social and Economic Organization*, trans. A. M. Henderson (New York: Oxford University Press, 1947); on the Victorians, see also Norbert Elias, *The Civilization Process*, trans. Edmund Jephcott (New York: Urizen, 1978).

dently regarding the interests of the other as opposed to their own . . ." (NS 165)

"Strange" because estranged from a natural Gemeinschaft, the society of the north is an aberration, a symptom of the Fall. As for Rousseau, *homo homini lupus* is not the description of a state of nature, but the very picture of modern society which the north symbolizes: people, here, "may be kind hearts, each separate; but once banded together, [they have] no more pity for a man than a wild hunger-maddened wolf" (NS 207). Yet, the old topos of "humane order and enduring values" which an agrarian south embodies[47] for the Victorians is evoked in *North and South* not to deny, in Rousseau's vein, a moral legitimacy to northern society, but to pacify it.

If the Industrial Revolution has raised "the idea of class" — which, as Matthew Arnold reckons, is a threatening and potentially revolutionary topos[48] — the antithetical idea of community (which rhetorical tradition recalls through the commonplace of the south), is called on to sedate social discontent and tension. Mr. Hale asks at one point, "Is there necessity for calling it a battle between the two classes?" (NS 125). Avoiding the rhetoric of class altogether, Margaret engages instead, for the instruction of both Higgins and Thornton, into nothing less than the hypothesis of a far-off, different south. The rhetoric of history and class is replaced by a rhetoric of place and community. A place — the south — offers an ethical alternative to the historical present. Margaret, in fact, quite often uses the topos of the south as a compensatory topos of the present — to remind master and worker, for instance, that "they never strike down there" (NS 182). She talks about the south, in other words, not to tell them that the society they live in is immoral and wrong but to teach them how to translate the values of community into their present society, for the general "improvement of feeling" (NS 512). The south becomes an ethical model in a rhetorical discourse aimed at the betterment of the north:

47. Richard Gill, "The Quest for Community," in *Happy Rural Seat: The English Country House and the Literary Imagination* (New Haven, Conn.: Yale University Press, 1972), 7.

48. Matthew Arnold, *Culture and Anarchy*, ed. Samuel Lipman (New Haven, Conn.: Yale University Press, 1994), 64.

though [such improvement] might not have the effect of preventing all future clash of opinion and action, when the occasion arose, would, at any rate, enable both master and man to look upon each other with far more charity and sympathy, and bear with each other more patiently and kindly. (NS 512)

The south is an invitation to dialogue, and to the piety of universal brotherhood. By the end of the story, Mr. Thornton has learned Margaret's lesson and, accordingly, has improved his feelings and manners a bit. He has become a new kind of master, indeed, sincerely concerned with the idea of an immediate and transparent unity between master and man:

> I have arrived at the conviction that no mere institutions, however wise, and however much thought may have been required to organise and arrange them, can attach class to class as they should be attached, unless the working out of such institutions bring the individuals of the different classes into actual personal contact. (NS 525)

Is this "actual personal contact" beyond the mediation of social "institutions" a reminiscence of Rousseau's southern rendezvous? In a way, it is. Yet, differently from Rousseau, there is no desire to return to the south in Gaskell's novel. Margaret's brief visit there risks to end — alas! — with a big disappointment: "somehow, this visit to Helstone had not been . . . exactly what she had expected. There was change everywhere; slight, yet pervading all" (NS 481). The change, of course, is all inside Margaret ("I change perpetually," NS 489), but her resolution to abandon the south is nonetheless final and clear: she has irrevocably "decided that she was very glad to have been there, and that she had seen it again, and that to her it would always be the prettiest spot in the world, but that . . . she should shrink back from such another visit" (NS 489–490). Her final acceptance of life in the north is total and unconditional: to the astonishment of her northern betrothed, she has become, in fact, "Miltonian and manufacturing in [her] preferences" (NS 413).

Along with Margaret's *Bildung*, which leads her to overcome all "prejudices" and to accept the north with its industries and its division of labor, there is, therefore, a parallel *Bildung* of the north, which begins with the general amending of Mr. Thornton's allegorical character. The brutal self-righteousness of his narrative exordium — his refusal, for instance, to negotiate with the workers — finally grows into a mature, if paternalistic, attitude. He yields, in the end, to the necessity of dialogue and, through dialogue, tries to make his men "feel and know how much his employer may have laboured in his study at plans for the benefit of his workpeople" (NS 525). In truth, simple dialogue may not be enough for such an arduous task: all the "tricks of tempers and modes of speech" (NS 525), which rhetoric alone can provide, will be necessary to him.

For this rhetorical upbringing of the north, Gaskell recovers the value of an ancient, classical *littérature du midi*. Like Arnold before her, she finds "the literature of ancient Greece . . . a mighty agent of intellectual deliverance; even for modern times, therefore, an object of indestructible interest."[49] She does so in a pragmatic epoch that threatens literature with its disappearance. This threat Gaskell dramatizes in classical Victorian terms: as a furthering of (modern) society from nature (or from Helstone, or from the south). Hazlitt, before Arnold, had already claimed that "arts hold immediate communication with nature. . . . When that original impulse no longer exists . . . all the attempts to recall it are no better than the tricks of galvanism to restore the dead to life."[50]

So, in the modern society of *North and South*, the ancient literature is quite on its way to extinction before Margaret's arrival: "What in the world do manufacturers want with the classics, or literature . . . ?" (NS 72). Northerners take their children away from school "at fourteen or fifteen years of age, unsparingly cutting away all off-shoots in the direction of literature or high mental cultivation" (NS 107). For these modern denizens of a progressive north, literature is a superfluity "for people who have leisure" and need not struggle for life. Newspapers can be read, but not the classics. "Classics may do very well for men who loiter away their lives in the country . . . but Milton men ought to have their thoughts and powers absorbed in the work of to-day" (NS 159). Not beauty and passion, but action and profit move and stir the north. Thornton, proudly, explains:

> Remember, we are of a different race from the Greeks, to whom beauty was everything, and to whom [one] might speak of a life of leisure and serene enjoyment, much of which entered in through their outward

49. Matthew Arnold, *Selected Prose*, ed. P. J. Keating (Harmondsworth, Eng.: Penguin, 1970), 58.
50. William Hazlitt, "Fragments on Art. Why the Arts are not Progressive?" in *Selected Writings*, ed. Jon Cook (Oxford: Oxford University Press, 1991), 258.

senses . . . I belong to Teutonic blood . . . we do not look upon life as a time for enjoyment, but as a time for action and exertion. Our glory and our beauty arise out of our inward strength, which makes us victorious over material resistance, and over greater difficulties still. . . . (NS 413–414)

Yet, is not this lack of interest in (southern) literature the very cause of all northern troubles? Is not it the cause, in fact, of the north's inability to engage in a dialogue and overcome the divisions of a strike? Matthew Arnold, in "The Literary Influence of the Academies," defined this peculiarly British inability to engage in a profitable, pacifying dialogue using the term of "provincialism":

the provincial spirit . . . does not persuade, it makes war; it has not urbanity, the tone of the city, of the centre, the tone which always aims at a spiritual and intellectual effect, and not excluding the use of banter, never disjoins banter itself from politeness, from felicity. But the provincial tone is more violent . . . it loves hard-hitting rather than persuading.[51]

"Provincialism" is the loss of a spiritual "centre" embodied by the virtues of southern "Attic prose"[52] and centered for Arnold in the academy. It is a fall, from classicist pastoralism to the "aggressive manner in literature" prevailing in newspapers. The miracle performed by Margaret Hale — a true Rousseauistic revolution, indeed — is therefore to cure the provincial brutality of the north through the recuperation of Attic prose. Such prose persuades and does not make war, and is now located not in Arnold's "centre" but in a British, provincial "south."

And so, the classics become for Margaret, just as many thesauri of past, examples that, "Out of the wisdom of the past, [will] help us over the present" (NS 415). They become repositories, in other words, of available and persuasive arguments. They deploy a strategic "knowledge of the past" (NS 221) that provides a profusion of commonplaces — from the Bible to "Plato's *Republic*" (NS 167) — to argue about equality and peace:

51. Matthew Arnold, "The Literary Influence of Academies," in *Lectures and Essays in Criticism*, vol. 3, ed. R. H. Super (Ann Arbor: University of Michigan Press, 1986), 249.

52. Arnold, "Literary Influence," 247.

"About the wages," said Mr. Hale [to Higgins]. "You'll not be offended, but I think you make some sad mistakes. I should like to read you some remarks in a book I have." (NS 292)

Margaret's arrival in Milton with a "great box of books" containing "well-bound little-read English Classics" (NS 51), and with her father "always reading, reading, thinking, thinking" (NS 178), is therefore some sort of messianic advent. Dispelling all northern prejudices about literature, she brings, in a society of practical ends, a *littérature du midi* that, beyond enjoyment and beauty, has been transformed into a practical means itself. Thornton, quite expectedly, becomes the first of his Teutonic race to realize the rhetorical and strategic importance of literature. As business takes a wrong turn because of the strike, he starts taking "books and papers into his own private room." He keeps reading there "long after the family were gone to bed" (NS 515). Do books bring him good counsel? Or do they simply offer him topoi and strategies to persuade his workers?

One way or the other, the strike, as the narrative approaches its conclusion, has been mastered. The workers are calmed and convinced, as described by Thornton: "I had a round-robin from some of my men stating their wish to work for me" (NS 527). It is, more than a happy ending, the marriage of the rhetorical powers of an ancient literature of the south with the progressive hubris of the north. The prophesied unity has been realized: "North and South has both met and made kind o' friends" (NS 112).

Here lies the epochal transformation of Rousseau's topos of the *midi* into the new Victorian one of the "south." Whereas Rousseau's commonplace of origins relentlessly denounces the injustice and decadence of a society that has reached, triumphantly, the heyday of its "progress," the Victorian myth of origins is intended only to amend or pacify society — with fables of its original wholesomeness — in the days of its crisis. A revolutionary project is absorbed into a fundamentally conservative one — one that, in fact, tries to fix what is already breaking at its seams. As the Romantic Age of revolutions comes to a close, the Victorian one of restorations begins: rising above the idea of class, the nation reunites around the idea of community — the unity, that is, of enlightened master and catechized men.

The mistake one should not make at this point is to confuse this melodramatic parable of national unity with something other than what we today call "regional literature." Because it is exactly the necessity to offer the nation — or the globe? — a topos of original unity and peace that produces the perspective of an "other" space, a "different" way of living that progress has not erased, and which remains a regional, marginal part of *our* culture. The ancient south is, like the new region, the hypothesis of difference. This difference is useful not as a negation of our way of living but as a possibility to improve it by offering us a "a much needed vision of life."[53]

Gaskell's vision is, as we have seen, that of dialogue. Her ideal catechism, like the multicultural dialogism that our literature of place proposes, is possible only insofar as divisions are glossed over as mere "differences" of opinion or, better, of prejudice. Difference is not a totally irreducible antithesis between those who enjoy the fruits of progress and those who pay the consequences for it. Like north and south, difference is a metonymic proximity, a regional idiosyncrasy, a spatial distribution of otherwise irreconcilable principles, and, in the end, the displacement of conflict into the topos of an organic community said to exist in a far off "region." Whereas historical divisions preclude dialogue, differences thrive on it.

A paternalistic warfare against prejudice has thus begun. All the regions are one: they are not the topos of the exotic, irreducible other but the commonplace of a difference — our past? our origin? — that we should be able to bring into our own society for its betterment. Here lies Gaskell's fundamental, ideological regionalism: our modern and "northern" industrial society can always recuperate the fragrance of difference into its otherwise fragrantless "loss of . . . fragrance" (NS 96):

"Do you know these roses?" [Thornton] said [to Margaret] . . .
"They are from Helstone, are they not? . . . Oh! Have you been there? . . ." (NS 530)

A piece of the south is transplanted into the north, bringing "a breath of country air, somehow" (NS 187). And while the floral wallpapers of arts and crafts start covering the walls of industrial England, the common-

53. Jim Wayne Miller, "Anytime the Ground is Uneven: The Outlook for Regional Studies and What to Look Out For," in *Geography and Literature: A Meeting of the Disciplines*, ed. William E. Mallory and Paul Simpson-Housley (Syracuse, N.Y.: Syracuse University Press, 1987), 11.

places of an older "country life" — the roses, its passionate communities, its naive literature — are put at the service of progress and commerce, of society and industry, so that life in the north can go on undisturbed. Whatever progress has been irremediably lost in history is recuperated by this displacement of the loss into a topical, regional "south" that can always be transferred into our north like a bunch of roses. We, like Margaret, might not even need to return to that south. Like Higgins, we had better not. All that we need, in fact, is the ambiguous art of translation — the belief that difference *can* be translated into our own. It is a belief so compelling in any regionalist utterance that I have devoted the next chapter to it.

Fifty Ways to Kill Turiddu

Lawrence, Translator of Verga

There are fifty ways . . .
— PAUL SIMON, "Fifty Ways to Leave Your Lover"

Ah . . . le canzonette? Roba che non
riempie la pancia, cari miei!
— GIOVANNI VERGA, *Mastro don Gesualdo*

England, 1912: The strike at Preston is over, and social unrest seems
under the control of reason and the spirit of the law. Class conflicts have
been partly sedated, and a rational peace now reigns over the vast stretches
of the north. With the marriage of southern humanism and northern capitalism, an urbanized dialogue has begun: the new reformatory parliaments
have, like Mr. Thornton, started to listen to Nicholas Higgins. The most restless souls have been brought to reason and convinced of the imperatives of
production. "The most outward features of a *modern* age," Matthew Arnold
declared in his 1857 lecture ("On the Modern Element in Literature"), "is the
banishment of the ensigns of war and bloodshed from the intercourse of
civil life."[1] The *homo homini lupus* has thus been sacrificed at the altar of

1. Matthew Arnold, *Selected Prose*, ed. P. J. Keating (Harmondsworth, Eng.: Penguin, 1970), 62.

progress, and his most egoistic passions — those of class and private interest — have somehow been tamed. From its ashes, a new social being has been born, perfectly and mathematically sociable — the curious specimen of a planned *Gemeinschaft*. Yet, the feeling has remained that individuals are mere functional cogs in the machinery of social relations that smoothly produces citizens at the price of the most intimate passions of class and self. Still trapped in the melancholia of instrumental reason — everything and everyone is a means to an end — the colder heart of the northerner feels a sense of loss haunting his brave new world:

> Our aim is a perfect humanity, a perfect and equable human consciousness, selfless. And we obtain it in the subjection, reduction, analysis, and destruction of the Self. So on we go, active in science and mechanics, and social reform. But we have exhausted ourselves in the process.[2]

While taking these bitter notes, Lawrence is already by the lake of Garda, in Italy for the first time in his life. Time and place seem all but casual in this little picture of the artist in his southern European exile. In that same year, David Herbert Lawrence, son of a poor British miner, had fallen in love with Frieda von Richthofen — German heiress, mother of three children, and wife of moneyed Ernest Weekley. The relationship had turned out to be somewhat different from the romantic bliss the couple had sought. As Emile Delaveney recounts, Lawrence's incipient phthisis, his latent homosexuality, the difference of class before him and the beloved, the social shame of adultery, and a fundamental dislike for the "weak sex," made him unable to live the fantasized carnal pleasures that the encounter with his premature Lady Chatterley had promised.[3] The consequences must have been disgraceful: "The night was a failure, why not?," Lawrence wrote in the morning in raging verses later to be collected in the *Unrhyming Poems*.[4] There, only the "Hymn to Priapus" stands sadly

2. David Herbert Lawrence, *Twilight in Italy*, in *D. H. Lawrence and Italy: Twilight in Italy; Sea and Sardinia; Etruscan Places* (Harmondsworth, Eng.: Penguin, 1972), 45. References to *Twilight in Italy* are given in the body of the text as "(TI 45)," for example.

3. Emile Delavenay, *D. H. Lawrence: The Man and His Work. The Formative Years: 1885–1919* (London: Heinemann, 1972).

4. David Herbert Lawrence, *Unrhyming Poems*, in *Complete Poems*, ed. Vivian De Sola Pinto and Warren Roberts (1964; reprint, Harmondsworth, Eng.: Penguin, 1993). The autobiographical tone of *Unrhyming Poems* is set by Lawrence himself in a fore-

in isolation, turgid witness of a rare moment of joy when "desire comes up, and contentment is debonair." But the poems that follow are all a wasteland of titles: "Mutilation," "Humiliation," "Misery" — and more bad beginnings.

Lawrence might have been precluded from the life of senses to the point of a true obsession with sexual impotence but was quick to see in his own inadequacies the result of social forces — what the poem "Welcome Death" called "our castrated society" — destroying his truest and inmost self. It is not that sensuality escapes *him* but rather that it escapes a whole northern society *with* him. The culprit is the dynamo of progress, which, beyond all the snowy Alps, advances, like Michael Ende's "Nothingness," to obliterate all natural impulses from the face of the world:

> There was London and the industrial counties spreading like a blackness over all the world, horrible, in the end destructive . . . Far away, beyond, beyond all the snowy Alps, with the iridescence of eternal ice above them, was this England, black and foul and dry, with her soul worn down, almost worn away. And England was conquering the whole world with her machines and her horrible destruction of natural life. She was conquering the whole world. (TI 53)

Echoing Arnold's warning about "that mechanical character, which civilisation tends to take everywhere,"[5] the failure of Lawrence's *homo eroticus* is thus an epochal one. Allegorical figure of the times, Lawrence's ailing sexuality is the catastrophe of postindustrial northern civilization, which has exhausted and worn away any spark of natural life in its mechanized individuals. The machine, Lawrence laments, has become "our master and our God" (TI 45).

England is too suffocating: it is a dissonance, a mechanical syncope in the natural symphony of the universe. Lady Chatterley herself, arguably the most representative of Lawrence's characters, would later comment on this musical aporia of England in the order of creation:

---

word reminding the reader that "[t]hese poems should not be considered separately" but rather as a spiritual narrative, and in the "Argument" to the series: "After much struggling and loss in love and in the world of man, the protagonist throws in his lot with a woman who is already married. Together they go into another country, she perforce leaving her children behind. . . ."

5. Matthew Arnold, *Culture and Anarchy*, ed. Samuel Lipman (New Haven, Conn.: Yale University Press, 1994), 33.

Anything more unlike song, spontaneous song, would be impossible to imagine. . . . It was not like savages: savages have subtle rhythms. It was not like animals: animals *mean* something when they yell. . . . What could possibly become of such a people, a people in whom the living intuitive faculty was dead as nails, and only queer mechanical yells and uncanny will-power remained?[6]

What can become of this machine out of tune with the passions that move the universe? Exile, no doubt, can be the only salvation! And where can Lawrence go to find another God to worship, a God in which the flesh will be resurrected? In what far place he thinks the powers of the machine will come to an end? There is no doubt, he must go south: "Let us go back . . . [to] enjoy our own flesh, like the Italians" (TI 45). Let us go down south, to the lake of Garda . . .

> Play on my shepherd's pipe what songs I will.
> — VIRGIL, *The Eclogues*

Higgins had been warned and dissuaded, and yet Lawrence's resolution to go south made, in line of principle and in the specific circumstances, quite a lot of sense. Lawrence, after all, did not need to work in the damp air of a rheumatic south. What he was looking for was not better wages but the return of passion. And was not Italy, of all the southern parts of Europe, the very topos of that passion? Already in 1697, Houdar de la Motte, in that thesaurus of national identities published as *L'Europe Galante*, had codified, along with the gallantry of the French and the faithfulness of the Spaniard, the commonplace of the Italian driven by the senses. In 1725, Ludwig von Murault, in the *Lettres sur les Anglais et les Français*, had also hinted at an "entirely sensual character" of the Italians. Winckelmann's commonplace of Italy as *Wiedergeburt und Neues Leben*, central to a work such as Burckhardt's *Kultur der Renaissance in Italien*, had acquired, by now, the imprimatur of medical science: Italy, in medicine too, had become the topos of renaissance, health, and new life. Already during the eighteenth century, the belief in the therapeutic virtues of the Mediterranean climates was widespread,

---

6. David Herbert Lawrence, *Lady Chatterley's Lover* (1960; reprint, Harmondsworth, Eng.: Penguin, 1990), 158–159.

but it is "in the Victorian era [that] 'ordering South' became a standard medical prescription."[7]

This curative aspect of Italy was well known to Lawrence's characters — especially to the numberless doctors who people his pages: "Take her way to the sun," one physician says to the ungratified husband of North American and frigid Juliet at the beginning of a typically Lawrencean short story. Helped by the timely prognosis, Juliet really becomes a new being under the southern skies of Italy: "Something deep inside her unfolded and relaxed, and she was given to a cosmic influence. . . . 'I am another being,' she said to herself, as she looked at her red-gold breasts and thighs." The "cosmic" rays of the southern sun, "penetrating" her at each page of the story, work miracles for Juliet: by the end, "[h]er womb was coming open wide with rosy ecstasy, like a lotus flower."[8] As someone were to say, "the fecundity of the Italian people, after all, is their only weapon"![9]

If the Italian sun could work so admirably for Juliet, there was no reason it would not benefit Lawrence himself. After all, had not John Ruskin, on his trip to Italy, abandoned his British prejudices and come to admire Michelangelo and the Italian Renaissance because of their sensual celebration of the body? Italy, as a commonplace of British fantasies at least, always had such an overpowering, liberating effect. Even Daniel De Foe, more than one century earlier, had noticed the "lustful"[10] character of all Italians. And nothing else than this "lust," this "phallic worship" of all the Italians, as Lawrence confesses, remains "the secret of Italy's attraction for us" (TI 44).

In other words, Lawrence determined, no other place like Italy could resurrect his flesh in the worship of a god other than the British machine.

7. John Pemble, *The Mediterranean Passion: Victorians and Edwardians in the South* (Oxford: Clarendon, 1987), 84.

8. David Herbert Lawrence, "Sun," in *Collected Stories*, ed. Craig Raine (New York: Everyman, 1994), 979, 986, 988.

9. This someone is one Professor Beonio-Brocchieri, and the place for the citation (translation mine) is a curious preface to an even more curious book by "Doctor" Richard Korherr: *Regresso della nascita: morte dei popoli* (Roma, 1928), also with an introduction by Benito Mussolini and Oswald Spengler!

10. See also Kenneth Churchill, *Italy and English Literature, 1764–1930* (London: Macmillan, 1980); and Hilary Fraser, *The Victorians and Renaissance Italy* (Oxford: Blackwell, 1992).

And more than Ruskin or De Foe, it must have been Virgil[11] who had seen a true cornucopia of fruitfulness and fecundity there, who took Lawrence and his lover exactly to the lake of Garda. In the unmistakable tone of the *Georgics*, the lake appears to Lawrence as the place where "[e]verything [is] clear and sun-coloured" (TI 34), and golden lemons and fruits grow in gardens "beautiful as paradise, as the first creation" (TI 52). This lake is a *locus amoenus* of fecundity and regeneration — a lost paradise of the senses to which Lawrence wants to return.

And yet, while the cattle breeds and lemon trees multiply their fruits, Lawrence starts to feel some sort of panic fear in front of this sensual south: it is, no doubt, "our habit of life, our very constitution" (TI 52) that makes the northerner fear what the Italian, simply, lives. It is not easy for someone who has made of life a planned, mechanical "habit" to accept now a primal way of life that so easily confuses itself with death: "the phallic principle is to absorb and dominate life . . . it is a desire to expose [oneself] to death, to know death" (TI 61). Eros *is* the other side of Thanatos. It is enough to look at any representation of Italian passion to realize this simple truth. Take Botticelli, for instance, and his emblem of a whole Italian renaissance of the senses that is his *Birth of Aphrodite*:[12]

> Aphrodite, the queen of the senses, she, born of the sea-foam, is the luminousness of the gleaming senses, the phosphorescence of the sea, the senses become a conscious aim unto themselves; she is the gleaming darkness, she is the luminous night, she is the goddess of destruction, her white, cold fire consumes and does not create. (TI 35)

Aphrodite is the genius loci of the south. She is destructive and egoistic, as any sensual and southern being must always be:

11. "Here is perpetual spring, and summer weather at other times: / The cattle breed twice, and twice orchards give their fruit." In Publius Vergili Maronis, *Georgicon*, in *Opera*, ed. R. A. B. Mynors (Oxford: Oxford University Press, 1969), II / 149–150; translation mine.

12. The reference is, of course, to the *Birth of Venus*. Greek Aphrodite, more than her latinate version of Venus, embodies a myth of sexual regeneration. As Hesiod tells the story in his *Theogony* (lines 188 to 200), after Cronus castrated the father Uranus by biting his genitals, he spat his seed into the sea. From the foam thus generated, Aphrodite was born, whose name literally means "foam-born." On the centrality of Aphrodite in Lawrence's mythology of "womanhood" and passion, see H. M. Daleski, "Aphrodite of the Foam and *The Ladybird* Tales," in *Modern Critical Views: D. H. Lawrence*, ed. Harold Bloom (New York: Chelsea, 1986), 201–214.

Compare a Botticelli Madonna, with all her wounded and abnegating sensuality, with a Hans Memling Madonna, whose soul is pure and only reverential. Beyond me is the mystery and the glory, says the Northern mother: let me have no self, let me only seek that which is all-pure, all wonderful. But the Southern mother says: This is mine, this is my child, my wonder, my master, my lord, my scourge, my own.[13]

Certainly, it was against this uncanny doubling of passion into possessiveness that Montesquieu had argued for the necessity of the law. Southern passion is an egoistic instinct: everything outside the self is just an obstacle standing on the way to a selfish satisfaction made into an absolute goal. In this sense, passion is the precondition of crime. Against it, the civilized north of the world has protected life under the wings of reason — in the exclusive interest, to say it with Freud, "of man's communal existence, which would not otherwise be practicable":[14]

So that now, continuing in the old, splendid will for a perfect selfless humanity, we have become inhuman and unable to help ourselves, we are but attributes of the great mechanised society we have created on our way to perfection. (TI 45)

The challenge, for Lawrence, becomes that of being able to understand and tolerate, instead, a selfish humanity — to accept passion in its deadly alliance with destruction. To do that, the northern man needs to do away with his petty bourgeois morality and learn to live, so to speak, beyond good and evil: "The English are 'good' because they are afraid, and the Municheners are 'wicked' because they are afraid, and the Italians forget to be afraid, so they are neither good nor bad, but just natural. *Viva l'Italia!*"[15]

13. David Herbert Lawrence, *Fantasia of the Unconscious*, in *Fantasia of the Unconscious and Psychoanalysis and the Unconscious* (1922; Harmondsworth, Eng.: Penguin, 1960), 38.

14. Sigmund Freud, *The Future of an Illusion*, trans. James Strachey (New York: Norton, 1961), 51.

15. D. H. Lawrence, letter to Ernest Collings of May 13, 1913, *The Letters of D. H. Lawrence*, ed. Aldous Huxley (New York: Viking, 1932), 126. The commonplace of a south beyond good and evil seems to be a consistent one in the memoirs of northern travelers to the south since the late seventeenth century. The south is beautiful and demonic at the same time; this is, at any rate, the kernel of its fascination. On this issue, see the erudite compilation by Benedetto Croce, "Un paradiso abitato da diavoli," in *Uomini e cose della vecchia Italia*, 3d ed. (Bari: Laterza, 1956), 69–87.

Viva l'Italia, then, and long live those good old demons beyond good and wicked, who "forget" the fear of love and death: "let me confess, in parenthesis, that I am not at all sure whether I don't really prefer these demons to our sanctified humanity!"[16] The determination is made. Garda, so close to the Alps, so civilized, is not enough. Lawrence wants to go in search of those very demons, remnants of a pristine humankind that the machine our god has forgotten at the margins of our civilized world. He will go more south than Garda, further from society and its simulacra, into a region more marginal than the margin, into the very locus of origin. The quest begins once again, and this time is a descent into Hades, which Homer located in the depths of the Sicilian Mount Etna, the volcano where Uranus confined the Cyclops who rebelled against his law. The odyssey is recorded in *Sea and Sardinia*.

> for they sit in a green field and warble him to death with the
> sweetness of their song.
>
> — *The Odyssey*

David Herbert and Frieda arrived in Taormina, Sicily, in March of 1920. If Garda's Spirit of Place was memento to a Virgilian bucolic world, the Spirit of Sicily, "outside the circuits of civilisation" (SS 3), was certainly of a more ancestral, visceral nature. Ann Radcliffe's gothic Sicily, "the seat of luxury and vice,"[17] was in wait for them, and Stendhal's "Sicilians, put on fire (*enflammés*) by love or hatred" were the authentic remnants of an original beautiful passion already dead anywhere else in the civilized north — absolutely dead, "*tout à fait morte*," from Paris to London.[18]

The kind of Sicily that appears to Lawrence is a truly demonic place: "terrible dynamic exhalations," "terrible vibrations," "demon magnetism,"

16. D. H. Lawrence, *Sea and Sardinia*, in *Lawrence and Italy*, 3. References to *Sea and Sardinia* are given in the body of the text as "(SS 3)," for example.

17. Ann Radcliffe, *A Sicilian Romance*, ed. Alison Milbank (Oxford: Oxford University Press, 1993), 1.

18. Stendhal, "La Duchesse de Palliano," in *Chroniques italiennes*, ed. Dominique Fernandet (Paris: Gallimard, 1973), 82. Leonardo Sciascia, *Stendhal e la Sicilia* (Palermo: Sellerio, 1987), argues that on July 22, 1838, the date of the alleged trip to Sicily, Stendhal was in fact somewhere else. Did he *ever* go to Sicily? Did he ever find *there* "le plaisir des yeux, qui est grand en ce pays singulier"? Or was the Sicily whose devouring passion he described with realistic zest a merely rhetorical commonplace?

"sulphureous" presences haunt the descriptions of *Sea and Sardinia* from the very beginning. From the western window of the rented Fontana Vecchia house, the Lawrences see "beautiful and wicked" Etna, geographic likeness of Aphrodite made stone and lava, and true emblem of the sublime threat that poets before Lawrence had called Sicily:[19]

> This timeless Grecian Etna, in her lower-heaven loveliness, so lovely, so lovely, what a torturer! Not many men can really stand her, without losing their souls. She is like Circe. Unless a man is very strong, she takes his soul away from him and leaves him not a beast, but an elemental creature, intelligent and soulless, like the Etna Sicilians. Intelligent daimons, and humanly, according to us, the most stupid people on earth. Ach, horror! How many men, how many races, has Etna put to flight? It was she who broke the quick of the Greek soul. And after the Greeks, she gave the Romans, the Normans, the Arabs, the Spaniards, the French, the Italians, even the English, she gave them all their inspired hour and broke their soul. (SS 2)

Reminiscent of Hardy's Egdon, Etna, too, is a genius loci. She protects and haunts the place. With her ghastly presence, she lures and repels at the same time; she terrifies[20] with beauty, like Circe, or like the Sirens who lived (according to Strabo in his geography) by the Sicilian cape Pelorus,

19. See chapter 35 of Longinus's *On the Sublime*, where Etna is cited as beautiful for its power to erupt. In Pausanias's *Description of Greece* (23.9), Etna is reported as being considered as a spirit to appease with sacrificial offers, which its "fire receives and consumes." In Appollodorus *Library* (1.6.3), Etna is "a huge mountain, from which down to this day they say that blasts of fire issue from the thunderbolts that were thrown" there by Zeus. Among more recent poets, see Henry Swinburne's description of Taormina: "Everything belonging to it is drawn in a large sublime style; the mountains tower to the very clouds, the castles and ruins rise on mighty masses of perpendicular rock, and seem to defy the attacks of mortal enemies; Aetna with all its snowy and woody sweeps fills half the horizon. . . ." (Henry Swinburne, *Travels in the Two Sicilies*, 2 vols. [London, 1783–1785], ii.169–170).

20. On volcanoes as sources of poetic terror, see John Dennis: ". . . that we may set this in a clearer Light, let us lay before the Reader the several Ideas which are capable of producing this enthusiastick Terrour, which seem to me to be those which follow, *viz.* Gods, Dæmons, Hell, Spirits and Souls of Men, Miracles, Prodigies, Enchantments, Witchcrafts, Thunder, Tempests, raging Seas, Inundations, Torrents, Earthquakes, Volcanos, Monsters, Serpents, Lions, Tygres, Fire, War, Pestilence, Famine, |&c.|." In John Dennis, *The Grounds of Criticism in Poetry* (London: George Straban, 1704), 87–88.

between Scylla and Charybdis, where Odysseus met them before Lawrence.

True *genius loci*, Etna shapes the human soul in its own "soulless" image beyond good and evil: "Like the Etna Sicilians," comments Lawrence. To this correspondence of place and personality, in fact, he had devoted the speculative efforts of "The Spirit of Place":

> every great era of civilisation seems to be the expression of a particular continent or continent region. . . . There is, no doubt, some particular potentiality attaching to every distinct region of the earth's surface, over and above the indisputable facts of climate and geological condition. There is some subtle magnetic or vital influence inherent in every specific location, and it is this influence which keeps the inhabitant stable. Thus race is ultimately as much a question of place as of heredity.[21]

And while a universalist sense of modernity and progress is "conquering the whole world with her machines and her horrible destruction of natural life" (TI 53), annihilating whatever is "distinct" about natural regions, Sicily — a true "region" indeed — instead remains under the influx of her "specific location" and *genius loci*:

> There must be something curious about the proximity of a volcano. Naples and Catania alike, the men are hugely fat, with great macaroni paunches, they are expansive and in a perfect drip of casual affection and love. But the Sicilians are even more wildly exuberant and fat. . . . (SS 7)

Like the Etna Sicilians, they are pure matter, pure bodily presence; huge masses, flesh gigantic and fat, wild and exuberant carnality, fiery like the Cyclops imprisoned there by cruel Uranus. Later, on the train to Syracuse:

> Enter more passengers. An enormously large woman with an extraordinarily handsome face: an extraordinarily large man . . . She has that queenly stupid beauty of a classic Hera. . . . She sends one's heart back to pagan days. And — and — she is simply enormous, like a house. . . . The husband of [this] Juno is a fresh-faced bourgeois young fellow, and he also is simply huge. (SS 14–15)

21. David Herbert Lawrence, "The Spirit of Place," in *The Symbolic Meaning: The Uncollected Versions of "Studies in Classic American Literature,"* ed. Armin Arnold (New York: Viking, 1962), 20.

Extraordinarily handsome faces, extraordinarily large men, and a plethora of gods and goddesses are the pagan denizens of this island. They are all *extraordinary* beings, first of all,[22] problematic referents for the civilized language of the north, which cannot even find a name for such extraordinary entities. Because the reader must have noticed, by now, the nonchalance with which Lawrence has dropped mythological names on these peculiar beings: the "large woman," for instance, is Hera — but also Roman Juno and, one moment later, a Cyclops as well, and Mother Earth. It is as if Lawrence's mythological structure, crossing the realistic surface of the *diario di viaggio* in an allegorical way, has obliterated each character and name behind their allegories: "Any person, any object, any relationship can mean anything else"[23] here, but no one — alas! — can ever remain himself or herself. The "macaroni paunches" become the personification of Sicilian exuberance, the "large lady" of Sicilian flesh, and everyone of the sublime passions that stir a classicist Olympus. Yet, no one remains oneself. And all, like Odysseus confronting the Cyclops in the mountain Etna, lose their name and become Nobodies, no-names. Here is a train conductor, there a policeman, and here again another large woman, or a group of soldiers singing the songs of the *Risorgimento*. But no one, peculiarly enough, seems to have a proper name. It is as if names — maybe tokens of a social, real existence — would compromise, for Lawrence, the allegorical depth of these personae. Or else, as if proper names were obstacles in the way of Lawrence's allegorical appropriation of these already "exuberant" figures.

In England, people are who they are; but there, estranged by geographic distance, in the extraordinary elsewhere of myth, the flower and seed of humankind are preserved as mere allegories of a Golden Age. Yet, if myth is estranged from England, which remains a reality principle of historical modernization, it has also to be estranged from Sicily, whose very presence is in fact erased, like its own name from the title page, and obliterated behind yet another allegory that tends to take its place. It is as

22. Like that Persian of Montesquieu's *Lettres Persanes* to whom the French could say only, in awe: "Ah, ah! monsieur is Persian? It's quite extraordinary! How can one be Persian?" In Montesquieu, *Lettres Persanes*, ed. Jean Starobinski (Paris: Gallimard, 1973), lettre XXX, 105; translation mine.

23. Walter Benjamin, *The Origin of German Tragic Drama*, trans. John Osborne (London: Verso, 1977), 175.

if Lawrence cannot see anything as it is: Sicily is already an expectation, a set of symbols alluding to an allegorical world — the region of a pristine humankind still stirred by the "indisputable facts" of nature:

> It seems as if Sicily, in some way, under all her amazing forms of so-phistication, still preserves some flower of pure human candour: the same thing that fascinated Theocritus.[24]

For Lawrence, novel Theocritus of the twentieth century, Sicily is the mythical home of idyllic creatures: Aci, Galatea, the Cyclops — all per-sonifications, in love and in vengeance, of pure human candor.

Reduced to the allegorical trope of Lawrence's own "necessity to move" away from the northern machine, Sicily exists as the allegorical set of co-ordinates necessary to define Lawrence's own quest for a space of purity. The island announces an allegorical sunrise, a renaissance, a new life for the world entire. And this renaissance, for the modern northerner, is noth-ing less than an Odyssey — the peripeteia of a return "back home" to the origin:

> There is something eternally morning-glamorous about these lands as they rise from the sea. And it is always the Odyssey which comes back to one as one looks at them. All the lovely morning-wonder of this world, in Homer's day! (SS 197)

And while Sicily becomes a citation — from Homer or from Theocri-tus — it also acquires the allegorical sense that Lawrence lends to it. Through *this* Sicily, the writer can now speak of his own Odyssey, of "Sicily" as the topos of *his* return to the pristine humankind of an heroic age: because "the Sicilians of to-day," as Lawrence will tell you, "are the nearest thing to the classic Greek that is left to us."[25]

Sicily exists as origin, then — the only origin, in fact, that is left to *us* — *our* origin, in a way! If Garda was the commonplace of a *locus amoenus*, is not Sicily — the most southern corner of Europe, already too close to Africa — the only commonplace left to the European north to claim an origin? Is not Sicily the place of the pastoral beginning of humankind sung in Theocritus's *Idylls*? Is not Sicily the place from where, sitting on a

24. David Herbert Lawrence, *Selected Literary Criticism*, ed. Anthony Beal (New York: Viking, 1966), 283.

25. Lawrence, *Selected Literary Criticism*, 276.

bench at the botanical garden in Palermo, Goethe had intuited "the clue to everything" contemplating the idea of the *Ur-Pflantze* — the "original plant"? Sigmund Freud, in a letter to Jung, wrote:

> Sicily is the most beautiful part of Italy and has preserved unique fragments of the Greek past, infantile reminiscences that make it possible to infer the nuclear complex.[26]

In this land of the unconscious, by the window opened in front of beautiful and wicked Etna, writing *Psychoanalysis and the Unconscious* and *Fantasia of the Unconscious*, Lawrence himself had hypothesized a "spontaneous, creative life" preceding the institution of the "supreme machine-principle."[27]

As the commonplace of origin, Sicily quickly becomes the allegory of a pristine, Janus-headed passion that bears with itself the duplicitous principle of life and death. Born, like Aphrodite, from the sea foam of the Mediterranean sea, Sicily is a locus where passion survives beyond good and evil:

> We think of ourselves, ah, how stupid . . . to have to go killing a man. . . . Was it worth it? . . . We ask the question with our reason, and with our reason we answer No!

But reason is the principle of a mechanical society. It is an invention, a cover up of natural passion:

> Is man a sweet and reasonable creature? Or is he, basically, a passional phenomenon? Is man a phenomenon on the face of the earth, or a rational consciousness? Is human behaviour to be reasonable . . . reasoned and rational? — or will it always display itself in strange and violent phenomena?[28]

---

26. Sigmund Freud, Letter of October 2, 1910, *Letters of Sigmund Freud*, ed. Ernst L. Freud (New York: Basic Books, 1975). For the reference to Goethe's *Urpflanze*, the original, or archetypal, plant, see Peter Sprengel, "Die 'Urpflanze'. Zur Entwicklung von Goethes Morphologie in Italien" and "Sizilien als Mythos. Das Sizilienbild in Goethes *Italienische Reise*," in *Un paese indicibilmente bello. Il Viaggio in Italia di Goethe e il mito della sicilia*, ed. Albert Meier (Palermo: Sellerio, 1987).

27. David Herbert Lawrence, *Psychoanalysis and the Unconscious*, in *Fantasia of the Unconscious and Psychoanalysis and the Unconscious* (Harmondsworth, Eng.: Penguin, 1971), 210–11.

28. Lawrence, *Selected Literary Criticism*, 284.

Whatever reason has repressed will always return as symptom: "Human behaviour is ultimately one of the natural phenomena, beyond all reason."[29] Sicily, situated in the south, is the allegory of that symptom. It is the phenomenon of a *genius loci* that brings life and death, passion and destruction at one time. It is an untamed origin. Loathing the boredom of the northern machine, Lawrence feels thrillingly closer to his goal. He is giddily approaching *our* origin, and he can already see traces of it in the gigantic and fierce descendants of the Cyclops that people the island — a shining knife in their hands, savage eyes, beautiful in their infernal radiance, violent phenomena: "A sort of sulphureous demons. *Andiamo!*" (SS 3).

> ... other than the sound of dance or song,
> Torment, and loud lament, and furious rage ...
>
> — JOHN MILTON, *Paradise Lost*

Andiamo, let's go! The object of the quest is near! And so we all go, elated, to Palermo, where it is "raining, raining hard. . . . Many human beings scurrying across the wet lines, among the wet trains, to get out in the ghastly town beyond" (SS 10). But in one moment, alas, Lawrence's euphoria vanishes while the rain still pours:

> Two convicts chained together among the crowd — and two soldiers. The prisoners wear fawny homespun clothes . . . No, but convicts are horrible creatures: at least, the old one is, with his long, nasty face: his long, clean-shaven, horrible face, without emotions, or with emotions one cannot follow. Something cold, sightless. I should loathe to touch him. Of the other I am not so sure. He is younger, and with dark eyebrows. But a roundish, softish face, with a sort of leer. No, evil is horrible. I used to think there was no absolute evil. Now I know there is a great deal. So much that it threatens life altogether. (SS 10)

If one puts aside for a moment Lawrence's distrust of Freudian analysis, it is difficult not to see in this description of the "horrible creatures" a rhetorical variation of Freud's *locus suspectus* — the uncanny. The description of the convicts uncannily parallels that of Hoffman's Coppelius: the "malicious sneer" of the latter doubles into the "sort of leer" of the for-

---

29. Lawrence, *Selected Literary Criticism*, 285.

mer; their "dark eyebrows" are reminiscent of the sandman's "bushy eye-brows." And then the convicts double into each other with their automa-ton-like — "cold" — lack of emotions. Is not their being "sightless" more of a reference to Olympia and the castration threat of the sandman than a descriptive necessity? Like the monster that plucks the eyes out of children who want to see too much, their very presence threatens, indeed, "life al-together."

Das Unheimliche is the title of Freud's essay written during the compo-sition of *Beyond the Pleasure Principle*. As a "primordial" word of the Ger-man language, *unheimlich* carries opposite meanings. Its root, the noun *Heim*, means "house." *Heimlich* is the familiar, the birth place, whatever protects and comforts. But *heimlich* also refers to the arts of black magic, of casting an evil eye, of plotting someone's death. The word carries op-posite meanings. Some people call *heimlich* what others call *unheimlich*. The homely, the place of origins and birth, is also the uncanny, the threat-ening, the place where one wants to return and that frightens with the promise of death at the same time:

> This unheimlich place, however, is the entrance to the former Heim [home] of all human beings, to the place where each one of us lived once upon a time and in the beginning. There is a joking saying that "Love is home-sickness"; and whenever a man dreams of a place or a country and says to himself, while he is still dreaming: "this place is familiar to me, I've been here before," we may interpret the place as being his mother's genitals or her body. In this case too, then, the unheimlich is what was once heimisch, familiar; the prefix "un" is the token of repression.[30]

Unheimlich is the *Heimat*, the place of our origins, a place qualified "by a certain lasciviousness — the phantasy, I mean, of intra-uterine exis-tence."[31] It is the place of a lost and immediate sensuality. But this sensual-ity of the origins is now threatening for our civilization, because, as Lawrence knows from Botticelli's Aphrodite (or is it *Totem and Taboo?*), sensuality is always a desire of death — the desire for the real mother, for the beloved that one chooses according to the image of the mother, and

30. Sigmund Freud, "The Uncanny," in *The Standard Edition of the Complete Works of Sigmund Freud*, vol. 17, ed. and trans. James Strachey (London: Hogart Press, 1955), 245. My analysis of the uncanny as a rhetorical trope is indebted here to Vincenzo Vi-tiello, *Elogio dello spazio. Ermeneutica e topologia* (Milano: Bompiani, 1994), 79–86.

31. Freud, "The Uncanny," 244.

for Mother Earth, the *Heimat* that will retake possession of man in the final moment of death.

This world of lost and "intra-uterine" passions is the place, the *Heim*, that precedes the intervention of the collective superego and its moral law, whither Lawrence would like to return in his Sicilian quest. But the sight of the original passion in the eyes of the outlaws in Palermo does not seem to deliver the promise. Passion, like the eyes of Olympia, remains "cold" and "sightless," "without emotions, or with emotions one cannot follow" — that is to say, extraneous, indifferent in its egotistic cruelty. It does not participate with the eager and civilized northerner, and remains *un-heim-lich*, without a *Heim* — without a home, that is, of security and comfort. The place of origins is a *un-Heim* — literally, a no-home, a no-place, or, put it differently, οὐ τόπος, a u-topia. The privative prefix (un-, no-, u-, οὐ-) is the token, to paraphrase Freud a bit, of a desire for origins that has always to be dis-placed, removed, and repressed from a home that has become threatening in its indifference. This desire can survive only, as Freud jokingly puts it, as "home-sickness," as nostalgia, as removal from a place of origins — that is to say, as Utopia, the *loss* of the place that we inhabited "once upon a time."

Certainly, Sicily, with its convicts, criminals, and passionate murderers, is the home where the fierce progeny of the Cyclops still dwells, untamed by the morality of good and evil. But for the northerner, in search of that lost past of savagery, Sicily is also the *unheimlich*, "something which is secretly familiar, which has undergone repression and then returned from it."[32] As the *unheimlich*, Sicily does horrify and frighten rather than please. Lawrence, the seeker of violent phenomena, cannot stand the horror:

> Away from abhorred Etna, and the Ionian sea, and the great stars in the water, and the almond trees in bud, and the orange trees heavy with red fruit, and these maddening, exasperating, impossible Sicilians, who never knew what truth was and have long lost all notions of what a human being is. . . . *Andiamo!* (SS 3)

Andiamo! Let's go! But where can we go this time? Back to England? No! Then Germany? Worse! Sardinia . . . perhaps . . .

Yet, Sardinia is not the place where Lawrence really intends to go.[33] Such

32. Freud, "The Uncanny," 245.
33. The *fact* that Lawrence leaves Sicily for Sardinia in the narrative of the journal is, allegorically speaking, a mere appearance. What Lawrence now calls Sardinia *is* the same

place must be, more literally than Sardinia, a place where "the world ends" (SS 55) and Utopia, untouched by reality, begins. The place is original Sicily of death and passion yet again. Only this time, it is a Sicily made exclusively of books, of words, where violence is still beautiful, blood is marvelous, "the sparks of the old, hardy, indomitable male still survive" (SS 61), and everything is a figure of speech.

"Ah!," urlò Turiddu accecato, "son morto."

— GIOVANNI VERGA, *Cavalleria Rusticana*

"Dear Catherine, Frieda and I have been reading Verga. . . . He exercises quite a fascination on me. . . . Do you know if he is translated into English? . . . It would be fun to do him — his *language* is so fascinating. . . ."[34] Thus wrote Lawrence to Catherine Carswell on October 25, 1921, while the celebrations for Verga's eightieth birthday were taking place in Palermo. No, he had not been translated. So, on February 20, 1922, the Lawrences leave Sicily for Ceylon, and then and there, at a secure distance from the horror of Sicily, by the Suez Canal and halfway across the Indian Ocean, David Herbert Lawrence takes *Mastro don Gesualdo* and *Cavalleria Rusticana* and "does" Verga. Sicily is now the nostalgia for a lost world of Man as "natural phenomenon, beyond all reason." It is a nostalgia, in fact, that Lawrence explicitly articulates: "the deepest nostalgia I have ever felt has been for Sicily, reading Verga. Not for England or anywhere else — for Sicily, the beautiful, that which goes deepest into the blood."[35] Only a few months have passed since Sicily was still "maddening," but now it can be desired again — as the nostalgia for something lost, as a phantasm evoked by a book. As a displacement. Love is home-sickness, says Freud half jokingly: the *Heimat* that Lawrence has lost, the origin of egotistic passions beyond good and wicked, was truly there, in Palermo, available to him in the convicts' eyes. The loss is not an ontological, or even an epochal, one

---

essence he used to call Sicily: "the uneasy sense of blood-familiarity [with Sardinians] haunts me. . . . It is something of the same uneasiness I feel before Mount Eryx [in Sicily]" (SS 60). And later: "Their [Sardinians'] proportion is so small that they make a boy walking at their side look like a tall man, while a natural man looks like a Cyclops . . ."(SS 60). While Lawrence becomes the Gulliver of his own travels, the thesaurus from which he takes is a fundamentally Sicilian one: the island, the Cyclops, the passion . . .

34. Lawrence, *Collected Letters*, 668; emphasis is Lawrence's.
35. Lawrence, *Selected Literary Criticism*, 278.

but a de-cision, a deliberate removal from something that can be desired only if it is lost. Nostalgia is the figure that Lawrence interposes between himself and Sicily — the land, that is, of pristine sensuality and homicidal ardor. As an apotropaic mask, Nostalgia wards off the fearful by attracting and comprehending it: the sinister is masked as desire.

Nostalgia is the mask provided by Giovanni Verga, whom Lawrence describes in the introduction to *don Gesualdo* as "a shortish, broad man with a big red moustache." Presaging already *Lady Chatterley's* Mellors — "with a red face and red moustache and distant eyes"[36] — Verga's red mask is, like Mellors's, the ritualistic disguise behind which Lawrence ventures in the uncanny territories of passion. The introductions to both *don Gesualdo* and *Cavalleria* are all punctuated by notations such as "he is Sicilian," "Verga himself is a Sicilian," "but he *is* Sicilian." The concept is reiterated endlessly, as if "Sicilian" were now not only something whose meaning we all know — "Sicily" as a metaphor?[37] — but also something pleasing and grand. This "greatest writer," in fact, is *so* Sicilian that he is not even Italian: there is something "unsatisfactory . . . about all Italian literature. . . . Italians have always borrowed . . . from the northern nations."[38] But Verga — regional Verga, peculiar and provincial Verga, the product of a *genius loci* called Sicily — does not borrow; he lends his face and signature as an apotropaic mask of lost southernness:

> he has a certain frankness, far more than an Italian. And far less fear than an Italian. His boldness and his queer sort of daring are Sicilian rather than Italian, so is his independent manliness.[39]

Through such a detour, whatever was disturbing about Sicily is represented through the mask of the desirable — the desire of a Sicilian "queer sort of daring," the desire to live in the elsewhere of the "northern nations," the desire to translate Sicily, the original.

As *Sea and Sardinia* obliterated Sicily behind the veil of allegory, so does Lawrence obliterate Verga's voice behind his own. Reduced to mere allegory, Verga now stands as the token of an "eternal Sicilian drawn-

---

36. Lawrence, *Lady Chatterley's Lover*, 49.

37. Leonardo Sciascia, *La Sicilia come metafora* (Milano: Mondadori, 1979). Aristotle calls Sicily a "metaphor" in *Rhetoric*, 1411a.

38. Lawrence, *Selected Literary Criticism*, 273.

39. Lawrence, *Selected Literary Criticism*, 277.

freshness."[40] Lawrence's lengthy and prescriptive preface, complemented by an abundance of footnotes directing and controlling the reading of the translated text, is an example of the method employed. Nothing like a preface could be more uncongenial to Verga's realist ideal of a story that "just happens by itself."[41] For Lawrence, instead, the story does not happen by itself but is produced by the *genius loci* of Sicily; and whatever may not be *genius loci*, the preface translates as such — Verga *is* Sicilian! Lawrence's foreword places into the reader's hands the threads necessary to (mis)read the text as a metaphor of our origins, and as the allegory of the "purely naive human being, in contrast to the sophisticated."[42]

Once both "maddening Sicily" and Giovanni Verga are eliminated from the scene of translation, only Verga's language — the dialect of Sicily, which Verga alleges to have "picked . . . up in the lanes among the fields, [and reproduced] more or less in the same simple and picturesque words of the people who told me"[43] — remains between Lawrence and his purely allegorical world. What is to be done with it? Elizabeth Mayer reports from an interview of September 1927:

> Lawrence said that the major problem in handling dialect is how to
> avoid the two oversimple and absolutely wrong solutions: the first, to

40. Lawrence, *Selected Literary Criticism*, 283.

41. In truth, Verga himself sometimes uses prefaces — but masked as dedicatory epistles, as in the dedication to Salvatore Farina introducing "L'amante di Gramigna." On the question of Verga's realism, already Croce had defined his *verismo* as an "observ[ation of] . . . nature and its laws," the painting of "earthly life and carnal love," and a rebellion "against all forms of mysticism." In Benedetto Croce, in *La letteratura della nuova Italia* (1914; reprint, Bari: Laterza, 1973), "I giovani poeti, 'veristi' e 'ribelli,' " vol. 5, 9, and "Giovanni Verga," vol. 3, 5–30. Croce, however, also begins the critical tradition that sees Verga as an outsider — or genius — who "thought" to be a *verista* without really being one.

42. Lawrence, *Selected Literary Criticism*, 283. Luigi Capuana, theoretical mind of the verismo and Verga's closest friend, had in fact remarked, in the *Fanfulla della domenica* of June 3, 1883, that "scientemente o inconsciamente, nei *Malavoglia* la nostra tradizione artistica si attacca forte, da un lato al Manzoni, dall'altro allo Zola" (knowingly or unknowingly, our artistic tradition becomes bounded, in the *Malavoglia*, to Manzoni on the one hand, and to Zola on the other). Verga, on his part, never understood such comparisons between him and the French as "abusive" of anything, and in fact thanked Capuana "dell'onore grande" (the great honor) in a letter written on the same June 3.

43. Giovanni Verga, "Gramigna's Lover," in *Cavalleria Rusticana and Other Stories*, trans. D. H. Lawrence (1928; reprint, London: Dedalus, 1987), 147.

translate the dialect of the original into another dialect which is spoken in a geographically existent region . . . and in a particular locality. For example, one can never have Sicilian fishermen talk like fishermen of the north or the Baltic sea, or have Sicilian peasants express themselves in the equivalent German or Austrian country idiom. Every dialect has inevitable overtones of the landscape, the character of the people and their native customs, inherent to their special locality and radically different from another and foreign region. Morals and manners, valid in Sicilian terms, would seem absurd when twisted into the sounds of a German way of life. On the other hand, it would be just as wrong to transplant the real Sicilian, together with his native peculiarities, into the German speaking ambiance and simply verbally reproduce his dialect: it would not ring true at all. Lawrence's advice, therefore, was to avoid both cheap solutions and to try to *invent* a new dialect, coined in German words but free from any reference, from any flavor of a special region, yet preserving the flavor of some sort of relaxed, uncitified, untutored mode of speaking.[44]

Lawrence's translation, then, seems inspired by the impulse to invent a language anew, "free from any reference, from any flavor of a special region, yet preserving the flavor of some sort of relaxed, uncitified, untutored mode of speaking." This language is, precisely, an allegory — it is the *idea* of dialect, a figure of what is "radically different" from a citified and tutored civilization. In Lawrence's allegorical world, accordingly, Verga's dialect becomes relevant only insofar as translation can, first, make it disappear and, second, replace it with the symbolic meaning bestowed on that displaced language. Benjamin's dictum that "a translation issues from the original — not so much from its life as from its afterlife"[45] — stands true here. Lawrence's translation stands for an absent dialect, which means, first, that "[e]very dialect has inevitable overtones of the landscape" and, consequently, that every dialect is a more natural — less mechanical and more passionate — kind of utterance.

To understand Lawrence's allegorical use of dialect, one should think of the ways author and translator, respectively, treat dialect. Verga's Turiddu,

44. Quoted in Jennifer Michaels-Tonks, *D. H. Lawrence: The Polarity of North and South — Germany and Italy in His Prose Works* (Bonn: Bouvier Verlag Herbert Grundmann, 1976), 29.

45. Walter Benjamin, "The Task of the Translator," in *Illuminations*, trans. Harry Zohn (New York: Schocken, 1969), 71.

returning from continental Italy to his native Sicily, speaks, or tries to speak, standard Italian. It is only when he realizes that he is no longer part of village life that he goes back to use the local dialect *with the villagers*, as if to ask for acceptance and reintegration: "addio, gnà Lola, *facemu cuntu ca chioppi e scampau, e la nostra amicizia finiu.*"[46] In Lawrence's translation, which renders the preceding passage in plain English ("goodbye, Ms. Lola, let's pretend that it rained and then made good, and all was over between us"), Turiddu's only recourse to nonstandard English is *in an aside*, which instead appeared in plain Italian in Verga's text: "'I'll show that bitch summat, afore I've done!,' he muttered to himself."[47] Dialect is no longer a token of belonging to a community. It is, instead, a private, personal — one would say "egotistic" — language, the language of "untutored" and "uncitified" passion or the allegory of such passion displayed exclusively for the reader's sake.

There is a problem, in short, with Lawrence's translation, but it is not a problem of translation. Sure enough, from the beginning of the story there are some factual mistakes: for example, Verga's *gnà* is contraction of the Spanish *doña*, lady or missis, but not "Mother" (VCR 33 and LCR 31). Yet, as Eduard Rod, French translator and friend of Verga, once noticed apropos *Cavalleria Rusticana*, "the greatest difficulty is not that of translation: it's that of interpretation."[48] What is at stake in Lawrence's *Cavalleria* is not the faithfulness of the translator but the possibility to appropriate a text and reinterpret it as an allegory. Verga's *verismo*, here, has become a morality play: Lola is Sensuality, Alfio is Pride and the Corruption of Money, Santa is Honesty. And Turiddu, as Lawrence puts it, is a principle of maleness as "natural phenomenon." His death stands to signify that manhood, "the vivid spontaneity of sensitive passionate life, non-moral and non-didactic," is threatened by "the vulgar and the greedy always destroying the sensitive and the passionate."[49]

46. Giovanni Verga, *Cavalleria Rusticana* (Roma: Salerno Editrice, 1990), 35; references to Verga's *Cavalleria Rusticana* are given in the body of the text as "(VCR 35)," for example.

47. D. H. Lawrence, trans., *Cavalleria Rusticana*, by Giovanni Verga, in *Cavalleria Rusticana and Other Stories*, 34; references to Lawrence's *Cavalleria Rusticana* are given in the body of the text as "(LCR 34)," for example.

48. Eduard Rod, letter to Giovanni Verga, Paris, 21 janvier 1908, in Giovanni Verga, *Lettere al suo traduttore* (Firenze: Le Monnier, 1954), 281; translation mine.

49. Lawrence, *Selected Literary Criticism*, 287.

Yet, where is this "vivid spontaneity," where is the "sensitive passionate life" in *Verga's* characters? From the very incipit, the story offers a rather different portrait of its would-be rustic and chivalrous hero:

Turiddu Macca, son of old Mother Nunzia (*gnà Nunzia*), when he came home from being a soldier, went swaggering (*si pavoneggiava*) about the village square every Sunday, showing himself off in his *bersagliere's* uniform with the red fez cap, till you'd have thought (*che sembrava*) it was the fortune-teller himself come to set up his stall with the cage of canaries. The girls going to Mass with their noses meekly inside their kerchiefs stole such look at him, and the youngsters buzzed round him like flies. And he'd brought home a pipe with the king on horseback on the bowl, simply life-like, and when he struck a match on his trousers behind, he lifted his leg up as if he was going to give you a kick. (VCR 33)

Already in his initial posture, parading like a peacock (*pavoneggiarsi* is the swaggering of the *pavone*, the peacock, which carries quite negative connotations and implies effeminacy), Turiddu strikes us as being quite far from any image of naivety or purity. He also displays, with pomp and circumstance, all the status symbols of his "continental" experience as a soldier — his uniform of the elite *bersglieri* unit, the pipe with the king of Italy, and the red fez. Affectation aside, the whole extended simile between Turiddu and the fortune-teller, sarcastic in Verga's text ("sembrava quello della buona ventura"), yet simply "objective" for Lawrence, who appeals to the authority of an impersonal readerly "you" ("you'd have thought it was the fortune-teller himself"), isolates Turiddu not as a hero of naive passions but as a charlatan. His very identity as Sicilian, which Lawrence takes as a guarantee of naivety, is put into question in Verga's narrative, which presents him, instead, first as a "continental" (the soldier with all the symbols of unified Italy) and later as an itinerant without a place (the fortune-teller of a circus). Turiddu is the pompous clown, the wandering charlatan who comes to the village to find himself an alien there.

Rather than the hero in uniform he would like to be, Turiddu is an outcast, because the village has a new champion to celebrate: *compare* Alfio, from the nearby town of Licodia, is the new hero in town. For him, Lola has even broken her promise to marry Turiddu. As the latter learns of the betrayal, his reaction becomes a tribute to Lawrence's southern man: "When Turiddu first got to hear of it, oh, devil! — he raved and swore! — he'd rip his guts out for him, he'd rip 'em out for him, that Licodia fellow!"

(LCR 31–32). In the euphoria for such abundance of passion, Lawrence even adds some extra exclamation marks to Verga's count but, caught in the fantasies of a pristine violence "beyond all reason," fails to realize that Turiddu's rage is merely that of a charlatan. Turiddu speaks, but hardly delivers: "But (*Però*) he never did a thing, except (*e si sfogò*) go and sing every slighting song he could think of under the beauty's window" (LCR 32). While Verga's sarcasm becomes derision, Lawrence attenuates the *però* ("instead") into a "but," and makes the ironic *si sfogò* (he found satisfaction by going to sing) disappear.

Verga is not the only one to dispense scorn and ridicule on Turiddu's broken heart: "'Has Mother Nunzia's Turiddu got nothing else to do but sing songs like a forlorn sparrow (*passera solitaria*), every mortal night?' said the neighbors" (LCR 32). Lawrence, intending to get the reference to the *passera solitaria* right in its allusion to a destiny of death[50] (but losing a new gender reversal that alludes again to the macho's effeminacy) does not realize that Verga speaks here the same sarcastic language as the villagers. The writer *has* disappeared in the chorus of popular wisdom, and Turiddu has become a laughing stock, a "[p]overaccio" (VCR 34) like the idiot of the village, not the "poor man" (LCR 32) of Lawrence's victimizing translation.

Idiot or symbolic victim, at any rate, the tragedy of passion is set with Lola's betrayal — were it not for the fact, overlooked by Lawrence, that the tragedy is not one of passion after all. Did Lola marry for love, or because *compare* Alfio had "four handsome Sortino mules of his own in his stable" (LCR 31)? Turiddu harbors no doubt: "Now you're going to marry that chap Alfio, as has got four mules of his own in his stable" (LCR 33). In fact, once she gets married, Lola wastes no time to show where her real passion lies: "the Sunday after [she got married], there she sat on her balcony, with her hands spread on her stomach to show all the great gold rings her husband had given her" (LCR 33). Turiddu, on the other hand, "si rodeva" (VCR 35), "it gnawed him inside himself to think that Lola's husband should have all that gold, and [in a subordinate sentence] that she pretended not to notice him" (LCR 33–34).

Playing the old game of jealousy, Turiddu starts courting another

50. In Leopardi's classical "Il passero solitario," the bird "cant[a], e così trapass[a] / dell'anno e di [s]ua vita il più bel fiore," sings, and so squanders the best part of the year and of his life.

woman, Santa, who lives, quite conveniently for the narrative's sake, across from Lola's window. Yet, more than a true effort to make Lola jealous, Turiddu's attentions to Santa seem to hide a more trivial interest in her father, who is "rich as a pig" (LCR 34). Turiddu's marriage proposal sounds like a financial negotiation:

"If I was rich, I should look for a wife like you, Miss Santa."

"Eh well! I shan't marry my Lord Tom-noddy, like Mrs. Lola, but I shan't come empty-handed neither, when the Lord sends me the right man."

"Oh ay! we know you're rich enough, we know that." (LCR 35)

To make a short story shorter, the passion that stirs the soul of Verga's Sicily has nothing primal or pristine about it. It is, more prosaically, a passion for *la roba*, the possession of "things," which, as Sciascia once said, are not "things" to enjoy but "things" to leave behind after one's death — and are therefore omens of death.[51] As an obsession for *la roba* is the displacement of a death wish — for instance in *Mastro don Gesualdo* — *la roba*, and not jealousy, prepares the tragic death set up by Verga on Easter day: the symbolic sacrifice of Turiddu at the altar of earthly possession. During the absence of *compare* Alfio, who is at the market with his precious mules, Lola has entertained Turiddu in her marital bed. Santa, jealous, awaits Alfio's return from the market "with . . . a good load of cash" (LCR 37) and informs him of the adultery: "You do well to bring her presents. . . . She's been adorning your house for you, while you've been away" (LCR 37).

Given the gravity of the accusation, it is curious that Santa notices the presents that Alfio brings for Lola. But the world of this rustic chivalry is hardly chivalrous at all, and the threshold between jealousy and envy is quite faint. On Easter day, the final duel puts an end to the story — not with the heroic composure one expects from such chivalrous titles but in an anticlimactic bathos of cold feet and subterfuge:

51. "Solo incidentalmente la roba è reddito e strumento: effettualmente non è cosa da *usare*, ma cosa da *lasciare*. È legata in eguale misura al sentimento della famiglia, all'apprensione per il futuro della famiglia, e al sentimento della morte. Col crescere della ricchezza cresce ciò che della vita lasceremo, cresce la nostra morte. Il ritmo dell'accumulazione è un ritmo di morte." In Leonardo Sciascia, *Pirandello e la Sicilia* (1961; reprint, Thilano: Adelphi, 1996), 29.

Come egli stava in guardia tutto raccolto per tenersi la sinistra sulla ferita, che gli doleva, e quasi strisciava per terra col gomito, [Alfio] acchiappò rapidamente una manata di polvere e la gettò negli occhi all'avversario.

— Ah! — urlò Turiddu accecato — son morto.

Ei cercava di salvarsi, facendo salti disperati all'indietro; ma compar Alfio lo raggiunse con un'altra botta nello stomaco e una terza alla gola.

— E tre! questa è per la casa che tu m'hai adornato. Ora tua madre lascerà stare le galline.

Turiddu annaspò un pezzo di qua e di là tra i fichidindia e poi cadde come un masso. Il sangue gli gorgogliava spumeggiando nella gola, e non potè profferire nemmeno: — Ah, mamma mia! (VCR 43)

Alfio, with the disloyalty that is proper to him, has won the duel, and Turiddu, with comic lack of decorum, has tried to run away from his murderer "facendo salti disperati all'indietro," with desperate leaps backward — to no avail. On the day of Easter, among the prickly pears of Canziria, without witnesses, Turiddu's throat is cut like that of a sacrificial lamb. The blood, frothing from his throat, will not even let him cry the name of the only person he has loved with no subterfuge — that of his mother.

But this is Verga. The following, instead, is D. H. Lawrence:

And as the carter stood on guard, doubled up so as to keep his left hand over his wound, which hurt him, his elbow almost brushing the ground, suddenly he seized a handful of dust and threw it full in his enemy's eyes.

"Ah!" screamed Turiddu, blinded. "I'm done!"

He tried to save himself by jumping desperately backwards, but Alfio caught him up with another stab in the stomach, and a third in the throat.

" — and three! That's for the house which you adorned for me! And now your mother can mind her fowls — "

Turiddu reeled about for a moment or two here and there among the cactuses, then fell like a stone. The blood gurgled frothing from his throat, he couldn't even gasp: Oh, Mother! (LCR 40–41).

It is not so much the elimination of Verga's most unheroic words that characterizes Lawrence's translation here — the "salti all'indietro" are a little more comical than Lawrence's "jumping desperately backwards," and

Alfio's arm that "quasi strisciava per terra" reminds us of snakes and sub-terfuge more than Lawrence's homely "brushing the ground." What is more peculiar is that Turiddu's final words have become an invocation to a higher principle; not "mamma *mia*" ("Ah, la mia povera vecchia!" in the first version of March 1880) but the eternal, transcendental, capital Mother — Mother Earth perchance, who gave birth to the Titans, ances-tors of the Sicilian indomitable Man! The use of dialect, which for Verga "makes everything sound smaller, whether you want it or not,"[52] is re-placed by a "pure" dialect that tends to make everything bigger — whether Verga wants it or not. A quite small, provincial "mamma," be-comes a big "Mother." The transformation is significant: capitalization, as Benjamin puts it, "is not only the aspiration to pomp" but the very "prin-ciple of the allegorical approach."[53] Is not this capital Mother the *Heimat*, the Spirit of Place that repossesses Manhood in its last days, while pre-serving it for a rebirth and a new Easter?

Lawrence's *Cavalleria Rusticana* is not a translation but the transfigura-tion of a story into an allegory whose meanings are already set in the pro-grammatic preface. In this appropriation of Sicily and its text, there is an attempt at internalizing the "other," the different-from-myself, as some-thing one's own. Sicily speaks English. Translation becomes anamnesis, the reminiscence of *our* past reappearing through the pure dialect of pas-sion. Significantly, after this appropriation, the locus of a regenerative, original passion, can be transposed from faraway Sicily to the British rus-tic region of Mellors's. At the beginning of *Lady Chatterley's*, the doctor — omnipresent figure in Lawrence's writings — diagnoses Connie: "There's nothing organically wrong [with you]. . . . Your vitality is much too low; no reserves, no reserves. The nerves of the heart a bit queer already; oh, yes! Nothing but nerves. . . . You're spending your life without renewing it." Connie's first lover, Michaelis, seems to have a solution for the renew-ing of her nerves: "Come down to Sicily! Go on, come to Sicily with me. It's lovely there just now. You want sun! You want life! Why, you're wasting away! Come away with me!"[54] Yet, Connie no longer needs to cross the

52. Paolo Maria Sipala, "*Cavalleria rusticana* tra Verga e Mascagni: dal dramma al melodramma," in *Poeti e politici da Dante a Quasimodo. Saggi e letture* (Palermo: Palumbo, 1994), 224.

53. Benjamin, *German Tragic Drama*, 208.

54. Lawrence, *Lady Chatterley's Lover*, 81.

strait between Scylla and Charybdis. Her regenerative Sicily has been, by now, translated into the mythical British countryside of Mellors. England has found and invented, by grace of D. H. Lawrence, its own mythical region — with its pure dialect, its culture, and its overflowing ardor.[55]

> I dance a tarantella on the rocks.
>
> — D. H. LAWRENCE, *New Poems*

Where does the regionalism of *Cavalleria Rusticana* begin? Did Sicilians read it as "regional literature"? Could its regionalism ever begin before translation? Verga, in truth, could hardly see anything "distinct" in his Sicily, devoured like the rest of the world by the cancer of possession — *la roba*. Nor did another Sicilian, Luigi Capuana, glimpse any allegory of "the uncitified and untutored" in Verga's Sicily. This does not mean that the kind of Sicily imagined by these Sicilians, and described according to the criteria of *verismo*, is the "real" Sicily as opposed to the symbolic one of Lawrence. Rather, this means only that "regionalism" is a mode of reading that begins exactly with a symbolic translation. The "original" region is, like the eyes of Lawrence's convicts in Palermo, essentially *unheimlich*: it is extraneous to "us," "cold," indifferent and inexplicable to our reason. That is why regionalism has had to appropriate this "origin," somehow, and translate it into something familiar and *heimlich* — into the allegory, notably, of *our* nostalgia. Regionalism, through translation, domesticates the "radically different" and housebreaks it: the potentially exotic becomes picturesque, a fragment of "our past." And by becoming "our past," by appropriating the "radically different" as something that is no longer *our* present, regionalism translates the original into its endless copies — Sicily, Egdon, Helstone, or Mellors's countryside.

How does *Cavalleria Rusticana*, an otherwise insignificant attempt by a Sicilian writer to mimic French naturalism and call it *verismo*, become a masterpiece of literary regionalism? Exactly by being removed from its

---

55. The emerging necessity of translation in industrial Britain, of which Lawrence's "Sicily" is just one episode, seems to answer the desire to find, in the "other" cultures, some models of communal sociability alternative to the class tensions of present-day England. On this point, see Wolfgang Iser, "The Emergence of a Cross-Cultural Discourse: Thomas Carlyle's *Sartor Resartus*," in *The Translatability of Cultures: Figurations of the Space Between*, ed. Sanford Budick and Wolfgang Iser (Stanford, Calif.: Stanford University Press, 1996), 247.

origin — by being translated. Published initially in *Fanfulla della Domenica* on March 14, 1880, *Cavalleria Rusticana*'s first success as a regionalist masterpiece is recorded at the time of its debut as a play at the Teatro Carignano of Torino, north Italy, on January 14, 1884. The theatrical adaptation had purged the original plot of any reference to money, thus yielding more easily to the nostalgia for pristine passions uncorrupted by capital. Sicilian difference, also, was exaggerated on the one hand, and translated away — so to speak — on the other. The duel proposed by Alfio, for instance, to which the story alludes when "Turiddu nipped the carter's ear between his teeth, thus promising solemnly not to fail him" (LCR 39), is supplemented by some kind of didactic explanation for the "radically different" public of Turin:

> ZIO BRASI (*piano*). Non hai visto, sciocca, quando gli ha morsicato l'orecchio? Vuol dire, o io ammazzo voi, o voi ammazzate me. (VCR 85)
> (ZIO BRASI (*whispering*). Didn't you see, you idiot!, when he bit his ear? It means: either I kill you, or you kill me).

Zio Brasi's whisper, obviously addressed to the public ("you idiot!"), is not a mere explanation of the symbolic meaning of Turiddu's gesture — it is mostly a remark on, and a highlighting of, the thrilling *difference* of a Sicily ruled by an awe-inspiring yet fascinating code of honor. It is the *unheimlich* made *heimlich*, the unhomely translated into homely terms.

This rustic chivalry, ambiguous expression of a desire and a repulsion for "our" original state of nature displaced onto "Sicily," was a success of regionalism. The public in Turin was impressed, as Silvana Monti summarizes, not by a "realistic play," which no longer existed, but by the picturesqueness of the scene — the savage and passionate nature of "the Sicilians."[56] The outbursts of such nature, not the adherence to some ideal realism, confirmed the success of the play in Paris, too, where "The Grasso Company plays with a violence which was liked by the public, at least in the folkloric scenes."[57] That is how *Cavalleria Rusticana* steadily acquired its European status as regional masterpiece — going more and more north every day, where everyone, furthered from the *unheimlich* of

56. Silvana Monti, "Il teatro di Verga e la società della Nuova Italia," in *Leggere Verga. Antologia della critica verghiana*, ed. Paolo Pullega (Bologna: Zanichelli, 1973), 238.

57. Eduard Rod, letter to Giovanni Verga, Paris, 21 janvier 1908, in Verga, *Lettere al suo traduttore*, 280; translation mine.

Turiddu's dead body, could feel nostalgia and cheer at the passion with which he had "bitten compare Alfio's ear."[58]

To put it differently, what is regionalist in *Cavalleria Rusticana* is its copy — the translation of an original plot into a set of expectations, symbols, or commonplaces. In this multiplication of copies, the fortune of the regionalist reading prospers: in 1899, Pietro Mascagni translates *Cavalleria* into an opera, and in 1907, another composer, Domenico Monleone, invited by Verga himself, writes yet another operatic *Cavalleria*. While Verga and Monleone are brought to court by Mascagni for infringement of copyright law, Monleone's opera is applauded in Budapest and Vienna as a regional masterpiece. In the midst of legal actions, Verga even lets his French translator, Julia Dembowska, sell the copyright for a film of *Cavalleria* to be shot by the Paris-based ACAD. Because the ACAD movie disappoints Verga, however, he sells the copyright to the Italian Tespi Film as well, which produces its *Scene Siciliane* (directes by Ugo Falena) in 1916. On April 10 of the same year, the magazine *Film* advertises yet another *Cavalleria Rusticana* produced by Flegrea Film, "all rights reserved" — "Which proves," as Verga might have said, "that each copy has its own special and original value"![59]

The "regionalism" of *Cavalleria* is in fact absolutely "original": it is a new value appended to the story by a peculiar kind of reading but extraneous to the story itself. This new "value" is the translation of Sicily into the allegory of an "original" passion dead and reborn. Not passion as *larmoyant* sentimentality, mind you, but passion as pristine, innocent and cruel, biting desire — and, precisely, in this cruelty, the only conceivable allegory of an idyllic humankind.

> Il faut méditerraniser la musique!
> — FRIEDRICH NIETZSCHE, *Beyond Good and Evil*

As desire for a primitive world of idyllic purity and epic passion, the regional reading tends, by its nature, to become more and more theatrical, more staged, and passionate to the point of melodrama. It is in fact

58. As Verga complained in a letter to Luigi Capuana, Milano, 7 luglio 1875, in Raya, *Carteggio*.

59. Letter of Verga to Luigi Capuana, Catania, 24 settembre 1889, in Raya, *Carteggio*. On the copious translations of *Cavalleria*, see Sarah Zappulla Muscarà, "Giovanni Verga e le 'brighe' di 'Cavalleria,'" *Foglio d'Arte* VI.1 (Giugno 1982): 24.

through works such as Bizet's *Carmen*, Rousseau's *Devin du village*, or Verdi's *Vespri siciliani*, that "the damp north" attempts to bring back its own passionate hypothetical "origin", to recover "a more southern, brown, burnt sensibility," and to "return to nature, health, cheerfulness, youth, virtue!"[60] Even more than *Carmen*, it is *L'Arlésienne*, inspired by a story by Alphonse Daudet and made into an opera by Bizet first, and then by Francesco Cilea (a *verista* himself), that realizes the perfect allegory for this doubling of regionalism into melodrama. Blue skies, pastoral peace, idyllic settings, the ponds of the Camargue region of southern France — *L'Arlésienne*, pure kitsch made music, is from its very outset a thesaurus of regionalist commonplaces. The story of the libretto unfolds as a love quest for the beautiful Arlésienne, and we soon realize that the desire for Woman here, like Clym's desire for Eustacia in *The Return of the Native*, is a metaphoric desire for the place that Woman personifies. One thing only is missing from this otherwise perfect regionalist stage: the southern *femme fatale* whom the tenor desires so ardently, whom the baritone claims as his lover, whom the mezzo-soprano wants to marry to her son, and whom the soprano hopes the tenor will forget. This obvious symbol of a passionate south-made-woman, half Aphrodite and half Etna, remains, throughout the opera, an absence. She does not sing or talk. She has no arias nor recitatives. She is not even hiding in the choir. She is, simply, not there. She is the pure nostalgia of southern passion — an emptiness, a void, a lack, a desire without an object but which stirs a melodramatic homesickness for a region that no longer is.

Opera, which Nietzsche saw as the decadence of tragedy, is also, in this sense, the closest referent to regionalism. Like the latter, opera is

> the yearning for the idyllic, the faith in the primordial existence of the artistic and good man. The recitative was regarded as the rediscovered language of this primitive man; opera as the rediscovered country of this idyllically or heroically good creature, who simultaneously with every action follows a natural artistic impulse, who accomplishes his speech with a little singing, in order that he may immediately break forth into full song at the slightest emotional excitement.[61]

60. Friedrich Nietzsche, *The Case of Wagner*, in *The Birth of Tragedy and The Case of Wagner*, ed. Walter Kaufman (New York: Vintage, 1967), 158, 159–160.
61. Friedrich Nietzsche, *The Birth of Tragedy*, in *The Birth of Tragedy and The Case of Wagner*, ed. Kaufman, 115–116.

We should not be surprised if, in Lawrence's regionalist translation of Verga, we find Turiddu singing to Lola "every slighting song he could think of" (LCR 31–32). The slightest emotional excitement, in truth, is put by regionalism into song!

How is one to understand the contiguity of regionalism and the rusticity of the *opera verista*? How else than by accepting the prejudice that in opera, as in regionalism, everything must be translated into allegory? In the world of opera, every person becomes a voice, every story a recitative, every feeling a note, every character a costume, every death a mood, every world a stage. Everything, in other words, is different from reality — not because, as Busoni once said, "people performing actions while singing" make sense only in the realm of "the incredible, the untrue, the improbable"[62] but because everything, in the *trompe l'oeil* that is the *opera verista*, is its own allegory. And everything is, on the stage of opera as within the "boundaries" of "region," more beautiful than reality, because all the difference, here, is the nostalgia for a lost *bel canto*.

Lawrence had seen Mascagni's opera in 1911. That was his first encounter with the Sicilian genius of Verga: "You never saw anything in your life more natural, naive, inartistic & refreshing,"[63] he wrote to Louie Burrows with words ostensibly borrowed from Nietzsche's praise of Bizet. The performance had taken place in London, where Sicily, needless to say, had the natural and inartistic essence of a melodramatic stage. Everything was positively refreshing, too, especially after the duo Giovanni Targioni-Tozzetti and Guido Menasci (both from Livorno, Tuscany) had eliminated from the libretto all references to a world corrupted by capital, while exaggerating instead the Christological symbolism of the Easter sacrifice and resurrection:

> Ora pro nobis Deum — Alleluja!
> Gaude et lætare, Virgo Maria — Alleluja!
> Quia surrexit Dominus vere — Alleluja![64]

62. Quoted in Robert Donington, *Opera & Its Symbols: The Unity of Words, Music & Staging* (New Haven, Conn.: Yale University Press, 1990), 151.

63. Lawrence, *Collected Letters*, 88.

64. Already in Verga's dramatization of *Cavalleria Rusticana*, the very first scene opens with the bells singing for the coming Easter. After that, there are sixteen references to Easter in the whole play, against one only in the story. The quotation from the opera is from G. Targioni Tozzetti and G. Menasci, "Cavalleria Rusticana: Melo-

In fact, the allegorical nature of the characters, which Lawrence would try to reenact in his translation, was already in that opera. Santa is, as her very name suggests, allegorical of a fallen sanctity; Alfio, in the cavatina that introduces him ("Il cavallo scalpita"), appears as the explicit personification of pastoral cheerfulness; and Turiddu, announced by the Siciliana "O Lola ch'hai di latti la cammisa," is instead presented as the unmistakable allegory of "Aphrodite's" passion: for love's sake, he says, "nun me mpuorta si ce muoru accisu," — I don't care if I will be killed. Sicily itself, moreover, appears as the allegorical locus of a time of resurrection. The bells toll for Easter and announce a symbolic spring, Virgilian in its bucolic tone:

> Gli aranci olezzano
> sui verdi margini,
> gli augelli cantano
> tra i mirti in fior.

Mascagni's Sicily, like Lawrence's, was one in which passion was pure and deadly, and where manhood was chivalrous and rustic, noble and natural at the same time. "Hanno ammazzato compare Turiddu!" — Turiddu has been killed. But the few seconds filled with the ominous chords that end the opera over cannot make one forget that it is already Easter. It is not difficult to glimpse, in this "musical mish-mash (*pasticcio musicale*) with clinking glasses,"[65] Lawrence's very nostalgia for regional Sicily. *This* is the regional Sicily of original passion that he will want to translate.

Ah! Passion! Pristine, consuming passion! You heal and destroy, seduce and horrify! *Hanno ammazzato Turiddu!* It is all as beautiful as the *opra di li pupi*, the puppet theater that Lawrence visits in Palermo in the last pages of *Sea and Sardinia*. In the puppet theater, Orlando and Rinaldo, the paladins of a world that is not, brandish their arms, and "Terrible is the smacking of swords, terrible the gasps from behind the dropped visors. Till at last the Knight of Spain falls — and the Paladin stands with his foot on the dead" (SS 203). How much better is the stage than the real world, how much better these puppets than real people! For desire, Lawrence ob-

dramma in un atto," in *Cavalleria Rusticana*, ed. Roberto Fedi (Roma: Salerno Editrice, 1990), 101.

65. Verga, letter to Luigi Capuana, Milano, 20 gennaio 1894, Raya, *Carteggio*.

serves, "is enacted by symbolic creatures formed out of human consciousness: puppets if you like: but not human *individuals*." And let us give these
puppets their stage, let us give them their Sicily, a splendid region where
blood achieves all. They love and kill, indomitable males, and a shiver
electrifies our senses, suspending for a moment our habit of life:

> But it is over. All is over. The theatre empties in a moment. And I shake
> hands with my fat neighbor, affectionately, and in the right spirit. Truly
> I loved them all in the theatre: the generous, hot southern blood, so sub-
> tle and spontaneous, that asks for blood contact, not for mental com-
> munion or spirit sympathy. I was sorry to leave them. (SS 204–205)

It is an incomparable moment. The contact with spontaneous blood is
back, as in the days of the first creation, but now no more than truly necessary. And Sicily is now beautiful, beautiful and terrifying, a real ecstasy,
but one which, we now know, exists only as an allegorical stage. It is a
stage, in fact, all too reminiscent of the one of regionalism, in which the
unheimlich extraneousness of a "picturesque" life is translated into the literary and familiar figure of "the regional" — *our* origin, that is, so "radically different" from our present. As beautiful as an *opra di li pupi*! We are
sorry for having left those "regional" origins. But it's over. All is over —
and just about to begin all over again. *Trasemu, ch'i ura!*

The Dialectic of Region and Nation

Giovanni Gentile, Particular Italian

Archimede, Empedocle, Teocrito, Diodoro,
sono glorie del genere umano, ma bisogna
confessare che un pochino sono pure siciliani . . .
— MICHELE AMARI, quoted by Giovanni Gentile

Professors and cardinals, ministers and friends, deputies and notables, scientists and hacks, philosophers and *mafiosi* — not even all the forces the Sicilian philosopher Giovanni Gentile could recruit, in 1898, in search of the ultimate *raccomandazione*, could gain him the coveted professorship at the prestigious "Liceo Garibaldi" of Palermo. Aurelio Covotti, a Florentine scholar of alleged great erudition, illustrious representative of the "historical method" — the *critica storica* — fashionable at the time, refused to leave the chair he was already occupying there — unless, that is, Gentile, "Sicilian and therefore mafioso," could obtain for him a professorship "in Rome or Florence, or at least Turin" in exchange.[1]

Writing to Donato Jaja, his beloved professor of philosophy in Pisa,

1. Gentile's letter to Jaja of August 17, 1898, in Giovanni Gentile and Donato Jaja, *Carteggio*, ed. Maria Sandirocco (Firenze: Sansoni, 1969), book 1, 146; all translations mine, unless otherwise noted.

Gentile vented his rage against the "mercantile" Covotti and all his idiotic stereotypes. Does he think Sicilians, mafiosi or not, are omnipotent and can move him to any corner of the world they please? And why would Covotti stay in Sicily if he thinks so lowly of its people? Why doesn't he leave the post to a Sicilian, who could truly stand life in "the province of gossip," in the kingdom of "provincial life, petty and chatty," in the "island of the sun [where] the heat is suffocating"?[2] Could Jaja please try to convince him?

Alas! — nothing could be done. Covotti stayed in Palermo, and Gentile, instead, was sent to the town of Campobasso, in the Abruzzi region, with an emigrant's suitcase and a sensibility badly bruised — the first Sicilian professor, perhaps, to have to leave his homeland according to the logic of the recently instituted system of *concorsi nazionali*. It was the price to pay to the unification of Italy! To console him, there were only the words of Professor Jaja still echoing in his mind: Covotti was only an egoist, and his "erudition, as it is natural to all erudition, makes his heart sterile. Or is it that sterile heart of his which has imprisoned him in erudition?"[3] No matter what, Gentile would seek revenge, and conquer the post that the Florentine had so unjustly usurped from him. Sicily to Sicilians!

To get back to Sicily, however, the Sicilian needed a few more publications to boost his curriculum — or rather his *punteggio* — a bit. Giovanni Gentile, with the thought of the lost *cattedra* of Palermo haunting his nights in Campobasso, began his pursuit by writing an article on the Neapolitan Francesco De Sanctis, whose essays on nineteenth-century Italian literature had recently been collected and published, in 1897, by the Neapolitan Benedetto Croce, under the title of *La letteratura italiana nel XIX secolo*. Croce, truly irritated by the positivistic vogue of the times, which debased poetry to the mere "pleasure of psychic associations,"[4] liked to oppose the passionate sensibility of Francesco De Sanctis to the collection of so called "facts" that, in the name of positivism, intended to transform literature and its criticism into science and vacuous erudition. As the reader can, at this point, imagine, Gentile's choice of De Sanctis as the object of an essay planned to question the famous erudition of Covotti and ease its author's return to Sicily was not entirely casual. De Sanctis, whose

2. Gentile's letter to Jaja of August 20, 1895, in *Carteggio*, ed. Sandirocco, book 1, 9, 10.

3. Jaja's letter to Gentile of August 21, 1898, in *Carteggio*, ed. Sandirocco, book 1, 156.

4. Benedetto Croce, *Primi saggi* (1919; reprint, Bari: Laterza, 1951), x.

writings remained for positivist historians nothing more than the "aesthetic, metaphysical, fantastic, and arbitrary criticism of a Neapolitan professor,"[5] was now becoming a symbol for a war that Gentile's generation was ready to wage, against positivism and erudition, in the name of "sentiment, passion, soul."[6]

Gentile's hostility toward positivism and erudition, in truth, had already begun in 1893, after Croce had pronounced his famous discourse[7] on "La storia ridotta sotto il concetto generale dell'arte" — "History Reduced under the General Concept of Art" — at the Accademia Pontaniana of Naples. Given that sciences elaborate general concepts that can be applied, indifferently, to different objects — as with the same mathematical calculation one can add either apples or oranges — Croce concluded that because history aimed at reporting *specific* and *circumstantial* facts only, it would hardly qualify as a science:

> Either one makes works of science . . . or one makes works of art. If one overlooks the specific for the general, one makes science; if one represents [*si rappresenta*] the specific as it is, one makes art. Now . . . historiography does not elaborate concepts, but reproduces [*riproduce*] specificity in its concreteness. That is why we have denied historiography the character of science. It is therefore an obvious consequence, and a perfectly legitimate syllogism, to conclude that, if history is not a science, it must then be an art.[8]

Against Croce's "legitimate syllogism," historians may, of course, be free to think that beyond the either/or of art or science there is still room for works of history. What Croce was trying to suggest, however, was that the "objective" and "scientific" facts collected with the method of positivism remained insufficient, in themselves, to make a history. Facts still need to be "represented" and "reproduced" into a sensible, linear discourse before they become "history." History, in fact, is the *telling* of facts — *il narrare i fatti* — elaborated by the poetic spirit that alone can transform them into

5. Benedetto Croce, *Gli scritti di Francesco De Sanctis e la loro varia fortuna* (Bari: Laterza, 1917), 102.

6. Giovanni Gentile, *La filosofia dell'arte* (1931; reprint, Torino: Utet, 1950), 317.

7. Returned to fame, in fact, after the attention devoted to it by Hayden White, *The Tropics of Discourse: Essays in Cultural Criticism* (Baltimore: Johns Hopkins University Press, 1978).

8. Benedetto Croce, "La storia ridotta sotto il concetto generale dell'arte," in *Primi saggi*, 23–24.

meaningful episodes in the epic of humankind. History, therefore, is a branch of the arts, and, as such, it ought to be subordinated to aesthetic and, more generally, to philosophy.

Croce's lecture, to be sure, was not meant to deny the necessity of "facts" in the historiographical work: before proceeding to the "representation," the historian certainly needs to collate facts. But for Gentile, a review of Croce's lecture for the journal *Studi storici* had become the pretext to rewrite Croce a bit and eliminate, once and for all, the centrality of facts in *any* discipline.[9] Anticipating a position characteristic of the later years of the "absolute idealism" — thought posits its objects and its "facts" to itself — Gentile wrote:

> [Historical facts] are "facts" for us [*son tali per noi*] inasmuch as they are represented in the spirit [*si rappresentano nello spirito*]; we can discuss them in philosophical terms as far as they have already been apprehended and elaborated by the spirit itself. . . . It is obvious that one cannot talk of pure facts, raw facts, as anything else than an abstract, ideal content, impossible to grasp or glimpse in the effectual reality — the reality exterior to the spirit.[10]

Still unable to give up a certain Kantian reality "exterior to the spirit," the young Gentile was already contending that the facts of historical erudition meant nothing at all. "Facts" are abstract ideas — unless, that is, they are "elaborated" by a philosophical spirit to which history has therefore to be subordinated.

The logic of this little deconstruction of the myth of factual evidence should not distract us from noticing that in the meantime Gentile was concocting a little theory of elective affinities between himself, Croce, and, above all, De Sanctis. Gentile's "*noi*" went beyond that conspicuous Italian habit of using a plural "we" in writing and was becoming instead the preparation to a lifelong project: the construction of something like a community of blood and intent between himself and the two Neapolitan writers. *We* know that, as facts must be internalized by the spirit, so is history to be subsumed by philosophy. Whereas Croce always remained a little skeptical of Gentile's attempts to talk so nonchalantly of "us" and

9. See Paolo Rossi, "L'attualismo gentiliano," in *Storia e filosofia. Saggi sulla storiografia filosofica* (1969; reprint, Torino: Einaudi, 1975), 31.

10. Giovanni Gentile, review of Benedetto Croce, "Il concetto della storia nelle sue relazioni col concetto dell'arte," *Studi storici* 6 (1897): 140–141.

"*our* origins,"[11] the universe for Gentile was already divided between "us" and "them." In those early years, before the trauma of Campobasso would trigger it all, Gentile distinguished between *their* historical positivism, dominant in the academies of northern Italy, and *our* "passionate" and "free southern criticism," inspired by Francesco De Sanctis.[12]

The difficulty of reconciling this splitting localism of north and south with the absolutism of Gentile's thought is one reason for overlooking this otherwise noticeable latitudinal fissure, and for the marginal place usually assigned, in the oeuvre of the *idealismo assoluto*, to the more "regional" studies of Gentile. The whole series of essays on Sicilian culture, which Gentile published in 1915 for the journal *La critica* and later collected as *Il tramonto della cultura siciliana* in 1919, remain for instance, according to Lo Schiavo's canonic introduction to Gentile, a simple "exception"[13] in the years of absolute formalism. The *Studi vichiani* of 1915, likewise, would be, from the same point of view, exceptional in their reconstruction of a local Neapolitan culture, "from whose tradition," as we read in the introduction, Vico "grasped some of his fundamental concepts." The fact is that, all but "exceptional," Gentile's interest in the local, which dates back to the doctoral thesis of 1898 on the philosophy of the "southern provinces," is the pendent to an absolutism in search of the possibility to posit a dialectic of "southern" and "northern" philosophy. As Gentile saw it, philosophy was characterized in the south [*quale si sviluppò nelle province meridionali*] by the passion of Vico's poetic reason; in the north, instead, it was tied to a historicist, positivistic method driven by a colder "need for science."[14]

11. Benedetto Croce, *Lettere a Giovanni Gentile (1896–1924)*, ed. Ada Croce (Milano: Mondadori, 1981), 585; Croce's emphasis. On the frictions between Croce and Gentile, see Jader Jacobelli, *Croce Gentile. Dal sodalizio al dramma* (Milano: Rizzoli, 1989).

12. Hegel's idea, transcending nature, had implicitly assumed a dichotomy between thought and nature, subject and object; the old dualism of spirit and matter had been revived. With Gentile's reform of idealism, which was a return to the "original" idealism of Vico, that very dualism was erased in the absolute immanence of the thought that posits itself and nature: "I agree with you [Croce] in your criticism of Hegel's Idea and Vico's Providence. I am convincing myself that Hegel did not discover the principle of immanence, and his Idea remained, therefore, transcendent." In Gentile's letter to Benedetto Croce, February 20, 1913, announcing the publication of *La riforma della dialettica hegeliana*, in *Opere filosofiche*, ed. Eugenio Garin (Milano: Garzanti, 1991), 241.

13. Aldo Lo Schiavo, *Introduzione a Gentile* (Bari: Laterza, 1986), 96.

14. Sergio Romano, *Giovanni Gentile. La filosofia al potere* (Milano: Bompiani, 1984), 35.

For the same Hegelian Gentile, who made of "thought" the only reality (*atto unico*);[15] who claimed that even matter is "a mode of the experience of thinking [*un modo dell'esperienza del pensiero*]";[16] who annihilated all kind of differences into the "absolute formalism" of logic;[17] who, as minister of education of the fascist regime, predicated the virtues of nationalism, of the absolute state, and of the linguistic unity of the country;[18] and who imagined "thought" as the "universal in the sense that, as necessity, it presents itself as thought not of a particular thinker . . . but as thought that thinks for everyone [*pensiero che pensa per tutti*]"[19] — for this same Gentile, who could see his own philosophy as the mere epiphany of one universal thought, the universal was still in need of a proper dialectic, which he saw, essentially, as an antithesis of local splits.[20]

The contradiction between local and universal is, in fact, only apparent. As the activity of the thinking spirit is a continuous and dialectical "differentiation of identity [*differenziazione dell'identico*],"[21] dialectics will of course subsume all differences into a new synthesis. Thought needs a space in which to represent its own objects of experience, and this space can be conceived neither as a Platonic emptiness where ideas fall and are "realized" nor as a unity. Space is not empty because thought posits it with the specific aim to represent its objects within it. Space is not a unity because it is a *relation* of objects that, all together, constitute "space." Space is, in fact, a "system of multiplicity,"[22] a multiplication of "here" (*hic*) within which we locate our objects of experience. All these "heres," these local points, do not exist per se but are posited by the thinking subject:

15. Gentile, *La riforma della dialettica hegeliana*, 319.

16. Giovanni Gentile, *Sommario di pedagogia come scienza filosofica. I: Pedagogia generale* (1913; reprint, Firenze: Sansoni, 1934), 26.

17. Giovanni Gentile, *Teoria generale dello spirito come atto puro*, in *Opere filosofiche*, ed. Garin, 653–654.

18. Gabriella Klein, *La politica linguistica del fascismo* (Bologna: Il Mulino, 1986), 82.

19. Gentile, *La riforma della dialettica hegeliana*, 315.

20. See, for instance, the chapter on "Il carattere storico della filosofia italiana," in Giovanni Gentile, *I problemi della Scolastica e il pensiero italiano* (1913; reprint, Bari: Laterza, 1923), 190–191.

21. Giovanni Gentile, *I fondamenti della filosofia del diritto* (1916; reprint, Firenze: Sansoni, 1937), 97.

22. Gentile, *Teoria generale dello spirito come atto puro*, 552; Cesare Luporini, "Il problema del rapporto fra spazio e tempo in Gentile e in Kant," in *Situazione e libertà nell'esistenza umana e altri scritti* (Roma: Editori Riuniti, 1993), 199–206.

"the multiplication, whereby this is not that, is my act." This separation of "this" from "that," of "north" from "south," is what Gentile calls "the spatializing [*spazializzatrice*] activity of the spirit, which does not presuppose multiplicity but generates it":[23] reality can only be conceived, as a later and more familiar jargon would put it, as an endless set of differences. These differences, for Gentile, are configured essentially as differences in space.

North and south, then, are the "multiplication" of the idea of philosophy into a first dialectic duplicity. They are the spatialization, in a sense, of two antithetical ideas that a thinking subject *needs* to imagine since "everything we discern and can discern, and therefore posit, in an actual experience, is spatial."[24] North and south become the necessary stages for Gentile's play on the mythical battle between the forces of positivism and the forces of idealism — the "spatialization," that is, of science and technique on the one hand, and of passion and sensibility on the other. Within this spatialization of positivism and idealism, Gentile could, in a way, create a space for himself, as a southern philosopher and therefore as a Sicilian.

Exactly with this "spatialization" in mind, Gentile must have begun his essay on De Sanctis, in Campobasso, in the year 1898. Although the piece never mentioned either north or south, it did allude quite explicitly to the two contrasting trends in the Italian academy: an idealistic aesthetic on the one hand (poietic thought creates the real) and a positivistic materialism on the other (facts are the matter of thought). If we can, for a moment, reduce philosophy (so to speak) to the concept of rhetoric, it should not be hard to see, behind Gentile's paralepsis, the desire to talk, albeit in elliptic terms, of his own personal drama. That a *northern* erudite like Covotti would teach philosophy in Palermo, and instruct a new generation of Sicilian intellectuals in the skills of historical criticism, was not only a personal affront to Gentile — it was an insult to the whole philosophical tradition of the "southern provinces"! What could Covotti ever know of Vico's poetic language? What could he say of De Sanctis? So, without ever mentioning Covotti in any explicit way, Gentile asked in his essay: Why is it that De Sanctis's great aesthetic intuition has been lost on a whole generation of philosophers? "Let's go back to De Sanctis!"[25]

23. Gentile, *Teoria generale dello spirito come atto puro*, 558–559.
24. Gentile, *Teoria generale dello spirito come atto puro*, 553.
25. Giovanni Gentile, "Torniamo a De Sanctis!" in *Memorie italiane* (Firenze: Sansoni, 1936), 173–181.

Gentile sent his article, so formulated, to Alessandro D'Ancona, once his professor of literature at the University of Florence. D'Ancona, one of the Italian masters of *critica storica* himself, was at the time chief editor of the *Rassegna bibliografica di letteratura italiana*. The journal, whose trend was admittedly historicist, was usually open to contributions from the opposing faction and gladly accepted "aesthetic" interventions, given that the tone would avoid "useless" polemics, and that the interest would remain the literary text rather than philosophical abstractions and other — in D'Ancona's colorful expression — "intellectual ejaculations."

The essay submitted by Gentile, Professor D'Ancona wrote back in a rather annoyed postcard, was far too polemical for a journal that was not interested "in the controversy of aesthetic and history [or] in the more trivial [*più balorda*] controversy between southerners and northerners [*meridionali e settentrionali*]." As much as Gentile had tried to curb his antinortherner *vis polemica*, D'Ancona was not a newcomer in these matters and clearly saw, in the revival of the querelle between positivism and aesthetic, something other than the spirit of pure scholarly speculation. The vindictive ghost of a dispossessed southern spirit was lurking from every page of Gentile's essay. It was a little too much for the old professor to bear! If Gentile would omit some unnecessarily polemical parts and correct some others. . . . Yet, this whole controversy — *balorda* as it could appear to D'Ancona — was central both to Gentile's philosophy, and to his self-promotion as a philosopher in an Italy that he saw as swarming with positivists and unfair to southerners. As for the corrections suggested by D'Ancona, Gentile let him know that he had no time to waste. The corrections were not necessary, and, if D'Ancona insisted, he could make them himself!

Would a less pretentious Sicilian philosopher ever have made a difference in the new Italy of the last *fin de siècle*? Or was it just this megalomaniac intransigence that launched Giovanni Gentile into synthetic immortality, as the godfather of southern regionalism on the one hand, and as the patron saint of fascist nationalism on the other?

> Oh Nordici, cui rende
> L'itala viltà sempre più alteri!
>
> — TOMMASO GARGALLO, *Le Veronesi*

Benedetto Croce, philosophical Masaniello, once fomented a little academic revolt when in 1901, in his essay on "Vico Discoverer of Aesthetic Science" (later to be included in the *Estetica*), he revealed that Baumgarten had not been the true Messiah — at most a John the Baptist — of the new age of aesthetic. German critics, he wrote, have managed to convince themselves that Baumgarten is the Copernicus of a modern "revolution": the one which has rescued art from Platonic disdain, and admitted it in the modern republic as a form of knowledge. But "What is Aesthetic for Baumgarten?" — asked Croce. For the German, "objects of Aesthetic are the facts perceptible by the senses (αἰσθητά)." Aesthetic is therefore, quoting Baumgarten, a "science of sensitive cognition, theory of the liberal arts, inferior cognition, art of small thinking."[26]

What bothered Croce about Baumgarten's definition was not so much the fact that aesthetic was reduced to a *gnoseologia inferior* but the fact that it was mistaken for *gnoseologia* at all. The very term coined by Baumgarten — αἰσθητά, sensual perception — implied the anteriority and precedence of the object to be perceived and known. In this way, however, the arts were reduced to yet another form of Platonic representation. To avoid the pitfalls of Platonism, Baumgarten claimed that aesthetic representation was not necessarily a "copy" of a "real" or "natural" object but rather the "fantastic" apperception of a "possible" one. The Aristotelian notion of verisimilitude, as Croce correctly notes, was back — and, with it, the subordination of the arts to what is, or may be, real: we are "back in the labyrinth without escape of verisimilitude, [of what] is and is not false."[27]

What has Baumgarten revolutionized? Croce's answer: nothing. As long as the concept of verisimilitude is not abandoned altogether, art must always be judged according to its degree of adherence to, and faithful representation of, a reality that precedes it. "Confused" aesthetic cognitions, accordingly, are to be subordinated to the "distinct" sciences which observe not the *verosimile* but the *vero* — the real against which verisimilitude must be evaluated. Baumgarten, in short, is for Croce a Platonist in

26. Baumgarten, quoted in Benedetto Croce, *Estetica come scienza dell'espressione e linguistica generale*, ed. Giuseppe Calasso (1902; reprint, Milano: Adelphi, 1990), 268; the preceding quotes in this paragraph are from Benedetto Croce, and come from the same page.

27. Croce, *Estetica*, 270.

Aristotelian disguise. He has invented not a new discipline but a name, and "the new name is empty of truly new content."[28]

As Baumgarten loses his insignia as messianic announcer of the age of aesthetic, Vico appears to Croce as the only, first, and true "revolutionary who, putting away the concept of verisimilitude and understanding fantasy in a novel way, penetrated the true nature of poetry and art and discovered, so to speak, the science of aesthetic."[29] Vico's *Scienza nuova* is, for Croce, nothing less than what Edward Said calls a "beginning": in the sense that it *begins* what we continue to call — *faute de mieux* — aesthetic; and in the sense that it understands aesthetic — poetry and the arts — as the founding ethical moment that institutes *human* reality.[30] Aesthetic cannot be a form of cognition for the simple reason that it *precedes* any cognition. It cannot be, either, the perception *of* a thing, because the thing is what is created by the aesthetic — poetic, in the etymological sense of the word — gesture. In the beginning it was the Word. As Croce reports from the *Scienza nuova* ("Elementi," LIII), sensation (Baumgarten's αἴσθησις) marks the first contact between the human being and the world. Αἴσθησις characterizes the moment in which humankind is thrown in a preexisting realm of physics, in the Aristotelian φύσει ὄντα — the existing things (*Physics*, 253a, 33–35). In this realm, humankind can feel only what there is to feel, and succumbs to the materiality of a world passively felt. It is only at a second moment, when the spirit perceives, in Vico's words, "with perturbed and moved soul," that poetry is born. This novel consciousness (*avvertire*), which Croce quickly translates as "conscience" (*coscienza*), is the true beginning of poetry. It is the moment in which the world becomes language and can be thought about and communicated. In the horizon of this linguistic conscience, things become meaningful, or, more simply, *become*: in Heidegger's maxim, *die Welt weltet, die Zeit zeitigt, das Ding dingt*. If language and poetry have thus instituted the world that is given to know and communicate, logical or scientific reflections (*riflettere*) can only follow — true Platonic mirrors! — this primordial moment of consciousness.

Poetry is not, as Plato had thought, the representation of an external

---

28. Croce, *Estetica*, 276.

29. Croce, *Estetica*, 277.

30. Edward W. Said, *Beginnings: Intention and Method* (New York: Basic Books, 1975).

world that always remains extraneous to the representing self but rather a *production* of that very world, an *inventio*. Poetry, therefore, cannot be, as Baumgarten thought, subordinated to the "clarity" of a science, since the very "real" on which science operates is, in fact, defined by a poetic gesture — the naming that originates conceptualization.[31] Poetry is, therefore, the beginning of any human cognition: it fixes the limits of the human world. The aesthetic revolution has begun: positivistic sciences, which once tried to define the territory and value of poetry in terms of what may be real and what may not, now find themselves absolutely dependent on a poetic act that has defined and named their very universe.

As Gentile summarizes Croce's reading of the *Scienza nuova*, he remarks with sincere enthusiasm:

> [Vico] denies the pre-existence of the object to the mind that knows it, and attributes to this mind an activity which creates this world. . . . Truth is thought, as Descartes maintained; yet, thought is not the spectator of what is represented, but its creator. One can debate whether we construct and create abstract geometries only, or something more tangible and real — how much, that is, our power resembles the one we attribute to God. For now, it is enough to say that the way is open. And Vico guides us in it.[32]

"One can debate" — Gentile concedes cavalierly — whether the world exists per se (as Croce in fact maintained) or whether it is the idea created by "our power" of thought (as Gentile's *idealismo assoluto* requires). Because one knows, as Vico's saying goes, only what one has created, the only thing *we* can ever know is what our original poetic fantasy had once created. Whether there is a world different from the one our fantasy constructed is, at this point, an insignificant question. For the time being, what matters to Gentile is that "the way is open": Vico is not only the beginning of aesthetic but also, and more radically, the beginning of a new philosophy — a philosophy that rises, with the *Scienza nuova*, to the understanding of the "concept of absolute spirit or idea, the same concept

---

31. On this point, consider the influence on Croce, and later on Gentile himself, of the Neapolitan Bertrando Spaventa, *Prolusione e introduzione alle lezioni di filosofia nella Università di Napoli* (Napoli: Vitale, 1862), 95–96.

32. Giovanni Gentile, *Studi vichiani*, in *Opere*, ed. Hervé A. Cavalletta, 3d ed., 55 vols. (Firenze: Casa editrice Le Lettere, 1992), vol. 21, 383–384; references to *Studi vichiani* are given in the body of the text as "(SV 383–384)," for example.

that Hegel will later painfully try to think [*si sforzerà di pensarlo*]" one century after Vico![33] The absolute reality is thought: all the rest — what positivists call "the world" or "facts" — is whatever thought has created.

The interest of Gentile in Croce's reevaluation of Vico's aesthetic, however, goes beyond Vico's aesthetic itself. Gentile, in fact, does not seem so much concerned with Croce's chronology — Vico comes earlier than Baumgarten — but with a radical relocation of the place of *origin* from Germany (Baumgarten's or Hegel's) to Neaples and the Italian "southern provinces." When Croce's article on Vico appeared in 1901, for instance, Gentile's enthusiasm took shape in the following words written for a review for the *Rassegna critica di letteratura italiana*:

> Croce's pamphlet *G. B. Vico scopritore della scienza estetica* can be called the discovery of a discovery; because no one, before Croce, had the idea to look, in this philosopher of ours . . . for the first principles of an aesthetic theory . . .
>
> . . . our Vico . . . truly disposed of the concept of verisimilitude, and understood fantasy in a radically new way. . . .
>
> The Neapolitan philosopher understands fantasy as a degree of the spirit. The first degree, as Croce remarks . . .[34]

If it is true that antonomasia replaces objects with attributes, we should notice that "the Neapolitan philosopher" and "Giambattista Vico" are not necessarily the same thing here. The attribute — the being Neapolitan — has simply taken over. How else are we to understand Gentile's insistence on *our* Vico, if not as the persistence of the "us and them" syndrome? It is, in a sense, the rebellion of "our" south to the evolutionism of German theory, which, as Croce had already remarked, always insisted — from Schiller to Hegel — on the idea of a *progress* from the "naive" Greek-Roman south to the "modern" northern "sentiment" of nature. Northern aesthetic, Croce concluded, was "weak": incapable of penetrating the true nature of poetry, it split the latter into two genres.[35]

33. Giovanni Gentile, "G. B. Vico nel ciclo delle celebrazioni campane," in *Opere*, ed. Cavalletta, vol. 21, 134. See also Benedetto Croce, *La filosofia di Giambattista Vico* (1911; reprint, Bari: Laterza, 1962), esp. 258–259, where Vico becomes the precursor of Marx and Sorel as well.

34. Giovanni Gentile, "I primi studi sull'estetica del Vico," in *Opere*, ed. Cavalletta, vol. 47, 60, 67.

35. Croce, *Estetica*, 607–608.

Gentile's enthusiasm for Croce's reevaluation of Vico cools down a little on this point, because this splitting and multiplication, which Croce was just trying to dismiss as a "weakness," was in fact at the very basis of Gentile's dialectics. Taking his cue from Vico, Croce had maintained that, although poetry had been the first "intuition" of truth, it needed now to make room for the superior "understanding" of truth, which is philosophy. In this sense, art was, for Croce as for Hegel before, "dead." But by imagining an *Aufhebung* [*superamento*] of art by philosophy, Croce — this was Gentile's accusation — had dismissed, with his half-dialectics, the negative term (art) in favor of the final synthesis (philosophy).[36] Croce, for Gentile, was not a dialectician but a mortician. An ideal "art," a creative moment, is for Gentile *always* necessary: the human world, social "reality," needs always to be renewed into novel forms. An ideal value of existence needs, at all times, to be postulated. That is why "art" can never die: it is our only way of inventing new meaning for life, beyond and above "facts." After liquidating Croce's idea of art as "a deficient concept," Gentile remarked:

> Art lives by dying, which means, by integrating itself with the other moments of the life of the spirit. . . . The death of art is not a factual and empirical death: rather, it is an ideal death, and therefore eternal life. Art is present and unavoidable in the fullness of the life of the spirit, in which the power of the subject, or of the sentiment if you prefer, is expressed via the mediation of thought.[37]

Art lives by dying — by becoming, that is to say, other than itself: art *becomes* thought, a philosophy that can institute a "world." The "immediate" truth of art therefore coexists, in the characteristic multiplicity of Gentile's dialectics, with the mediated truth of philosophy: there is no philosophy without art, no idea without sentiment, no thought without "aesthetic" creation, no reason without a poetic origin — no north without a south.

In the end, what Gentile takes from Croce is not an aesthetic theory, which he sees as distorted by a false dialectic of *superamento*, but only the

36. Dino Formaggio, "La 'morte dell'arte' e la filosofia dell'arte — G. Gentile," in *L'idea di artisticità. Dalla "morte dell'arte" al "ricominciamento" dell'estetica filosofica* (Milano: Ceschina, 1962), 105–106.

37. Giovanni Gentile, "Arte," in *Opere filosofiche*, ed. Garin, 882, 885.

southern origin of aesthetic with Vico. A rhetoric of latitudes, which we have seen developing from Montesquieu, is still at work behind Gentile's philosophy. It is from *southern* Vico, not from northern Hegel, that the "concept of absolute spirit or idea" begins. The south still appeals as an origin. And it is in the return to this origin that Gentile sees the possibility to "reform" an already decayed Hegelian dialectic, and revive idealism again in the age of positivism.

La riforma della dialettica hegeliana is the title Gentile gave to a collection of essays he had written written between 1898 and 1915. The necessity of such "reform" was felt by Gentile not only because he was convinced that "Hegel had not really discovered the true principle of immanence,"[38] and had ended up proposing a "world" on the one hand and a transcendent "thought" that thinks the world on the other, but fundamentally separated from it. Moreover, this felt necessity was the fruit of Gentile's discomfort with left-wing Hegelianism, and with Marxism in particular. Had not Marxism suggested that thought is the product of material circumstances? Had not Marx himself, after all, been part of the materialistic decadence of the west that proposed that matter is all? And how, then, could a Marxist praxis ever change the material circumstances from which it allegedly depended? Was not the proletarian revolution something produced instead by the "moral" idea of Marxism?[39]

Ideas — and Marxism is the paradoxical proof of it — move history and create material circumstances — not the other way around. That is why Hegelian dialectic, revolutionized by Marx, needs now to be reformed and brought back to its true origin — which is not Hegel but Vico himself. An idealism properly understood — *Vico's* idealism — is the only philosophy that can "overcome [*supera*] a reality to create another."[40] And this new reality is, first of all, an ethical ideal: a "resurrection of the ideal."

The south, in other words, presents itself once again as a topos of ethical exemplarity: it is an ethical origin, an ideal that can renew a world corrupted by materialism and positivism alike. The north, forgetful of the poetic creation of reality on the part of the absolute spirit, less naive and

38. Gentile's letter to Croce of February 20, 1913, quoted by Eugenio Garin, introduction to *Opere filosofiche*, ed. Garin, 241.

39. This is an admittedly sweeping summary of Gentile's works on *La filosofia di Marx*, in *Opere filosofiche*, ed. Garin, 85–233.

40. Gentile, *La riforma della dialettica hegeliana*, 257.

too modern, itself an emblem of modernity, has imprisoned itself in the study of a reality mistaken as something independent from poetic creation. Whereas an original, southern idealism creates reality anew, the north explains facts, collects details, and amasses data. Pragmatic reason — technique — is the final outcome of this false idealism of the north. Its philosophers

> no longer create novel ideas; they repeat, and comment, and defend, and attack. They act on behalf of society, not of knowledge. . . . But there is no trace of the artistic life, the philosophical life of the spirit, in which every instant is a new position and a new creation — in which, in other words, the spirit truly lives. (SV 4)

Gentile's "resurrection of the ideal," coinciding with the longed for "renaissance [*rinascita*] of idealism," needs therefore to begin from the south once again — from the place where all began. It has to start, today as yesterday, from "*this* university [of Naples]," where Vico was taught — "*here*" — by a professor such as Neapolitan Bertrando Spaventa.[41] Professor Jaja, Gentile reminds us, was right: a "regenerative" philosophy cannot be conceived if not "in our southern provinces" — *nelle nostre meridionali province!*[42] And it is in this southern principle that Gentile — southern Gentile — starts seeing not only a way to "reform" dialectics but a way, indeed, to overcome the epochal "crisis of modernity" — the *Untergang des Abendlandes*, the twilight of a West bent under the burden of technique, and with no ideal in sight.[43]

The new liberal democracies of the West, enmeshed in all sort of scandals and corruptions, find themselves in an unprecedented crisis. Europe, divided by the scars of World War I, seems already heading toward an imminent disaster. While international tensions worsen, even national unities are shattered by a resurgence of class tensions. One feels everywhere "a trivial utilitarian spirit" that debases the fiber of modern societies.[44] Lib-

41. Gentile, *La riforma della dialettica hegeliana*, 247; emphases are mine.
42. Gentile's letter to Jaja, *Carteggio*, ed. Sandirocco, book I, 6.
43. On the reception of *The Decline of the West* — and of Spengler in general — in fascist Italy, see Rita Calabrese-Conte, "Recezione di Spengler in Italia," in *Il tramonto dell'Occidente. Lineamenti di una morfologia della Storia mondiale*, ed. Calabrese-Conte, Margherita Cottone, and Furio Jesi (Parma: Guanda, 1995).
44. Giovanni Gentile, *La riforma della scuola in Italia*, in *Opere*, ed. Cavalletta, vol. 41, 157.

eral democracy, as Gentile remarks, "has generated the egoism of a class."[45] Gentile's felt necessity is that of a resurrection of the ideal from the ashes of matter, a *risorgere* that crystallizes, during the years 1915 to 1919, around the essays that form *I profeti del Risorgimento italiano*.

The only attempt to answer the crisis of the West, as Gentile sees it, has been, so far, that of Marxism. As the actual order of liberal democracies — corrupted, decayed, and *trasformiste* — cannot be maintained, Marxism has proposed a renewal of society through the proletarian revolution. Yet, this revolutionary break with the existing order can hardly be a final solution for Gentile: "the liberation of a people is not simply a work of destruction; on the contrary, it is, mainly, a work of edification [*edificazione*]" (PRI 75). Marx's destructive logic — the antithesis of an ideal "creation" — is, for Gentile, the last episode of an age begun with the French Revolution, and which has now reached its twilight: "Now, that age is over. . . . Today we should aim at a higher goal. . . . Politics is no longer enough" (PRI 141).

"Ideas precede facts and make them" (PRI 41). But Marxism claims to be the mere product of circumstances. The limit of Marxism is the limit of politics itself. "Politics affirms men as they are: it defines their tendency, and attunes their action" (PRI 35). Marxism, like politics, is a technique, an administration of the real. It is not a creative moment but the last exhalation of an idea born with the French Revolution. What is needed now to *transform* tendencies is the ability to create a new idea for a new society — a new idealism, in short.[46] Ideals should be restored for humankind: "'restoration' is the key word today."[47] But who, or what, can teach us the way? The answer is simple: Italy can. If, in the *Riforma della dialettica hegeliana*, Italy was singled out as the only place where idealism could be reborn, in *I profeti del Risorgimento*, Italy appears, quite literally, as the very locus of a Risorgimento — a new ideal sunrise after the twilight of the Age of Politics.

Here, Gentile insists that the Risorgimento is not a historical fact, but rather an idea, a "prophecy" that, as stated in the introduction, "has not been totally accomplished on September 20, 1870, with Vittorio Eman-

45. Giovanni Gentile, *I profeti del Risorgimento italiano*, 3d ed. (1923; reprint, Firenze: Sansoni, 1944), 31. References to *I profeti del Risorgimento italiano* are given in the body of the text as "(PRI 31)," for example.

46. See Augusto Del Noce, *Il suicidio della rivoluzione* (Milano: Rusconi, 1978).

47. Gentile, *La riforma della scuola*, 71.

uele." As an "idea," the Risorgimento is a new creative beginning, a sunrise after the twilight brought by the aging of the "ideals of the French Revolution" — an aging that has brought, in turn, to "the absolute end of history." These last words are Hegel's, who in his *Lectures on the Philosophy of World History* had also remarked that "world history travels from east to west" and that "[northern] Europe is the absolute end of history."[48] For Gentile, it is the whole of Hegel's geography that must be reformed now: if northern Europe is the *Untergang*, the twilight of the west, than southern European Italy will be, with its Risorgimento, a new sunrise and a new beginning of history. "Italians, having begun a new history [with the Risorgimento], begin a new history not only for themselves, but for the whole world."[49] This new history is nothing less than the overcoming of politics in the ultimate synthesis — as Gentile quotes from his prophets — of

> "stability and motion, conservation and progress, unity and variety, authority and liberality, centralism and diffusion, property and community, capital and labor, proletariat and bourgeoisie, city and family, town and country, nationalism and cosmopolitanism, concentric and eccentric action, private law and public law, and so on." All the principles, in other words, which clash in the political struggle. (PRI 102)

As the proletariat in tatters used to crowd the streets of revolutionary Europe, the new Europe of the prophesied southern sunrise will be peopled by a new, sublime humankind: "not the debased people of the present, but a different sort of people, the sublime one of the future [*quello sublime dell'avvenire*]; the people that will be, but that is not a reality" (PRI 51). It will be an ideal people, indeed, that fascist idealism, after the prophecy of the Risorgimento, will in fact create. "A new era has begun" (PRI 171): it is an Italian era, and a southern one.

In this displacement of philosophy and history from a decadent north to a rising south, much more than a shift from the French Age of Revolution to a new "moral and civil primacy of Italy" (PRI 86) is at stake. The movement south, for Gentile, reformer of Hegel, is not simply a "return"

---

48. Georg Wilhelm Friedrich Hegel, *Lectures on the Philosophy of World History: Introduction: Reason in History*, trans. H. B. Nisbet (London: Cambridge University Press, 1975), 197.

49. Gentile, *La riforma della scuola*, 73.

to idealism, sensibility, and passion in the age of cold technique and pragmatic reason. It is also a movement away from that "maturity" of world history that Hegel saw embodied in the ultimate synthesis — the *stasis* — of the state made absolute. A movement south, in other words, is the undoing of the state, and a return, in Hegel's words, to a "liquid," regionalistic south. Parted at its center by the sea, Hegel had seen this south as something that "does not have a clearly defined nucleus of its own, but is oriented outwards, looking towards the Mediterranean." Without a center, Hegel's south was not a unity: its "costal territory . . . encourages individual autonomy."[50] Gentile's problem with Hegel's state is that the latter is — yes! — an ideal unity but one without any content, still torn by class egoism and strife. This state — this idea — needs now to realize itself into something concrete, into a reality. And this ideal unity, to become real, has to become something other than itself: it has, in other words, to realize itself as difference — a difference that can exist only as coexistence of the regional "individual autonomies" of the south.

That is why the ideal unity of the Italian nation — a southern nation, indeed — will be realized by Gentile, Minister of Education, as a pervasive form of regionalism. The new, idealist school imagined by Gentile for the instruction of Italy has to "renew, reinforce, and promote the beautiful local traditions [*le belle tradizioni locali*] . . . in order to free Italians from foreign teachings."[51] As Gentile laments (in the *Studi vichiani*, for instance) the corruption of Italy by "all dominant ideas coming from beyond the Alps" (SV 104–105), his goal becomes that of recuperating "the good local tradition [*la buona tradizione paesana*]," and of replacing a "generic Italianness [*generica italianità*]" with an original, "particular Italianness [*italianità particolare*]" (SV 194). It is a form of Italianness

> implanted, so to speak, in the language and folklore of the land to which
> it belongs, in the region [*regione*] in which language and folklore have
> the first appearance of a determinate configuration; [it has to spring]
> from the regional dialect and culture. . . .[52]

As French Revolutionary theories, disguised in new Marxist attire or in the materialistic method of positivism, have penetrated the Italian acade-

50. Hegel, *Lectures on the Philosophy of World History*, 195–196.
51. Gentile, *La riforma della scuola*, 77.
52. Gentile, *La riforma della scuola*, 345.

mies, the possibility of a Risorgimento coincides, then, with the quest for the "sources" of *italianità*, for a "particular" italianness "isolated [*isolata*] and opposed to a general Italian spirit [*generale spirito italiano*]" (TCS 28).

Can it be mere chance that Gentile, while working on the idea of a redeeming Italian Risorgimento, also starts to write that "curious regionalist book"[53] published with the intriguing title of *Il tramonto della cultura siciliana* — "The twilight of Sicilian regionalism"? Or is not Sicily — regional and isolated Sicily — the very emblem, for Gentile, of an "Italy which did not suffer at a social level the impact of the French Revolution" (TCS 17)? Is not this Sicily a model for the "origin" (TCS 99) of an otherwise lost *italianità*, a "primal island [*isola iniziatrice*]"[54] closer to the source? The most southern of the southern provinces, further from a north where "stronger [is] the influence of French thought" (TCS 29), Sicily is not *an* island, but *the* Island, "*l'Isola*" as Gentile calls it with a capital "I." It is, quite allegorically, a geographical "Island always sequestered [by] the sea . . . from the rest of the world" (TCS 5), and a symbolic one: "it is not merely the geographical configuration . . . which sequesters the Island from the remaining Italy" (TCS 13), but an allegorical destiny makes it into a "particular nation [*nazione particolare*]" (TCS 4–5) that will serve as an example to the entire nation.

In the quintessence of "regenerative" southern philosophy that is Sicily, Gentile then tries to find the idea from which the fact of a European Risorgimento can begin. And in the rhetorical tradition of conservative *meridionalismo*, he finds the tropes for a southern sunrise venomous and hostile to all trans-Alpine influences — to *liberté égalité fraternité*, to northern industrialism, to machines, to plebeian revolutions, and to *communes*.

The history of *meridionalismo* begins no later than with the unification of Italy in the 1860s — when, from Piedmont, the south, appearing "so different from Torino" (Scialoja), started looking already like a problem: *la questione meridionale*, as it came to be known. Urged by his minister Count Cavour, and preoccupied that the southern provinces liberated by Garibaldi might become a "nest of red republicans and socialist dema-

53. Augusto Del Noce, *Giovanni Gentile. Per una interpretazione filosofica della storia contemporanea* (Bologna: Il Mulino, 1996), 13.
54. Giovanni Gentile, "Il fascismo e la Sicilia," in *Opere*, ed. Cavalletta, vol. 45, 58.

gogues,"[55] Vittorio Emanuele II, King of Piedmont, quickly took the southern provinces away from Garibaldi's control and unified them to his Piedmontese kingdom. However, as apple and oranges never add up nicely together, the product of the unification was, as the Sardinian Guido Dorso once put it, "a Piedmontese State bigger in terms of territory, but . . . as confining"[56] for the south as the occupying Burbon state had been.

Pupil of Francesco De Sanctis, illustrious historian in his lifetime, fervent patriot, deputy and minister of the new state, Pasquale Villari became the inspirator of a vast *meridionalista* movement with the publication of his *Lettere meridionali*, which begun in 1861 in the journal *Perseveranza*. Villari's observation of the singular poverty of the southern masses led him to believe that an "enlightened despotism," rather than the parliamentary system of Cavour, could ease the south's condition. A parliament, for Villari, could only worsen the endemic corruption of the south and remained the main cause of southern underdevelopment. With Villari begins a quite masochistic southern tradition that dreams of endless punishments and strong rule for the south.[57] But it is only with the news of the Parisian experience of the *commune*, in 1870, that the observation of southern poverty starts nourishing, in Villari's followers, an authentic fear for what indigent masses can do, and a parallel invocation for authoritarian government and "special measures" to repress the delinquency — actual and potential — of the south.

As the (northern) criminal anthropology of Lombroso — indebted to Montesquieu's climatic theories — proposed a racial propensity of southerners for crime,[58] *meridionalismo*, accepting southern criminality as a fact, blamed it on the "social conditions of this [southern] race."[59] Such so-

55. Cavour's letter to Nigra, quoted in Massimo L. Salvadori, *Il mito del buongoverno. La questione meridionale da Cavour a Gramsci* (1960; reprint, Torino: Einaudi, 1976), 24.

56. Guido Dorso, *La rivoluzione meridionale. Il mezzogiorno d'Italia da Cavour a Mussolini* (1925; reprint, Milano: Il Saggiatore, 1969), 68.

57. Salvadori, *Il mito del buongoverno*, 35–42.

58. Cesare Lombroso, *In Calabria (1862–1897)*, ed. Paolo Crupi (1898; reprint, Reggio Calabria: Casa del libro, 1973); Salvadori, *Il mito del buongoverno*, 184–205.

59. Napoleone Colajanni, "Razze a confronto," in *La questione meridionale. Scritti e testi*, ed. Pietro Borzomati (1897; reprint, Torino: Società editrice internazionale, 1996), 110.

cial conditions were determined, primarily, by the import of northern models — parliamentary democracy, industrialization, urbanism — into an essentially different south.[60] The topic of a *meridione* in need of an iron fist and the reestablishment of authoritarian law and order, along with the parallel blame of the perverting democratic principles of the French Revolution, are elaborated within this context by a conservative *meridionalista* such as Giuseppe Turiello. Turiello's *Il secolo XIX* explicitly advocates the necessity of what he calls a "virile" state to save the south from corruption. The same commonplace of a strong state as corrective of a fundamental corruption was the common denominator of the *meridionalismo* of Sydney Sonnino and Leopoldo Franchetti's *Sicilia nel 1876*, and of Giustino Fortunato's *Il Mezzogiorno e lo stato italiano* (1911) — but also of the liberal Benedetto Croce, who concluded that a reformation of the *meridione* could not be a achieved with the gentle methods that usually suffice "in fairy tales."[61]

Even if distant from Lombroso's "science"[62] and from Turiello's portrait of a delinquent south, Gentile's thought is, at heart, framed in the rhetorical tradition of the *discorso meridionalista*. His friendship with Giustino Fortunato, like anything else concerning Gentile's "regionalism," is hardly acknowledged by his critics.[63] Yet, in a speech occasioned by the political elections of 1924, speaking in Palermo, Gentile exalted the virtues of the "strong State" to be realized by Mussolini's Fasci in the very rhetorical tradition of *meridionalismo*: virile Fascism only can correct the damages caused, in the south, by northern liberalism, under which the corruption of "*la raccomandazione*" prospers and thrives.[64] Specifically, *meridionliste* are also Gentile's allusions to the deleterious effects of the "rigid political and administrative unification" (TCS 21) imposed on the south by Cavour's north, and the dating of the "dissolution of [Sicilian] regional culture," in *Il tramonto della cultura siciliana*, "just after 1860" (TCS 28–29). But absolutely proper to the *meridionalismo conservatore* is, most

60. Salvadori, *Il mito del buongoverno*.

61. See Salvadori, *Il mito del buongoverno*, 146.

62. See, for instance, TCS 11.

63. On Gentile's friendship with Fortunato see, for instance, Gentile's letters to Jaja, *Carteggio*, ed. Sandirocco, book 1, 118, and book 2, 354. A rather deluding treatment of Gentile in relation with *meridionalismo* (or, at least, Sicilian culture) can be found in Antonino Infranca, *Giovanni Gentile e la cultura siciliana* (Roma: Gangemi, 1990).

64. Gentile, "Il fascismo e la Sicilia," 49.

of all, Gentile's belief, in spite of the present corruption, in an ideal nature of the south.

The south, depicted by the *meridionalista* discourse as a den of crime, a demonic place "full of hardships and risks" (TCS 7), a locus of utter corruption, preserves in the same discourse and time an ideal quality. It is probably the very idea of corruption that needs to posit, as a logical necessity, the hypothesis of an original, uncorrupted, and ideal south — as if corruption were the product of northern political, economic, and cultural influence but also something extraneous, at heart, to the nature and essence of the poor but happy south of the origin. From this fertile soil, as Gentile notices in the *Tramonto*, is born the *meridionalista* epic of an original place adulterated by a "trans-Alpine contagion [*il contagio oltramontano*]" (TCS 62). Gentile does not withhold irony and scorn against a certain naive chauvinism that depicts the north as a space of contagion for the entire "Italian character," perverted by "the ice of the North [*geli del Norte*]" (TCS 57). He does not refrain from some little criticism, either, for the southern dream of the Island — to the desire, that is, to be "close on itself" (TCS 16). In fact, what the naive *sicilianista* sees as northern corruption Gentile even evokes, at times, as a "beneficial wind" that "purifies a close environment, in which the air stagnates and putrefies" (TCS 28). Dialectic, after all, is a confrontation with the other!

Yet, despite this scorn for the excesses of *meriodionalismo*, "the soul of Sicilian culture" remains for Gentile the example of a "negative attitude [*atteggiamento negativo*]" to contrast the import of northern models. Sicily is exemplary because its negative attitude is typical "not only [of] Sicily, but [of] every Italian province" (TCS 49). It is an ideal, "particular" *italianità*. Its "negative attitude" is the "antithesis [*l'antitesi*] to what one can consider as the dominant character of the general Italian culture [*generale cultura italiana*]" (TCS 29). "Ideal," "antithesis," "negative attitude" — in the terminology that Gentile applies to his "particular" and southern Sicily, the jargon of dialectic idealism renders explicit the ideal of a Sicily that is not. Sicily is in fact a pure negation, an antithesis in the triadic movement Gentile learned from Hegel's dialectics. Gentile's idealism, against materialism and positivism, does not consider "the fact for the fact's sake, the document for the document's sake" (TCS 111), and Sicily for Sicily's sake: it instead considers Sicily only for what it is — an ideal, a negation of what exists, a principle and a prophecy of regeneration.

By relocating the topos of an original and regenerative purity from central Rome to provincial Sicily, Gentile thus subverts a classic Italian tradition that, beginning with Dante's *De Vulgari eloquentia*, had placed cultural purity in the center — *mediastinis civibus* — of the city, and saw in the periphery the results of a decadence — *rusticitas* — increasing progressively with distance from that center.[65] At the moment in which the city — *mediastinis civibus*, center of civilization — is contaminated by foreign and trans-Alpine fashions, Gentile feels the necessity of relocating a topos of purity and perfection from the center to the periphery of Sicily. Nor was Gentile alone in this effort of relocation, to which the Italian culture of the time, on the contrary, zealously participated. Giovanni Papini wrote, for instance, in *Fiera letteraria* of January 15, 1928, some sort of manifesto of Italian provincialism that curiously shares many of Gentile's anxieties. After the observation that "the city does not create — it destroys," and that "all cities are sterile — there are statistically very few newborns, almost never genial," he explains what is to be understood as an Italian "provincialism":

> first, a firm opposition to all forms of civilization extraneous to ours, or that would damage, being undigestible, the classic qualities of the Italians. Besides: a defense of the universal meaning of the village [*senso universale del paese*], which is, to spell it clearly, the natural and immanent relationship between the individual and his land. Finally, exaltation of our own characteristics [*caratteristiche nostrane*] in every field and activity of life: that is, Catholic foundations, a religious sense of the world, fundamental simplicity and sobriety, adherence to reality, control of fantasy, and a balance between spirit and matter.

By virtue of a providential linguistic ambiguity, the *paese* (understood as the countryside, the province, the region, the peripheral village) becomes the particular commonplace — the land — in which, as Papini comments, "the universal sense of the *paese*" (understood as the country, the nation) is sheltered. The immortal principles of Italian identity have taken refuge in the province, safe within all-too-Italic pigsties and among the poultry.

65. Dante Alighieri, *De Vulgari Eloquentia* (Milano: Mondadori, 1982), book 1, chapter 17, 3; and book 1, chapter 11, 6. Quintilian also had identified *urbanitas* with "learned diction" (*conversatione doctorum tacitam eruditionem*), and *rusticitas* with peripheral ignorance. See Quintilian, *Institutio oratoria*, trans. H. E. Butler (Cambridge: Harvard University Press, 1920–1922), book 6, chapter 3, 17.

In the same year in which Gentile had pronounced his discourse on "Il Fascismo e la Sicilia," and while the socialist deputy Matteotti was kidnapped and killed by the black shirts of Mussolini, Mino Maccari, in a black shirt himself, presented his new journal — *Il selvaggio* — as the voice of a wholesome Italian provincialism that he called *strapaese*: "[*Il selvaggio*] has been tailored [*fatto apposta*] to defend, up and at them!, the rural and provincial [*paesano*] character of the Italian people." It was 1924, and as the Italian city was seen by some as "the instrument of communist economic power and the proletarian dictatorship," and by others as "the ideal principle" of capitalism,[66] the province was taking instead the consistency of a Fascist *terza via*, different from both bolshevism and capitalism, and closer to the ideal of a pure, particular, and original *italianità paesana*.

This *paese* was, *compensatio* to the communist and capitalist ideal of the city, an all-Italian ideal province — a *strapaese* in Maccari's neologism, a "hyper-country" whose essence the same Maccari outlines, with his penchant for coinage of words, in *La Stampa* of May 4, 1929:

> This *strapaese* is opposed to the import of modernities . . . [it] tries to avoid damaging contacts . . . [and] the corruption of the integrity of the nature and features of the Italian civilization, as it was quintessenced [*quintessenziata*] in the centuries.

As the *paese* is the quintessence of *italianità*, and identity subsists in the particular, the province, metonymic of Gentile's south, becomes the ideal place not for a discourse of decentralization and the recuperation of the marginal but for a metaphysic of immanence. As this province is the center of a true, uncontaminated *italianità*, there is nothing different from it, and outside of it, but only a no-center — a pure negation, that is — of the absolute metaphysical immanence of provincial Italy: this negation is, in Maccari's provincialism as in the theology from which it derives, nothing less than diabolic corruption.

The project, in other words, was to turn the idea of the *strapaese* — *paese, meridione*, south, province, or region — into a synonym of "truly, unadulterated Italian," or "particular" Italian, in Gentile's words. In this

66. Respectively, Antonio Gramsci, "The Historical Role of the Cities," in *Selections from Political Writings*, ed. and trans. Quintin Hoare, vol. 1 (1978; reprint, Minneapolis: University of Minnesota Press, 1990), 150; and Carlo Cattaneo, "La città considerata come principio ideale delle istorie italiane," in *Storia universale e ideologia delle genti. Scritti 1852–1864*, ed. Delia Castelnuovo-Frigessi (Torino: Einaudi, 1972), 79–126.

way, the *paese* could inspire a delirium of nationalist pride, in which practically every region could claim to be the most Italian. In the south, Hegel's nuclear center is always shifting and always immanent — nowhere but, for the same reason, everywhere.

Giovanni Gentile, like his contemporaries,[67] believed in both the possibility and the necessity of synthesizing the "tender affection of the mother island" with the "more vast horizon of the Italian nation" (TCS 26–27), the "big country [*la patria grande*]" with "the small one [*quella piccola*]."[68] Without an anchor in the love of the particular land, a love for the nation remained for him a plain abstraction. The region is the "rightful originating motive [*motivo originario*]," the "deep root" from which the sense of "nationality" may grow (TCS 85). On this principle he had built, as Minister of Education, the whole linguistic policy of fascism: accepting the thesis put forward by Sicilian linguist and pedagogue Lombardo-Radice, Gentile had proposed that the teaching of Italian language and culture in the first years of elementary school be based on "translations" from dialect into Italian.[69] Regionalism, after all, was for him a microcosm containing in itself "the problems of the other regions . . . the history of the nation, or, better, of the world" (TCS 108). This was an ideal "particular" Italy whose example was "to be incorporated and fused into the national unity" (TCS 103), just as his Sicily could have become the "instrument and center of a new, superior, and universal culture" (TCS 81).

Yet, this example and this south, as the title of *Il tramonto della cultura siciliana* implies, is now at its twilight: a Sicilian culture is at its sunset. The 1917 preface of the *Tramonto* opens with an unmistakably elegiac tone: it mourns the death, between March 19 and April 10, 1916, of "the triad of the

---

67. Benedetto Croce, for instance, saw a regional "literature in dialect not [as] a fight against the national spirit, but, on the contrary, [as] a participation in the formation and consolidation of the national spirit." In Benedetto Croce, "La letteratura dialettale riflessa, la sua origine nel seicento e il suo ufficio storico," in *Uomini e cose della vecchia Italia*, 3d ed. (1926; Bari: Laterza, 1956), 225. Also Luigi Sturzo, the founder of the antifascist Partito Popolare and a strong believer in the virtues of decentralization, maintained that "a regional life is local life in the spirit of unification," and that the goal of regionalism was not to fragment national unity but "to insert . . . the region into the nation." In Sturzo, *La regione nella nazione* (1949; reprint, Bologna: Zanichelli, 1974), 108.

68. Gentile, *La riforma della scuola*, 43.

69. Klein, *La politica linguistica del fascismo*, 82.

most illustrious and representative writers of Sicilian culture in the nineteenth century": Salvatore Salomone-Marino, Gioacchino Di Marzo, and, above all, the beloved and revered Giuseppe Pitrè. Especially the last had been, for Gentile, the emblematic figure of a Sicily that "yielded to local trends" but "always looked at the Italians beyond the Lighthouse [of Messina]. . . ."[70] With his death, elevated to symbol, nothing will remain of Sicilian culture on the face of the earth: Sicilian culture is "a closed chapter . . . in the modern history of Italy." From now on it "will be available only in the books of the dead."

What has caused this twilight, this *tramonto*, this *Untergang* of a particular, redeeming *italianità*? Augusto Del Noce, arguably the highest Italian authority on Gentile, has suggested that the causes of a Sicilian *tramonto* are in a way the same in Sicily as elsewhere: "materialism . . . naturalism, scientism, verismo . . ."[71] have corrupted all cultures. Yet, Gentile's own answer to the question is rather more explicit than that: "the rigid political and administrative unification" (TCS 21) of Italy begun with the Risorgimento — he claims with *meridionalista* zest — has initiated "the dissolution of [Sicilian] regional culture . . . just after 1860" (TCS 28–29). The very same idea of a destructive national unification, in fact, recurs in a speech of 1923, devoted to yet another twilight — that of the local culture of the Abruzzi:

> After 1860, Italian patriotism depressed and almost erased the regional sentiment [*il sentimento regionale*]; but in the present reawakening of the Italian soul the need is felt to awaken all the sleepy local energies, stimulating the particular capabilities [*capacità particolari*] of the different provinces, to give the national soul, in the end, a concrete content consisting of all the memories and glories of the various regions.[72]

It is as if, in Gentile's dialectic of region and nation, there can be no nationalism without the "concrete content" of a regionalist "particular" identity — but there can be no nationalistic "patriotism" and no Risorgimento, *de facto*, if not after the *tramonto* of regionalism's "particularity" itself. Because also regionalism, in Gentile's vision, has to be overcome [*superato*] in the vision of the "big country": "our entire life is a continuous

70. Giovanni Gentile, "Profilo di Giuseppe Pitrè," in *Opere*, ed. Cavalletta, vol. 30, 199–200.
71. Del Noce, *Giovanni Gentile*, 163.
72. Gentile, *La riforma della scuola*, 137.

death . . . our life is a continuous sacrifice, a continuous denying our particular being."[73] Neither nationalism nor regionalism, in fact, can exist if not through their continuous dying of one into the other. While regions supply their "concrete content" to the nation, they sit at the horizon of history; and while nationalism rises as a concrete entity, it instead dies into localism. Every *risorgimento* is a *tramonto*, every sunrise a sunset. There cannot be one without the other. The beginning is always the darkest moment. Life is a liminal moment, a twilight between two ideal absences.

How can one "orient" oneself in the darkness of this twilight?, Gentile asks, alluding to Kant's question, *Was heißt sich im Denken orientieren?*[74] In the eternal crepuscule, Gentile has promoted his own "reformed," southern, and "particular" idealism as the sole light capable of "orientating" the new youth of postnational Italy: "our youth, looking for an orientation [*per orientarsi*] turns to the philosophy of idealism" (TCS 176). The creation of an ideal nation "beyond the Lighthouse" (TCS 89) remains a project that has to begin from the concreteness of a regional culture. But, as of yet, neither one exists: the ideal nation is still to be created, and the region is already dead, awaiting for a new resurrection.

In the wait for an ideal Risorgimento, it is still darkness all around. In this obscurity, the lighthouse of Messina, built like Gentile's own philosophy on the very soil of regional Sicily, casts some light to orient fascist Italy in the path of nationalism. For a moment, as the light turns outward, it enlightens, beyond the sea, a beautiful nation. Yet, the vision of the nation lasts only one moment. The turning light, veering inward again, now illuminates the region. The continuous circling of the light reminds the reader — what in a nice Italian expression is called *fare mente locale*, "to make local mind"[75] — that regions and nations are, after all, projections of the same, rotating center. Both regions and nations are, in a sense, ideas, as Gentile would say, illuminated for a moment by the flickering light of the ideal. They are not facts, nor are they realities. They are simply inventions, poetic acts, metaphors.

73. Gentile, *La riforma della scuola*, 55–56.

74. Maria Teresa Catena, *Orientamento e disorientamento. Il sublime come luogo sistematico della filosofia di Kant* (Milano: Guerini Scientifica, 1996), 23–24.

75. Franco La Cecla, *Mente locale. Per un'ntropologia dell'abitare* (Milano: Elèuthera, 1996).

After Strange Gods

Conclusions on the Literature of Place and Region

> Because I know that time is always time
> And place is always and only place
> — T. S. Eliot, *Ash-Wednesday*

A famous chorus from the *Antigone* begins as a praise of man: many things on earth are wondrous but none more wondrous than man. He crosses the wild seas, captures the birds, overcomes the beast in every aspect; he has learned speech, too, and the art of building cities to escape the inhospitable hills; he never meets his destiny without resource:

> Skillful beyond hope is the contrivance of his art, and he advances sometimes to evil, at other times to good. When he applies the laws of the earth [χθονὸς] and the justice the gods have sworn to uphold he is high in the city [ὑψίπολις]; outcast from the city [ἄπολις] is he with whom the ignoble consorts for the sake of gain.[1]

1. Sophocles, *Antigone*, in *Antigone. The Women of Trachis. Philoctetes. Oedipus at Colonus*, vol. 2, ed. and trans. Hugh Lloyd-Jones (Cambridge, Mass.: Harvard University Press), 37.

Man is a wondrous creature indeed when inclined to what is sanctioned by the law; but when inclined to evil, he becomes an outcast, ἄπολις. This happens, as Hölderlin had observed while translating Sophocles before Heidegger, because the "natural" authority (*Naturgewalt*) to which man obeys is the law of *his* native land, νόμους ... χθονὸς. This law is Ethic in the sense of ἦθος, ethos, a local custom. The law is therefore obedience sworn (*Beschwornes*), in a sense, to the place of one's ancestors. For Heidegger, too, the law that institutes "good" and "evil" is the law of the *polis*: whoever breaks it will also destroy the very order and foundation of the city-state, and will remain not only an outlaw but also, literally, one without-city, ἄ-πολις, *un-städtisch*.[2]

Heidegger's suggestion that Sophocles' second chorus of *Antigone*, along with Hölderlin's interpretation of it, should be considered as the foundation of western metaphysics is, as George Steiner correctly notices, a "plausible" idea. It is "plausible" because a reading of it entails a discussion of nothing less than the relation of man, nature, and the law. With this sense of a high mission in mind, Heidegger begins discussing the chorus with a tribute to Hölderlin's "eccentric" translation, and with a deconstruction of the "traditional" readings of the *Antigone*. In what sense is man "wondrous"? "Many things are formidable, and none more formidable than man!" reads a traditional translation of verses 332 and 333 such as, for instance, the one provided by the Loeb Classics. But δεινότερον is, Heidegger observes, an ambiguous word in Greek. Δεινόν is "formidable" only because it connotes what is "terrible," what inspires fear, like the "gray sea beneath the winter wind." Many things are terrible in nature because nature is sheer power (*Gewalt*) and is violent (*gewalt-tätig*) in its indifference to living beings; against this overpowering (*Überwältigende*) violence of nature, man can be only "more formidable" — but in the sense of "more terrible."

Already Hölderlin had seen, in the δεινά of *Antigone*, an echo of Clitemnestra's horrible crime and of her gruesome punishment — both δεινὸς — in Aeschylus's *Choephori*. Accordingly, he had translated the Greek word as *Gewaltige* (brutal, violent) in the first draft, and as *Ungeheuer*

2. Friedrich Hölderlin, "Antigonae," in *Antigone di Sofocle nella traduzione di Friedrich Hölderlin* (Torino: Einaudi, 1996), 384–386; see also George Steiner, *Antigones* (Oxford: Clarendon Press, 1984).

(a monster) in the final version: there are many monsters on earth, and none is more monstrous than man. Quite an eccentric deviation, in fact, from the usual reading but not enough, yet, for Heidegger, because "monstrosity" is absolute extraneity and total difference, and with such translation Hölderlin misses altogether the *familiarity* of man with nature. Is not nature, after all, the familiar surrounding of man, his environment? And *yet*, this familiar surrounding is hostile and terrible to him. Against it, man has to be "more terrible" and build houses against the cold winter, sail on ships against the sea that separates him from fertile lands, and hunt the bird and the terrible beast against hunger and for his own survival. Nature, at once familiar and terrible, could be conceptualized in the times of Sophocles with a perfectly ambiguous Greek word: δεινά The problem of translation is the problem of the decadence of that primordial language — Greek — into Latin and the other romance languages. Yet, German conserves for Heidegger, in a very Romantic way, a sense of the "original." Closer to the primordial root, German, the only language that can still speak metaphysics, like Greek possesses a perfectly ambiguous word to think of nature and translate δεινά— *unheimlich*, uncanny: therefore, "Uncanny is the universe with all of its creatures, and nothing is more uncanny than man."

If nature *is* uncanny, in what sense is man "most uncanny"? Heidegger explains:

> We are taking the strange, the *unheimlich*, as that which casts us out of the "homely," i.e. the customary, familiar, secure. The unhomely [*Unheimische*] prevents us from making ourselves at home and therein is overpowering. But man is the strangest of all, not only because he passes his life amid the strange understood in this sense [i.e., as *unheimlich*] but because he departs from his customary, familiar limits, because he is the violent one, who, tending toward the strange in the sense of the overpowering, surpasses the limit of the familiar.[3]

The distance from Hölderlin (and Sophocles?) on this point may be unbridgeable: it is not *the* man who breaks the law of the city who becomes without a city, but *every* man is, in his essence and nature, without

3. Martin Heidegger, *An Introduction to Metaphysics*, trans. Ralph Manheim (New Haven, Conn.: Yale University Press, 1959), 150–151.

a place — *un-heim*. He has no choice but to be "unhomely," without a city and without a place.

Without a home, *unheimlich*, man needs also to "build" a place for himself, a "house" and a *polis*, with its law, for "grounding (*begründen*) [his] historical existence."[4] Homeless by nature, man is *unheimlich* — extraneous — to his own nature: he wills what is unnatural to him — having a place — and then becomes *unheimlich* twice. In this sense, too, man is the most *unheimlich*, *der unheimlicheste*, the most terrible. By creating his place he rises above his homeless nature, becomes ὑψίπολις in the place he has thus created; but exactly by doing this, he will lose his nature, his placelessness, his u-topic essence — he will become ἄπολις, without a city.

The key to Sophocles' *Antigone* is to be found, according to Heidegger, in verse 370, and especially in the two contiguous attributes that here define man, the creator of his place, as ὑψίπολις ἄπολις: "When he applies the laws of the earth . . . he is high in the city [ὑψίπολις]; outcast from the city [ἄπολις] is he" who does otherwise, as we usually read. But is it in man's nature to obey earth and the laws of nature? Or is it not his nature, exactly, to break those laws and build *his* city? The syntax of the whole translation needs to be amended here, and the absence of any punctuation should be restored in Heidegger's quite original translation: it is exactly by "raising above his place" and his environment, for Heidegger, that man "loses his place in the end." He is ἄπολις when he elevates himself ὑψίπολις, placeless when he is higher in his place. The law that Creon has instituted giving his Thebes the consistency of a human *polis* has elevated him among his peers, has made him into an "authentic" man, a creator — but has in the meantime estranged him from nature, whose law, the natural law of the burial, he has violated by replacing it with a human one:

> as violent men [who] use power . . . become pre-eminent . . . they become at the same time ἄπολις, without city and place, lonely, strange, and alien . . . at the same time without statute and limit, without structure and order, because they themselves *as* creators must first create all this.[5]

---

4. Martin Heidegger, *Nietzsche*, 4th ed., vol. 1, trans. David Farrell Krell (San Francisco: Harper San Francisco, 1991), 90; see also Martin Heidegger, "Building, Dwelling, Thinking," in *Poetry, Language, Thought*, ed. and trans. Albert Hofstadter (New York: Harper and Row, 1971).

5. Heidegger, *Introduction to Metaphysics*, 152–153; Heidegger's emphasis.

The institution of a community around a *polis* is, as Gentile had already warned us, an invention, a poetic act. This act estranges "man," Heidegger remarks, from a violent (*gewalt-tätig*) and uncanny (*unheimlich*) nature. By doing so, it makes man more violent (*Überwältigende*), and the most uncanny being of all — *der unheimlicheste*, indeed. But does he have any choice?

As a matter of fact, man *does* have a choice: modernity, with its gusto for cosmopolitanism, is one such choice. "Modern man," Heidegger observes looking at a bunch of stereotypical tourists staying at some American hotel in Mikonos, Greece, "feels at home anywhere":

> So much so, that who speaks of the loss of the place [*Heimatlosigkeit*, also loss of the Country, or of the original place, or of the home] would be accused of lying, and his words would be considered as an escape into vacuous romanticism. But what if this being-at-home [*Zuhause*] with no roots, made possible only by technique and information, would mean a renunciation to the search for a place [*Heimat*]? . . .⁶

It is not that placelessness is an impossibility for man. Simply, the possibility of placelessness, offered for instance by modernity, remains for Heidegger a debasement of what *ought* to be authentic and rooted — namely, the *unheimlich* will of man to found his *polis* — in some unspecific and indistinct technical standardization. Placelessness is not only possible: it is the real and actual threat of an Americanization of the Old Continent — the uprooting of culture, that is, from its own ground.

The defense of man's place — a place in which the "grounding" of his "historical existence" remains possible in its specificity — becomes then for Heidegger an ethical imperative. But what else can this imperative be if not an invitation to that most *unheimlich* violence (*Gewalt*) through which man establishes, time and again, his *polis* as identity of place (ethos) and community — what Heidegger calls *die höchste Gemeinschaft*?⁷ The controversial rectoral address of 1933 points exactly to the way in which the ethical necessity to "define" a "common rootedness" of the nation implies, on the part of an otherwise "homeless" Germany, the necessity to become "most uncanny" in order to establish its own place:

6. Martin Heidegger, *Aufenthalte* (Frankfurt: Klosterman, 1989), 43.
7. Heidegger, *Introduction to Metaphysics*, 199.

Out of the resoluteness of the German students to stand their ground while German destiny is in its most extreme distress comes a will to the essence of the university. This will is a true will, provided that German students . . . place themselves under the law of their essence and thereby first define [*bestimmen*] this essence. To give oneself the law is the highest freedom. The much-lauded 'academic freedom' will be expelled from the German university: for this freedom was not genuine because it was only negative.[8]

The assertion concerning the elimination of an "academic freedom" already imprisoned within quotation marks, so difficult for us to come to terms with, should not distract us from noticing what remains instead the most disturbing element of the rectoral address: its echo, namely, of the *unheimlich* violence of Creon's law.

Germany, in the moment of "its most extreme distress," needs lawgivers. The mission of its university is exactly to form "the leaders and guardians of the destiny of the German people."[9] These leaders will have, first, to give a law to themselves. This is their highest freedom. This is what will raise them ὑψίπολις: by defining their *unheimlich* nature first, they will define the very essence of the German national community (*Volkgemeinschaft*). But this definition is, first of all, a decision, *bestimmen*, a separation of these people "high in the city" from the "city" itself. It is the decision of "violent men [who] use power [to] become pre-eminent" and "become at the same time ἄπολις, without city and place, lonely . . . without statute and limit, without structure and order." Like Creon, indeed — or like Hitler, hailed as the first lawgiver of the nation in the infamous end of the rectoral address.

The *unheimlich* monstrosity of man is, after all, as Heidegger learned from that foundation of Western metaphysics that is the *Antigone*, his will to *decide* a community with its law of rootedness: *unheimlich* is a will of separation that, alone, is capable of instituting a *polis*. With *unheimlich* violence, the law of man eliminates what exceeds it. *Gewalt*, which ambiguously refers to law and force at the same time, gets rid of the "other" that does not belong to this decided community, it excludes the uprooted, the inauthentic — or, as in Sophocles' tragedy, it eliminates and buries away

8. Martin Heidegger, "The Self-Assertion of the German University," in *Martin Heidegger and National Socialism: Questions and Answers*, ed. Günter Neske and Emil Kettering (New York: Paragon House, 1990), 10.

9. Heidegger, "Self-Assertion," 6.

Antigone herself, the "figure of Woman" as the "concrete realization of the crime" perpetrated against the *polis* of Man.[10]

Nations *are* monstrous inventions, and, to judge from a number of recent publications, the spirit of the times has little doubts about that. It might be redundant to insist here on this point. We have heard much, in recent years, about the violence of nationalism, and the stress has fallen quite properly on the equation of invention with imposition. We speak, however, as if nationalism in itself, not an archaic and more pervasive dream of placeness founded indeed at the center of Western metaphysics, were the actual danger. We seem to forget that the nation, in the moment of its "most extreme distress," when the placelessness brought about by modernity starts throwing its weight around, has in turn produced that historical invention that we start now to call regionalism. "Situated in the center," writes Heidegger, "our nation incurs the severest pressure. It is the nation with the most neighbors and hence the most endangered."[11] At the very center of Europe, Heidegger's Germany suffers, as Franco Cassano has noted, the paranoia of all centers: that of being surrounded, penetrated, and deflowered by the foreigner.[12] This center of Western civilization "lies today in a great pincers, squeezed between Russia on one side and America on the other," between the placeless internationalism of bolshevism on the one hand and the technological one of capitalism on the other.[13] It is to escape the threat of these pincers, and to elude the force of this advancing, all-erasing technique, that a new search for place has begun, with Heidegger, from some "eccentric" energies that unfold, literally, "from out of the center."[14]

This eccentric search begins, then, from nowhere else but the isolated periphery, the province, the region "out of the center" — not because this region is "marginal" in respect to some hegemonic center but because, simply, it is, different from a surrounded center, a *Heimat* untouched by technique, and left out of the pincers of modernity. The essence of a Ger-

10. Alexandre Kojève, *Introduction à la lecture de Hegel: lecons sur la Phenomenologie de l'esprit professées de 1933 à 1939 à l'Ecole des hautes etudes*, ed. Raymond Queneau (1947; reprint, Paris: Gallimard, 1979), 105.

11. Heidegger, *Introduction to Metaphysics*, 38.

12. Franco Cassano, *Il pensiero meridiano* (Bari: Laterza, 1996), 37; see also Jacques Le Rider, *La Mitteleuropa* (Paris: Presses Universitaires de France, 1994).

13. Heidegger, *Introduction to Metaphysics*, 37.

14. Heidegger, *Introduction to Metaphysics*, 38–39.

man place, in other words, and the kernel of its national *Volksgemein-schaft*, is recovered by Heidegger from the blood-and-soil rootedness of a "province" in which Heidegger's thought, like the *Heimatlitteratur* from which it derives,[15] tries to invent its origin:

> philosophical work . . . belongs right in the midst of the peasants' work. . . . My work is of the same sort. It is intimately rooted in and re-lated to the life of the peasants. . . . The inner relationship of my own work to the Black Forest and its people comes from a centuries-long and irreplaceable rootedness in the Alemannian-Swabian soil.[16]

The sort of province thus depicted in an essay such as "Why Do We Live in the Province?" is, as Farias correctly notices, "the homeland in its most local sense"[17] — an uncorrupted origin of German-ness away from the "big-city and [its] decadent ways of thinking"[18] that Heidegger always tried to escape.

"We" live in the province because thought, like man, is driven by an *un-heimlich* will to be "intimately rooted" in the place, to feel organic to it: that is, in one word, what makes thought and man "authentic," against the inauthenticity of modern man and industrial technology. In his *Jargon der Eigentlichkeit*, Adorno can easily show how Heidegger's "authenticity," like his Lederhosen and his alleged life among the Swabian peasants, are "manufactured"[19] in some industrial way themselves — they package the

15. On the *Heimatlitteratur* and its search for an "original" German-ness, see Marino Freschi, *La letteratura del Terzo Reich* (Roma: Editori Riuniti, 1997), 69–140.

16. Martin Heidegger, "Why Do We Live in the Province?" in *Heidegger: The Man and the Thinker*, ed. Thomas Sheehan (Chicago: Precedent Publishing, 1981), 28.

17. Victor Farías, *Heidegger and Nazism*, trans. Joseph Margolis and Tom Rockmore (Philadelphia: Temple University Press, 1989), 4.

18. Max Müller, with Bernd Martin and Gottfried Schramm, "Martin Heidegger: A Philosopher and Politics: A Conversation," in *Martin Heidegger and National Social-ism: Questions and Answers*, ed. Günter Neske and Emil Kettering (New York: Paragon House, 1990), 178; see also Federico Chabod, *L'idea di nazione*, 3d ed. (1961; reprint, Bari: Laterza, 1979), 29–32.

19. Theodor W. Adorno, *Jargon der Eigentlichkeit: Zur deutschen Ideologie / The Jar-gon of Authenticity*, trans. Knut Tarnowski and Frederic Will (Evanston, Ill.: North-western University Press, 1973); see also Hans Jonas's recollection of Heidegger: "yes, a certain 'Blood-and-Soil' point of view was always there: He emphasized his Black For-est-ness a great deal; I mean his skiing and the ski cabin up in Todtnauberg. . . . He had thought up a kind of traditional costume that accentuated the landscape: knee breeches with long socks, a vest, I think it was an Alemannic one, a costume, which he

philosopher as the spokesperson of a Nazi cult of blood and soil. Lacou-Labarthe also clearly sees the idyllic "province" of Martin Heidegger as the "invention" of a place "which has never actually seen the light of day."[20] Is not this "invention" of a province or a region, however, the *unheimlich* gesture of Creon? And is not this gesture, like the gesture of nationalism, the "most violent," the most uncanny of all?

We are too ready to accept as a fact the *unheimlich* violence of nationalism, and of Hitler's national socialism in particular. With the innocence of literature virginally protected from the temptations of an evil nationalism, we have proceeded, confidently, to simply give literature a new place in the new, "changed ecology" of regionalisms. What remains sadly untouched is, nonetheless, the very metaphysical assumption of rootedness, purity, *Gemeinschaft*, and authenticity that transfer so easily from nation to region, and back again. Far from being an aberration of an otherwise respectable desire for place, Heidegger's provincial nationalism — like Gentile's own particular nationalism — is nothing less than the logical product of a metaphysics of place.

Behind the rhetorical lure of a *locus amoenus* sheltered in some hypothetical region, and behind the metaphoric discontent that we moderns feel for modernity, technique, and industrialization, a true loathing for what modernity and industrialization historically *stand for* should now be taken into consideration. Not machines, but that "population . . . imported from any sources whatever"[21] that characterizes modern industrial life is the recurrent, if sometimes implied, foe of regionalist aesthetics. The nostalgia for what is authentic, communal, and organic, is nothing else than a pendant to the hostility for what is extraneous and disturbing of a "natural" order — of an ethos. This hostility for the "foreign" is the fruit not of nationalism, or of the ultimate perversion of nationalism that is fascism, but of a resilient rhetoric of place.

While Heidegger was smoking his pipe amid his authentic Swabian

---

also wore during lectures, that was half thought up by him and half copied from the Black Forest peasants." In Hans Jacob, "Heidegger's Resoluteness and Resolve," in *Heidegger and National Socialism*, ed. Neske and Kettering, 200.

20. Lacoue-Labarthe, *Heidegger, Art and Politics*, 56–58.

21. John Crowe Ransom, "The Aesthetic of Regionalism," in *Selected Essays of John Crowe Ransom*, ed. Thomas Daniel Young and John Hindle (Baton Rouge: Louisiana State University Press, 1984), 55.

hills, in another continent, speaking from a podium at the University of Virginia, T. S. Eliot, whose abhorrence for Nazism was earnest and undisputed, was lovingly addressing the agrarian movement. The speech, published as *After Strange Gods* in 1934 but soon withdrawn from the bookstands by Eliot himself, begun with the following articulation of a logic of place:

> May I say that my first, and no doubt superficial impressions of your country — I speak as a New Englander — have strengthened my feeling of sympathy with those authors [the agrarians]: no one, surely, can cross the Potomac for the first time without being struck by differences so great that their extinction could only mean the death of both cultures. . . . I think that the chances for the re-establishment of a native culture are perhaps better here than in New England. You are farther away from New York; you have been less industrialised and less invaded by foreign races. . . .[22]

Virginia is more of a place than New England: as we know already, some places are regions, while others are not. Virginia is more of a region because the "difference" that regionalism wants to preserve from extinction, and reestablish at the same time, is a resistance against industrialization just as much as it is a resistance against its "foreign races" that have occupied New York and New England alike. Regionalism, in Eliot as in Heidegger, is the beautiful discourse of what we *ought* to be; it is a commonplace free from the multicultural aporia of modern times. This region is, as Eliot spells it clearly for a moment, a commonplace of homogeneity. In the region, accordingly,

> The population should be homogeneous . . . reasons of race and religion combine to make any large number of free-thinking Jews undesirable. . . . And a spirit of excessive tolerance is to be deprecated.[23]

22. Thomas Stearns Eliot, *After Strange Gods: A Primer of Modern Heresy* (London: Faber & Faber, 1934), 16–17.

23. Eliot, *After Strange Gods*, 20. In "defense" of Eliot, one could quote his Post-War "repentance" regarding the regionalist question. Revising the thesis of a totalitarian regionalism of "purity," Eliot, "Notes Toward a Definition of Culture," in *Christianity and Culture* (1948; reprint, San Diego: Harcourt Brace & Company, 1988), develops a more dialectic understanding of culture, as interrelation between the "ancestral ties" (p. 125) or "old roots" (p. 127) of the community (which he never renounced) and the confronting "enemy": "One needs an enemy" (p. 133) because "of the vital importance for society of *friction* between its parts" (p. 132).

Because nations could no longer mention their cultural unity with the ostentation that was proper to them in the Golden Age of their fantasies, regions — strange gods, indeed — have started to people their books with imaginary communities, happy and beautiful in their orthodox and pristine purity. The ideal of a multicultural society in which the desire for unity would be appeased, as in a Platonism perfectly realized, does not discard the wish for "purity," which every now and then reappears as the counter-ideal of local *Gemeinschaft*. The "region," the elusive essence of a Western desire "less firm than the historical or geographical . . . boundaries" (Mandel) is pitted against the entire universe. All regions do smilingly revolt. "Regionalism is a more appropriate frame within which to read literature than is nationalism," said New. The danger, apparent already in New's formulation, is that regionalism is merely taking the place and role that once was given to nationalism: they speak the same language, they foster the same desires, menacing and *unheimlich*, of purity and authenticity.

Index

Derrida, Jacques, 11, 29
dialect, 31–32, 121–123, 128, 153, 160
dialectics, 16–19, 25, 29, 32, 63, 77, 88,
    140–142, 148–150, 157, 161
Dorso, Guido, 155
Dupin, Charles, 34–35, 38, 40, 42

ecology, 4–5, 8, 27, 171
Eliot, Thomas Stearns, 16, 25, 172
environment, 15, 17, 19, 29, 35, 47, 63,
    66–67, 86, 87, 157, 165–166
ETA, 26. *See also* Basque Countries
ethnicity, 6, 20, 22

Fanon, Frantz, 16
Farias, Victor, 170
fascism, 32, 33, 141, 143, 152, 160, 162, 171
Foucault, Michel, 24, 27, 49
Frampton, Kenneth, 16
Frémont, A., 8
Freud, Sigmund, 18, 70, 109, 115–119

Gadda, Carlo Emilio, 23
Gaskell, Elizabeth, 29–32, 75–79, 84, 89,
    93–101
Gemeinschaft, 32, 94–96, 104, 167–168,
    171, 173
Gentile, Giovanni, 32, 136–162, 167, 171
geography, 1, 3, 4, 8, 12, 14, 28, 30, 35, 40,
    75, 111, 152, 154, 173
Gissing, George, 53
globalization, 4, 22, 24
Goethe, Johann Wolfgang, 115
Gramsci, Antonio, 26–27

Hardy, 12, 15, 30–31, 40–47, 51–54, 59–60,
    65–72, 83, 111
Harley, J. B., 40
Hartman, Geoffrey, 12
Hazlitt, William, 59, 98
Hegel, Georg Wilhelm Friedrich,
    147–149, 152–153, 157, 160
Heidegger, Martin, 2, 33, 145, 164, 165,
    166, 167, 168, 169, 170, 171, 172

historicism, 2–3, 8–20, 25–35, 46, 49,
    51, 52, 56, 70, 75, 78, 86, 87, 90, 94–96,
    101–102, 113, 136, 138–139, 140, 142–
    143, 151–154, 160–162, 166, 167, 169,
    173
Hölderlin, Friedrich, 164, 165
Horne, Donald, 82
Hoskins, W. G., 38
humanism, 4, 31, 56, 59, 80, 103

identity, 4–5, 7, 10, 12–13, 16, 19, 21–22,
    25, 28–31, 33, 47, 68, 141, 158–159, 161,
    167
idyll, 66, 74
immigration, 22–23, 52–53
industrialization, 17–19, 22, 28, 31, 38,
    51–52, 70, 77–79, 81, 83, 87, 92, 95, 97,
    101–102, 105, 156, 170–172
INTEREG, 21
inventio, 40–42, 146
isolation, 9, 16, 61, 70, 93, 154, 169

Jauss, Hans Robert, 77
Jordan, David, 9, 11, 29

Kant, Immanuel, 2, 162
King, Jeannette, 48

Lake District, 17, 22, 38
Lawrence, David Herbert, 31–32, 104–129,
    133–134
Lefebvre, Henri, 2, 40
Lo Schiavo, Aldo, 140
Lombard League, 5, 20
Lombroso, Cesare, 155–156
London, 17, 82, 105, 110, 133

Mandel, Eli, 8, 12, 173
Manning, Susan, 71
mapping, 4, 16, 30, 35, 38–40, 42–47,
    51–52, 65–66, 72–74, 85; thematic
    mapping, 39–40. *See also* cartography
margins, 3, 5, 9, 17, 24, 27, 72, 88, 92, 101,
    110, 140, 159, 169

Sollors, Werner, 7
Sophocles, 163–169
Spaventa, Bertrando, 150
Staël, Madame de, 87, 88, 89, 91, 92
Starobinski, Jean, 92
Steiner, George, 164
Stendhal, 84, 110
Stephen, Leslie, 54, 55
supplement, 18, 19, 25, 28, 90. *See also*
  compensatio
Swabia, 170–171
symbol, 38, 55, 56, 57, 61, 132–133, 138,
  161
synecdoche, 51

Taine, Hyppolite, 88
Theocritus, 9, 114
Thiesse, Anne-Marie, 21
Tönnies, Ferdinand, 94–95
topos, 19, 22–23, 25, 28, 30, 32, 38, 42,
  46–47, 51–52, 54, 58, 61, 69–70, 84, 87,
  91, 94–96, 100–102, 106, 114, 149, 157,
  158. *See also* commonplace

trains, 51–52, 70, 112–113, 116. *See also*
  railway
translation, 5, 31, 32, 86, 88, 94, 96, 102,
  119–125, 127–135, 145, 164–166
Tuan, Yi-Fu, 8

unheimlich, 106, 109, 116–118, 120, 129,
  130, 135, 165–173
utopia, 3, 49, 90

Veblen, Thorstein, 30
Verdi, Giuseppe, 20, 132
Verga, Giovanni, 31, 119–133
Vico, Giambattista, 140, 142, 144–150
Virgil, 110, 134

Walker, Scott, 5, 10, 12, 19
Welty, Eudora, 13
Wessex, 15, 30, 40, 42, 51–52, 54, 68–
  70
Williams, Raymond, 17, 28, 70
Wing, George, 71
Wordsworth, William, 12, 22, 38, 57–59